NATIONALISM, COMMUNISM, AND CANADIAN LABOUR

IRVING MARTIN ABELLA

Nationalism, Communism, and Canadian Labour
The CIO, the Communist party, and the Canadian Congress of Labour 1935-1956

UNIVERSITY OF TORONTO PRESS
Toronto and Buffalo

© University of Toronto Press 1973
Toronto and Buffalo
Reprinted 1975
Printed in Canada
ISBN 0-8020-1893-9 (cloth)
ISBN 0-8020-6150-8 (paper)

Preface

This is a history neither of the Canadian Congress of Labour nor of the CIO in Canada, but rather a study of the interaction of the two. Two basic conflicts –one internal, the other external–pervaded this relationship: the internal struggle of both organizations to rid themselves of their Communist-dominated affiliates, and the external battle of the Congress, and to a lesser extent of its CIO affiliates, to achieve and then defend their autonomy in the face of the aggressive incursions of the American unions to the south. A corollary to this latter conflict was the desperate struggle of the Congress to maintain its authority over its international affiliates. These two themes–the internal threat from the Communists and the external threat from the Americans–dominate the entire history of the Congress from its creation in 1940. Besides these two issues, all others seem insignificant.

It is worth noting, that to most rank and file union members at the time, even these two problems were irrelevant. It was amongst the leadership and not the rank and file that these two battles were fought. The average union member, as almost all studies of the labour movement have shown, plays an unimportant role in the affairs of his union. Only at times when his own economic well-being is at stake–during strikes and collective bargaining negotiations–does he take more than a passing interest in the activities of his union. And this, of course, was especially true of the unionist in the 1930s and 1940s, when his immediate, and indeed sole concern was to achieve financial security.

Most labour leaders did not see the expansion of American unionism into Canada as a problem. Indeed, except to a few nationalist labour leaders, the Americanization of the Canadian labour movement was of little concern. In fact, the majority of Canadian union members saw the American connection as both necessary and beneficial. To be part of a continent-wide labour movement with a huge treasury and membership at its disposal was such an obvious advantage that few Canadian unionists considered the drawbacks of being forced to accept policies made for them by men in another country. Few saw the problems involved in having Canadian unionists subject to the whims and wishes of an American leadership. But there were some who did. And this is largely a study of how these few labour leaders attempted to curb American control of the industrial union movement in Canada.

The other issue, that of the Communist threat, was of course a more obvious problem. But again most Canadian workers–except for those in the unions most directly affected–were indifferent. To them the Communists were no threat. To their leaders, however, the Communists and their left-wing allies were indeed a menace; the possibility of a Communist takeover of the Congress –though highly unlikely–was never far from their minds.

I should point out that throughout this book I have used the terms "left wing" and "Communist" almost interchangeably. There were two major political factions within the CCL, one dominated by the CCF, the other by the Communists. In each of these groupings there were men who were partisans of neither organization. Certainly in the faction dominated by the Communists, there were a large number of unionists who were not party members. For the sake of accuracy, therefore, this group was most usually called the "left wing." At the price of accuracy, however, the other faction was ordinarily identified as the "right wing." For the sake of brevity and for the want of an acceptable alternative, I have reluctantly adopted these classifications.

This study is based largely on the files of the Canadian Labour Congress and its affiliates. Interviews have filled in whatever information was not available in this voluminous correspondence. Because of the vastness of the topic and the dearth of research concerning it, I have been forced to ignore some issues and skim over others which are undoubtedly important but which were extraneous to the themes of this study. For this, I ask for the indulgence of the reader.

For their co-operation and assistance in permitting me to see the records and files of their organizations, I would like to thank Donald MacDonald, Arthur Hemming and Senator Eugene Forsey of the Canadian Labour Congress; Eamon Park, Margaret Lazarus and Ed Norton of the United Steel Workers; Clifford Scotton of the NDP; Fred Dowling of the Packinghouse Workers; C.S. Jackson of the United Electrical Workers; Sam Fox of the Amalgamated Clothing Workers; Carrol Coburn and Jerry Hartford of the United Auto Workers; Paul Phillips late of the British Columbia Federation of Labour; Grant McNeil of the International Woodworkers; and Emil Bjarnson of the Trade Union Research Bureau. In addition, for allowing me to see his private files on the Canadian Brotherhood of Railway Employees, I am most grateful to the late J.E. McGuire. And for permission to peruse some of the records of the British Columbia Communist Party I am indebted to Nigel Morgan.

I am also grateful to those who read this work and gave me the benefit of their comments–John Crispo, Harry Crowe, Peter Hunter, C.S. Jackson, J.B. Salsberg, and especially to the two elder statesmen of the Canadian labour movement, Pat Conroy and Senator Eugene Forsey, both of whose insights and criticisms were of inestimable value. My good friends, Professors Craig Brown and Kenneth McNaught, under whose supervision this study first took shape as a doctoral thesis, have been extraordinarily generous with their advice and encouragement. To all of these people this book owes much of its strength; its weaknesses and errors, however, are naturally my responsibility.

Throughout the many years of research that went into this study I have been supported at various times by the Canada Council, the Canada Department of Labour, the Ontario Department of University Affairs, and Glendon College. This book has been published with the aid of a grant from the Social Science Research Council using funds provided by the Canada Council.

Finally, I am profoundly thankful to my wife Rosie. Without her, this book would not have been possible. To her it is dedicated.

IMA

Contents

NATIONALISM, COMMUNISM, AND CANADIAN LABOUR

1

The CIO comes north

1935 was the key year in the history of the Canadian labour movement; it was then that the future course of the trade union movement in Canada was determined. In that year it became apparent that the Canadian labour movement would probably never be Canadian, that it would – for the foreseeable future – continue to be dominated by American unions.

When 1935 began, Canadian unionism, ironically enough, was at the peak of its strength. For the first and only time in this century nearly half the organized workers in Canada belonged to Canadian unions. To most observers at the time, it appeared that at long last Canadians were about to recapture control of their own labour movement. National unionism seemed on the rise and international unionism on the wane. Canadian unions were growing for more rapidly than their American counterparts. The former were plainly more militant, more vigorous, more imaginative, and thus more successful than the latter. The craft unionism to which the international unions were wedded belonged to another generation. The industrial unionism of the national unions was clearly more appropriate for the assembly lines of the 1920s and '30s. The national unions were confident that it was only a matter of time until they replaced the international unions as the dominant force in the Canadian labour movement.

For the Canadian labour movement, no period was more dismal than the 1920s. Organization was at a standstill, membership declined drastically, and union leadership was divided and paralysed. Torpidity and acrimony seemed the dismal hallmark of labour activity in this period. Though this was a decade of rapid economic development, the Canadian labour movement was unable to capitalize on these propitious circumstances. It simply could not cope with the new economic challenges of the period.

Canadian labour was then dominated by the craft-obsessed Trades and Labor Congress, an affiliate of the American Federation of Labor. Both organizations seemed moribund in the face of the rapid advances in size, scale, and technology being made in such relatively new industries as electrical appliances, automobiles, chemicals, and rubber. These new industries could not be accommodated within their existing craft structures, and the AFL and the TLC were not willing to change their organizational policies.

The rise of mass-production industries and new modes of production called for new and more aggressive methods of organization. To both the AFL and the TLC, dominated by conservative craft unionists, the very thought of organizing unskilled workers was anathema. Since the beginning of the century the AFL and the TLC had beaten back all attempts to introduce industrial unions into the mainstream of the North American labour movement. They doggedly refused to organize along industrial lines and attempted to exorcise those unions which did. They believed, and continued to believe throughout the 1920s and '30s, that only the most skilled, and thus least replaceable workers should be organized. With the exception of unions in the mining and clothing industries, the AFL and TLC consisted almost entirely of skilled workingmen in craft unions. They were select organizations whose membership made up the elite of the labour movement; they wanted nothing else but to maintain their status and be left alone.

The industrial work force in Canada had proliferated rapidly throughout the 1920s and was demanding to be organized. Yet, hidebound, the TLC perversely clung to its craft mentality. It launched no organizing campaigns, hired few organizers, and spent little money. In a time of rapid economic expansion, the TLC consciously chose retrenchment and consolidation. It succeeded in neither. By the end of the decade it had lost much of its membership and was on the verge of bankruptcy. It was impotent, rudderless, in total disarray, and its very survival seemed in the balance.[1]

To compound the TLC's problems, new labour organizations had sprung up in the 1920s and early '30s, challenging its control of the Canadian union movement. The first of these – the Canadian and Catholic Confederation of Labour – appeared in 1921 in the province of Quebec. It was a confessional union dominated by the Catholic Church and was strongly nationalist. Because of its connection with the Church and its opposition to international unionism, the CCCL was able to attract a substantial number of Quebec workers who felt that the American-dominated TLC was not paying sufficient attention to the unique problems of the French-Canadian workingman.

In 1927, the second new labour centre – the All-Canadian Congress of Labour – was founded by unions expelled from the TLC for their advocacy of industrial unionism and their unyielding antagonism to international unionism. Led by the powerful Canadian Brotherhood of Railway Employees, these unions, the tiny Canadian Federation of Labour, the remnants of the One Big Union, and a host of smaller national unions, began a campaign against the TLC. They denounced international unionism, and condemned the TLC for its docility and its opposition to industrial unionism. The ACCL also launched a mildly successful campaign to seduce other unhappy TLC affiliates into its ranks and to organize new unions.

The third new national union – the Workers' Unity League – was founded in 1930 and was the most radical and aggressive of the TLC's competitors. It consisted of industrial unions in the mining, clothing, lumber, and textile industries. The WUL was the only labour centre committed to organizing not only the unorganized but the unemployed as well, and it was also the only one willing to use the strike as a weapon against both employers and governments. Though its leadership was Communist, most of its membership was not. The WUL was a national union made up entirely of Canadian workers in Canadian unions. Yet, significantly, important policy decisions affecting it were not made in Canada, by Canadians, but in Russia, by Russians.[2]

In 1935 the combined membership of these three national union groups – the CCCL, the ACCL, and the WUL – equalled that of the TLC. As the depression deepened and the TLC remained immobile within its obsolete craft structure, it seemed only a matter of time before the national unions would eclipse the international unions and alter the balance of power within the Canadian union movement. Labour in Canada would finally be truly Canadian.

Then, suddenly in 1935, the national union movement was felled by two crushing blows. Though few realized it then – and even fewer cared – two decisions made that year, one in Moscow, the other in Washington, destroyed Canadian unionism. Since then, national unions have never again been numerous or powerful enough to challenge American unions for control of the Canadian labour movement.

The first of these blows was struck at the Seventh Congress of the Communist International. The Communist party sounded the cry for a united front of the working class around the world to destroy fascism. On instructions from Moscow, the party in Canada ordered the dissolution of the Workers' Unity League. Unions affiliated with the WUL were instructed to join the TLC "to strengthen the trade union ranks and to lay a solid foundation for a broad united front movement against fascism and against another imperialist war."[3] There was fierce opposition to this 'ukase' from many quarters both within the Canadian Communist party and the Workers' Unity League.[4] But the party leadership was inflexible. It ordered even the most unyielding opponents of international unionism to return to the fold of the TLC; there could be no exceptions. Thus, on orders from Moscow, the most militant national union in Canada unilaterally disbanded and turned over its entire membership to the American-controlled Trades and Labor Congress. It was a blow from which the national union movement was not to recover.

The second ruinous step was taken in Washington. There, immediately following the annual AFL convention, a handful of frustrated union leaders met to discuss their problems. They were enraged and humiliated by the convention's contemptuous rejection of their attempts to get the AFL to launch organizing campaigns in the mass-production industries. Called together by John L. Lewis of the United Mine Workers, these unionists decided to create a new organization within the AFL which would facilitate organizing along industrial lines. Thus the Committee for Industrial Organization – the CIO – was born. It would not become apparent for several years that the formation of the CIO doomed whatever possibility there remained of creating in Canada a labour movement, the majority of whose members belonged to Canadian unions.

Immediately on its creation, the CIO became the voice for the millions of workers in the United States crying out for organization – cries that previously had been disdainfully ignored by the AFL. Led by John L. Lewis and his United Mine Workers, and propelled forward by the New Deal labour legislation, these "new unionists" successfully defied the regressive leadership of the AFL. Under the aegis of the CIO, vast organizing campaigns were launched in the mass-production industries and within months several million unorganized and largely unskilled workers were brought into the AFL. Aghast at this influx into the organized labour movement of what the AFL Teamster president, James Tobin, called "riffraff ... good for nothings ... and ... rubbish",[5] and fearful of the radical ideas of these aggressive, militant new members, the AFL at first suspended and then finally expelled the CIO. But it was all to no avail. The CIO continued its massive organizing campaigns in the steel, automobile, rubber, smelting, and electrical industries. And, sparked by victories in the sitdown strikes in the rubber plants in Akron and the automobile plants in Flint, by April of 1937 it had a membership approaching four million.

In Canada, however, during this same period, the CIO accomplished little. In fact, it had no intentions of moving into Canada – at least not until it had completed the formidable tasks confronting it at home. But Canadian workers were impatient and restive. Captivated by the glamour, the excitement, and the monumental breakthroughs of the CIO campaigns in the United States, they desperately pleaded with it to come into Canada. On their own, without informing the CIO, scores of ex-WUL organizers began organizing CIO unions in Canada. The director of the Communist party's trade-union section, J.B. Salsberg, travelled to New York and Washington and begged the CIO leaders to launch campaigns in Canada. He returned empty-handed. There was just too much to be done in the United States, he was told, before the CIO could think of funnelling any of its resources and efforts into Canada.[6]

Disappointed but determined, Salsberg and other party stalwarts accelerated their efforts on behalf of the CIO. Within months these men, and a handful of others, had organized hundreds of new workers and scores of new CIO locals. Yet not one CIO organizer or one cent of CIO money had crossed the border. All the organizing had been done by Canadians with no help – or even encouragement – from the CIO. Indeed the CIO was not even aware of what was being done in its name in Canada.

Finally, midway through 1936, bowing to the relentless pressures from north of the border, John L. Lewis agreed half-heartedly to allow some CIO activity in Canada. He appointed the director of the United Mine Workers in Canada, Silby Barrett, to organize the Nova Scotia steel workers into the Steel Workers Organizing Committee (SWOC). Concentrating on the Dosco plant in Sydney where he was well known and where the employees already had a plant council, Barrett succeeded in signing up 2600 of the 2900 workers in Local 1064 of SWOC.[7] Though Dosco refused to bargain with the new union – and did not until the Nova Scotia Trade Union Act, passed in April of 1937, compelled it to recognize the SWOC bargaining unit – the CIO had gained its first real foothold in Canada.

In the rest of Canada, however, except for locals of the United Mine Workers in Alberta and the Amalgamated Clothing Workers in Toronto and Montreal, there was no official CIO organization. But at the request of the Communists, in August 1936 Lewis sent a SWOC director, Leo Krzycki, to address a meeting of steelworkers in Hamilton. Somewhat disingenuously, Krzycki told his audience of the great breakthroughs made by the CIO in Canada. After Krzycki's speech, the steelworkers voted to join SWOC and to ask Lewis to set up a SWOC office in Hamilton.

Within a few months, the SWOC under the direction of an active young Communist, Harry Hunter, claimed to have organized locals in every steel plant in the Hamilton area. Unfortunately, this claim was not true. Hunter and other party members had indeed attempted to organize all the steel plants in the Hamilton area – but with no success. By the end of 1936, no steel plants had been organized and the SWOC organization in Hamilton had collapsed.[8]

Similarly, efforts to organize the miners in Northern Ontario were ineffectual. George Anderson, the organizer for the Mine-Mill and Smelter Workers and a prominent Communist, had succeeded in forming locals in Sudbury and Timmins, but the total membership of both amounted to less than thirty. An organizer for the United Rubber Workers was active in Kitchener, but by the end of the year only twenty-one workers were signed up. The United Automobile Workers had succeeded in organizing the small Kelsey Wheel plant in Windsor, but John Eldon, the UAW organizer, reported that since the company refused to negotiate with the new union there was no possibility of signing a contract. Thus by the end of 1936 the CIO membership in Canada was concentrated in the two established unions – 16,600 in the United Mine Workers and 7000 in the Amalgamated Clothing Workers – though SWOC reported a membership of 3140, mostly in the steel plants in Nova Scotia. Even the locals organized by the Communists had, after the first flush of enthusiasm, largely disappeared. So hopeless did the CIO task seem at the end of the year that John L. Lewis announced that the only CIO activity in Canada for the foreseeable future would be to continue organizing the steel workers in Nova Scotia.[9]

But Lewis had not taken into account the growing demands of Canadian workers for organization. These were most evident in Ontario. With the worst of the depression over, industry after industry began announcing record profits and issuing optimistic reports for the new year. Workers, on the other hand, were still being paid depression wages and were growing increasingly more restless. With the example of the CIO sit-downs just across the border, it was only a matter of time before Ontario workers would rebel both against their deplorable working conditions and their overcautious union leadership. The flash point was reached in March of 1937 at the Holmes foundry in Sarnia.

In early February, a SWOC representative in Ontario, Milton Montgomery, was invited by several of the employees of the Holmes foundry to organize the plant into SWOC. Montgomery was dubious but agreed to see what could be done. His efforts were doomed from the start. Though the plant seemed ripe for organization – low wages, long hours, no security, and unsafe working conditions – there were several factors which made Montgomery's task impossible. A large minority of the workers were immigrants of Slovak, Polish, and Ukrainian descent and the native-born majority would have nothing to do with them. But even more discouraging, the Holmes management threatened to close the plant rather than negotiate with a CIO affiliate. In addition, the recent violent sit-downs across the lake in Michigan had turned public opinion in Sarnia against the CIO. Montgomery was therefore able to sign up less than one quarter of the workers – almost all of them foreigners.

Enraged at the slow progress of organization and at the recalcitrance of the management, and encouraged by the success of the recent sit-down in Flint, on March 2 some seventy of the workers, without informing Montgomery, decided to sit down at their machines. As soon as word spread of the sit-down, a mob of enraged citizens of Sarnia – only a few of whom were employees of the plant, but all united in their hatred of the foreigners – descended on the foundry with an assortment of anti-union devices – crowbars, baseball bats, bricks, and steel pipes. A bloody battle ensued, and within an hour the union was broken, as were the arms, legs and heads of many of the "sit-downers." During the entire incident, the Sarnia police force refused to intervene, claiming that the plant was located in Point Edward, which was across the road from Sarnia, and therefore not in its jurisdiction. The first CIO sit-down in Canada was an ignominious failure. The battered and bloodied strikers were taken – some were carried – to court and convicted of trespassing. No charges were laid against the strike-breakers.[10]

Many people in Ontario were shocked at this apparent injustice. Sam Lawrence, the lone CCF member in the Ontario Legislature, asked Attorney-General Arthur Roebuck in the House what the government intended to do about the treatment of the strikers. Before Roebuck could answer, Premier Mitchell Hepburn jumped to his feet and shouted emotionally, "My sympathies are with those who fought the strikers ... Those who participate in sit-down strikes are trespassers, and trespassing is illegal in this province ... There will be no sit-down strikes in Ontario. This government is going to maintain law and order at all costs." Several days later Hepburn amplified his warning in a veiled threat to the CIO. "We are not going to tolerate sit-down strikes," he stated, "and I point that out to those people now in this country – professional agitators from the United States – who agitate and foment unrest in our industrial areas ... I shall put down these sit-down strikes with the full strength of the provincial police if necessary and other resources at the government's disposal."[11]

There is little doubt that Hepburn's warning was aimed, not at Sarnia where the CIO had been bloodily repulsed, but much closer to home, to the bustling industrial city of Oshawa, less than forty miles from Hepburn's office in Queen's Park, where some local men were actively organizing a union, which in a few short weeks, would more than anything else mark the birth of industrial unionism in Canada.

In the early 1920s the giant General Motors Company of America had purchased the McLaughlin Carriage Works of Oshawa and had built a huge new plant on the outskirts of the town. By 1929 the company employed more than 3000 men and produced more cars for the Canadian and Empire market than the rest of Canada combined. A plant union had been organized in the early 1920s and in March of 1928 the entire work force had walked out protesting a 40 per cent wage reduction. The strike lasted for three days and was settled only when the General Motors management agreed to the demands of the strikers, and referred the wage question to a conciliation board. It was a great victory for the union. As the *Canadian Labour Monthly* exulted: "Oshawa is a demonstration that the spell of industrial slavery can be broken down even in the automobile industry."

Because of the determination of the AFL and the TLC to break the union up into its component crafts, however, it began falling apart. At the same time, the union came under the control of the Communist-led Auto Workers Industrial union, and when it applied to affiliate with the All-Canadian Congress of Labour, the TLC began a rival union in the Oshawa area. Taking advantage of this inter-union dispute, the company began offering better wages and working conditions. By 1935 there was no union in any of the General Motors facilities in Oshawa.

As the union disappeared however, so did the company's largesse. In January 1937, General Motors announced that the 1936 profit of $200,000,000 had been the highest in the company's history. In the same month, the company's employees in Oshawa underwent their fifth consecutive wage cut in five years. Worse than the low wages, however, was the lack of job security. The company had insured the men with the Metropolitan Life Assurance Company and all workers were required to undergo periodic examinations by the insurance company's doctor. Those men not considered good risks by the company – that is, those over fifty – were fired. In this way the company maintained a steady supply of strong, young workers.[12]

With the increasing ferment in the auto plants below the border, labour activity was beginning again in Oshawa. In 1936 a "Unity Group" was formed by one of the workers, Malcolm Smith, an old-country Independent Labour Party advocate. It was a clandestine group of about twenty men who met periodically to discuss ways to improve working conditions. Some of the members were Communists, though most of the organization adhered to the principles of the Independent Labour party. But its existence was unknown to most of the workers and nothing was achieved. There was also a group organized by the Communist party which attempted, unsuccessfully, to organize a union. Even the regular visits of such active party functionaries as J.B. Salsberg accomplished little.

Eventually the company itself finally aroused the men to action. On 15 February 1937, acting on the advice of efficiency experts and engineers from the United States who had toured the plant, the General Motors management posted new work schedules that would speed up production from 27 to 32 units an hour with a concomitant increase in wages of 5 cents. The workers who already felt they were overworked were furious, and the men in the body shop decided to strike. One of them, Allen Griffiths, an active member of the CCF and opponent of the Unity Group, took it upon himself to phone the UAW office in Detroit for help. At the same time a call went out from Communist party headquarters to the UAW pleading for an organizer to be sent to Oshawa. On 19 February, the body shop workers, about 250 men, laid down their tools and walked out, thus tying up production in the entire plant. On that same day, a UAW organizer from Detroit, Hugh Thompson, arrived in Oshawa.[13]

Within minutes of his arrival, Thompson was taken by Griffiths to a meeting of the 250 strikers which was being addressed by Louis Fine of the Ontario Department of Labour who had been invited to mediate the dispute. Fine urged the men to go back to work and give the new system a trial. When he learned of Thompson's presence he pleaded with the men to ignore the "outsider" since the dispute was simply a matter between General Motors in Oshawa and its employees. The strikers rebuffed Fine and invited Thompson to speak. Within half an hour Thompson had signed all 250 men to UAW cards and had collected a $1.00 initiation fee from each. They also agreed, on Thompson's suggestion, to go back to work for two months to give the new system a trial.[14]

On the following morning Thompson rented an office and set up Local 222 of the UAW. By holding nightly meetings with every department in the plant and explaining to the workers the advantages of belonging to the CIO, Thompson succeeded in signing up most of the 4000 workers within a month. Even the mayor of Oshawa, Alex Hall, and most of his council, were enrolled as honorary members. Charlie Millard, a forty-year-old war veteran and an active member of the CCF, was elected president of the local, and stewards were nominated from each department to represent the men on the union bargaining committee.

The first meeting between the General Motors management and the new union was held on the afternoon of March 18 in the office of Colonel Highfield, the company's personnel manager. George Chappell, a company vice-president, told the union representatives that the Canadian company was in no way bound by the union contract signed in the United States, and Highfield made it clear that the company would negotiate only with its own employees in Oshawa. None of the union negotiating team led by Millard had ever before been involved in negotiations; in their own words, they were "simply a bunch of amateurs." They listened, said nothing, and then suggested another meeting for the following week. On the next day, concluding that a show of strength was necessary to intimidate the company, Thompson called a meeting for March 20 to install the union's officers. But he found it impossible to rent a hall large enough for the meeting. The Oshawa arena refused to accommodate the union as the president of General Motors, Colonel R.S. McLaughlin, owned a large share of its stock. The school board refused to rent the collegiate auditorium, as Thompson was not a "local man," and the Department of National Defence refused to rent the Oshawa armouries. In desperation, Thompson announced the union would hold its meeting at the "four corners" – the busiest intersection in downtown Oshawa – at the height of the rush hour on Saturday afternoon. Eventually the meeting was held in the school auditorium, and the several thousand union members attending the rally applauded joyously as Thompson recounted his adventures and difficulties in attempting to rent a hall.[15]

The first showdown between the UAW and management occurred the following day at the Coulter Manufacturing Company, a General Motors supplier in Oshawa, whose entire staff of 260 was organized by Local 222. When the company announced on 21 March that it was laying off the night shift, a strike was called. Within a week the company agreed to the union's terms and a contract was signed in the office of Ontario Labour Minister David Croll, in which Local 222 was recognized as sole bargaining agent for Coulter's employees. With union morale at a new peak, at the next bargaining session Millard demanded that Thompson be permitted to sit in on negotiations. Highfield peremptorily refused, arguing that Thompson was not an employee of the company. Millard countered that neither was Louis Fine who had sat in on previous negotiations. Highfield stated that this was a completely different matter and that the company would never negotiate with Thompson. On that note, Millard and the committee walked out, barely ten minutes after the meeting had started.[16]

On Friday, 26 March, UAW vice-president Ed Hall – the "Bull of Detroit" as he was appropriately called – addressed a large rally of workers in the school auditorium. He promised the men the complete support of the International and announced that Millard had been appointed a full-time CIO organizer. Privately, however, Hall warned Millard that the UAW treasury was empty and could offer Local 222 nothing more than moral support.[17]

Negotiations were at a standstill despite the efforts of Croll to bring both sides together. The company was adamant in its refusal to negotiate with Thompson; Local 222 was equally stubborn in its demand to choose whomever it wished as its representative. On 31 March, Chappell and Thompson met with Fine and Croll in the latter's office in Queen's Park. After Chappell reiterated his company's stand on Thompson, Croll turned to the UAW organizer and said: "Well this narrows the issue down to one thing. It looks as if the people would get along nicely if it were not for one person, and I would suggest that you withdraw out of the picture." Thompson stated that it was the wish of Local 222 that he be its representative, but he agreed that Millard should do the negotiating for the union. Chappell consented and a meeting was scheduled for the following day at Croll's office.[18]

Early the following afternoon Chappell and Highfield came to Croll's office to discuss Millard's new status. Highfield protested that all that had been done "was change the name of Thompson to Millard," and that the company would have no dealings with the CIO or any of its representatives. Croll reproved them for their "childish stubbornness"and then remarked: "I can read men, and as I look at that bunch in the next room [the union negotiating team], I can tell by the eyes of most of them that they are a bunch of fanatics ... as for Millard ... I think he's a weakling who can't do anyone any harm ... I don't want a strike and they shouldn't either, because I'll have to feed them and they won't get fat on what they get from this Department."[19]

With that, he ushered Highfield and Chappell into an adjoining room where Fine and the union committee were waiting and the meeting began. Millard spoke first and presented Chappell with a list of the union demands. These included an eight-hour day with time and a half for overtime, a steward and grievance system, a seniority system, abolition of the new efficiency system, a minimum wage, rest periods, and an agreement that would terminate at the same time as the UAW contract with General Motors in the United States. Chappell agreed to study these proposals and present the company's position on the following Monday. Fine then adjourned the meeting, optimistically adding that he was sure that an agreement would be reached shortly, so that Croll who was leaving on Friday for a two-week vacation would not have to postpone his trip. Yet for the following three nights the company shipped an average of 1500 cars – more than ten times the usual number – from the Oshawa plant to an emergency storage depot on the grounds of the Canadian National Exhibition in Toronto.[20] Evidently General Motors did not share Fine's optimism.

On Monday, 5 April, another meeting was held in Highfield's office. Chappell announced that the company had accepted some of the union's demands but would institute neither the minimum wage nor the new seniority system proposed by the union. Highfield added that the company did not accept Millard as a representative of the CIO, nor would it sign an agreement "that recognizes the international union." An angry Millard immediately stalked out of the room.[21]

The union then invited Fine to act as mediator. The meeting next day was once again held in Highfield's office, but this time it was chaired by Fine. Chappell, who had been in contact with the General Motors head office in Detroit, announced a change in management's policy and stated that the company would now negotiate with Millard "as representative of Local 222." He agreed to negotiate all the union's demands and offered the men a 44-hour week with time and a half for overtime. The union negotiating team was jubilant. Millard said he would present the company's offer to the men and that he expected an agreement could be reached by the end of the week. Fine concurred, and adjourned the meeting until the following day.[22] It seemed that the CIO would win its first and biggest engagement in Canada without a struggle. But such was not to be the case. Mitchell Frederick Hepburn would see to that.

From the beginning Hepburn had taken an unusual interest in what went on in Oshawa. As early as February, without informing his cabinet, Hepburn had phoned his close friend Ian Mackenzie, Minister of National Defence, to ask him to pressure Thomas Crerar, the minister in charge of immigration, and Norman Rogers, Minister of Labour, to take "deportation action" against Thompson. Mackenzie wired back that the federal cabinet decided that no action could be taken against Thompson until he had committed a crime. Hepburn then ordered Roebuck to make a file on Thompson, in the hope that something would be discovered that could be used to deport Thompson as an "undesirable immigrant." Several days later Hepburn phoned Crerar and demanded that Thompson be deported, but Crerar promised only to investigate Roebuck's dossier on Thompson before making a decision. Finally on 5 March, Crerar forwarded to Hepburn his report on Thompson, showing that Thompson had entered Canada legally and had not acted "criminally" since coming into the country and could not therefore be deported.[23]

Thwarted by the federal Liberals, Hepburn was kept fully informed of the situation in Oshawa and when a settlement favourable to the CIO seemed imminent, Hepburn suddenly ended a Florida vacation and hurried back to Toronto. Nor was it too surprising that on the day Hepburn returned, General Motors once again changed its stand and refused to negotiate with Millard as long as he was "a representative of the CIO."[24]

With Hepburn's return, the worst was now expected at Queen's Park. Roger Irwin, Croll's secretary, warned Acting Labour Minister Harry Nixon that a strike was now inevitable.[25] Hepburn meanwhile had contacted both Fine and Chappell urging them to resist the union's demands. This Chappell did at the meeting that evening with the union negotiating team. Predictably, on the following morning, Thursday 8 April, the entire work force walked out. For the first time in nearly ten years, the General Motors plant was closed by a strike.

The news of the strike spurred Hepburn to even greater efforts. He wired the Federal Minister of Justice, Ernest Lapointe, asking for RCMP assistance on the grounds that the Oshawa situation was becoming "very acute and violence [was] anticipated" at any moment. He then ordered General Victor Williams, chief of the provincial police, to cancel all leaves, put his entire force on 24-hour alert and mobilize one hundred constables from the areas surrounding Oshawa. In turn Williams informed him that the OPP had an undercover constable in Oshawa "to keep an eye on developments." E.G. Odette, chairman of the Ontario Liquor Control Board, acting on the recommendation of Mayor Hall and the union's executive, received Hepburn's permission to close all liquor and beer outlets in Oshawa for the duration of the strike. Hepburn also ordered the Department of Welfare not to issue relief to the strikers because "these employees are rejecting the opportunity to work at fair wages and fair hours and as a result they need not look to the government for relief assistance." It was only after all this was done that Hepburn considered consulting his cabinet, and even then he only spoke to Harry Nixon, Paul Leduc, Minister of Mines, and Duncan Marshall, Minister of Agriculture. He then called a news conference and stated that he believed that now was the time for a "showdown" with the CIO before its "ever-increasing and impossible demands" would hurt Ontario's "ever-increasing export trade." He warned that "the entire resources of the province" would be used to keep the CIO at bay, because Oshawa was "the first open attempt on the part of Lewis and his CIO henchmen to assume the position of dominating and dictating to Canadian industry."[26]

Later that day Lapointe agreed to send one hundred RCMP officers, though the province would have to bear all the expenses. Hepburn immediately phoned the RCMP commissioner, J.H. MacBrien, to alert him that he would need many more reinforcements as he did not expect the "main crisis" for two or three days. The commissioner informed him that he had already dispatched 67 men and 33 others would be "moving up by fast freight and passenger train" by the morning. Another fifteen men from the Toronto division, he added, would also be made available. On Lapointe's instructions, MacBrien ordered the RCMP commanding officer in Toronto to keep his forces "in the background as much as possible" so that they would be used only to support provincial and municipal police.[27]

To help keep order, Chief Owen Friend of the Oshawa police force had wisely enlisted fifty strikers as deputies "to keep peace" on the picket line. And, indeed, the only unusual activity in Oshawa was the continuous procession of cars along the road to the nearby town of Whitby where the beverage rooms were reporting a record business.[28]

Aside from the *Toronto Star* and the *Ottawa Citizen* all the Ontario press supported Hepburn's strong anti-CIO position. Most echoed the *Globe and Mail* editorial which praised Hepburn for quashing the CIO before it could "extend into all the major industries of Ontario and wreak havoc in its wake." On the other hand, Mayor Hall of Oshawa, condemned Hepburn for his "impulsive and irrational action." But in the same breath he refused to grant relief to the strikers as this would mean "taking sides" in the strike. The one newspaper which perhaps most clearly understood Hepburn's motives was the organ of the Communist party, the *Daily Clarion*. It commented that "Hepburn fears the CIO unionism will mean the ultimate invasion of the mines ... Hepburn's close association with certain big mining magnates of Northern Ontario has been the source of much gossip during the past year." As if to prove the prescience of the *Clarion,* on the following day, after a conference with the OPP chief, Hepburn stated: "We now know what these agitators are up to. We were advised only a few hours ago that they are working their way into the lumber camps and our mines. Well that has got to stop, and we are going to stop it! If necessary we'll raise an army to do it."[29]

Hepburn had also taken upon himself the rather unlikely role of mediator. On 10 April he called a meeting of the union and management negotiating teams in his office. Characteristically, he abruptly called off the meeting when he discovered Hugh Thompson on the union team. He coldly informed the union representatives that he refused to sit in the same room as Thompson. The Premier also informed the press that he would never negotiate with Thompson, nor with "any of those men who are trying to dominate Canadian industry." "Thompson is the issue in the strike right now," he added.[30]

Later that same day, the union negotiating committee conferred at the office of a Toronto lawyer, J.L. Cohen, who had recently been appointed the union's legal adviser. From there they went to the Toronto airport to welcome the UAW president, Homer Martin, who had flown in from Detroit to inspect the Oshawa situation. In a cavalcade of a dozen cars, Martin was conveyed from Toronto to the battleground, forty miles distant, where he paraded down the main street crowded with thousands of cheering, jubilant people. It was, according to Police Chief Friend, the largest demonstation in Oshawa's history. As a veteran labour reporter, Felix Lazarus, rapturously described it: "Labour leaders almost wept when they saw this amazing display of enthusiasm. Never in all the history of the Canadian labour movement had a town been so completely captured by the sentiment of unionism." At a huge rally that night, Martin, the slight bespectacled, ex-Baptist minister from Kansas, railed against "Herr Hepburn ... the puppet of General Motors ... a little two by four who is trying to sweep aside the tradition of a thousand years." He publicly vowed that "if General Motors of Canada doesn't make cars in Canada, under union conditions, they won't make cars in the United States at all."[31]

Language of this kind was not meant to ingratiate the union with Hepburn, but it did serve to stiffen the resolve of the strikers. Their morale was also kept at a peak level by the unusually warm spring weather, by the encouragement and material support – free milk, bread, and pastries – offered by the Oshawa business community, and by the letters and telegrams of support arriving daily from various labour groups, churches, and individuals throughout Canada. The men were also heartened by the large number of tourists from Toronto and the surrounding districts who drove though Oshawa "to take a peek at the strike" and who stopped to talk and encourage the pickets.[32]

The competition between the Young Communist League and the Co-operative Commonwealth Youth Movement also benefitted the strikers. Every day, a truck from Toronto arrived at the picket line, carrying that day's edition of the *Daily Clarion,* which was handed out free to the strikers. It also brought a host of active young Communists eager to help wherever they could. Similarly, cars and trucks bearing equally enthusiastic young CCYMers from Toronto arrived regularly to add to the number of young people anxious to help the pickets by marching, making coffee, and doing odd jobs.[33]

Meanwhile, on Saturday 10 April, the federal Minister of Labour, Norman Rogers, wired Mayor Hall offering the services of his department to settle the dispute. The infuriated Hepburn angrily informed Mackenzie King that he "deeply resented the unwarranted interference" of Rogers, and that he believed that the General Motors Company would "not be a party to such treachery." He added gratuitously that "this action is quite in common with the treatment that this government has received from most of your ministers." After consulting with Rogers, King apologized, claiming that Rogers' offer "had been misunderstood and misconstrued," and that the federal government had no intention of intervening "so long as the matter is being dealt with by the authorities of the Province of Ontario." Not content with embarrassing King and in effect forcing him to repudiate one of his cabinet ministers, a man whom Hepburn considered "unfit for any political position," the Ontario premier then turned his attention to Lapointe.[34]

Despite the fact that Oshawa seemed relatively peaceful, Hepburn informed Lapointe that the situation in Oshawa was desperate and that at least another hundred RCMP reinforcements would be required, as he had received word that the Communists were about to foment "disturbances." On the following day, Lapointe coldly rejected Hepburn's request for more police. The angry premier then sent Lapointe a vitriolic telegram condemning the federal government for its "vacillating attitude" and demanding the removal of all dominion police. Since he could "no longer depend on federal aid" he would use other resources available to him as premier of Ontario.[35]

At a press conference later that day, King and Rogers reiterated their intentions not to intervene, though the latter issued a statement stressing the government's support "of the right of workmen to organize for lawful purposes." "The right of association for legitimate purposes should not be denied," he added, "and labour should not be refused the means of organizing for collective bargaining." This statement in turn so angered the Ontario premier – in the words of the *Toronto Star* it "made Hepburn's pot boil over" – that he called his own press conference, excoriated the federal government, and explained that since he had been informed that the RCMP were ordered to "take no active part until it was shown that provincial police were unable to cope with the situation," he had asked to have them removed and had set up his own special police force.[36]

Previously, Hepburn had ordered the provincial police "to enrol 200 or if necessary 400 special officers." These "Hepburn's Hussars," or "Sons of Mitches" as they were irreverently dubbed in Oshawa, were placed under the command of Colonel Fraser Hunter, a Toronto Liberal MPP, and were to be used to back up the regular police if the "Oshawa situation got out of hand." Hepburn explained that these special police were necessary because he had received reliable secret reports that the "Reds were massing in great numbers in Oshawa." In actual fact however, the secret reports he received several times daily from the "undercover" police officer in Oshawa, Constable Wilson, indicated that "the strike is proceeding smoothly ... with no violence in sight" and that there was no evidence at all of any Communist activity. In any case Hepburn informed his new recruits that he would continue to use their services even after the strike was over, as he could no longer depend on the federal government to maintain law and order in the province.[37]

During these manoeuvres, Hepburn still found time to fire two members of his cabinet who had opposed his actions during the strike, Arthur Roebuck and David Croll. In fact, both Roebuck and Croll were out of Toronto for the first few days of the strike and when they returned several days later, Hepburn refused to meet them. Immediately upon his return Croll had contacted Chappell to learn what had gone wrong with the negotiations which had been proceeding so smoothly. He was informed that with the Premier's return on April 8, the company had decided to break off negotiations as Hepburn had promised that he would do all in his power to "break" the union in Oshawa.[38]

On Wednesday 14 April, Hepburn sent both ministers letters asking for their resignations as they were "not in accord" with his policy of "fighting against the inroads of the Lewis organization and Communism in general." At the same time, Hepburn called in the press, informed them of his dismissals of Croll and Roebuck and added, "this is a fight to the finish ... If the CIO wins at Oshawa it has other plants it will step into ... it will be the mines, demoralize the industry and send stocks tumbling." Later that day Croll and Roebuck sent Hepburn their letters of resignation. Both complained that they had not been consulted before they were fired. They both expressed support for the strikers; in Croll's memorable phrase, "my place is marching with the workers rather than riding with General Motors."[39]

With all these activities in Queen's Park, the workers in Oshawa must have wondered whether anyone remembered the strike. Certainly Hepburn seemed to have had other things on his mind, at least until he was informed that at a meeting with General Motors executives in Detroit, Homer Martin had agreed that the strike "should be settled on a Canadian basis without recognition of the CIO ... and that it should be settled between company officials and the various representatives of the local unions involved." The ecstatic Ontario Premier termed Martin's statement "a surrender by the CIO of its attempt to extend its mass product industrialization drive into Canada" and a victory for his own attempt "to root Communism out of the Canadian labour movement." He then phoned Millard and invited him to resume negotiations in his office. The latter demurred until Martin, who was due in Oshawa that same day, could explain to the angry members of his union why he had reneged on his promises.[40]

Martin arrived in Oshawa to face a hostile union negotiating team. He explained to them that he had accepted a four-point program to settle the strike. This involved opening negotiations at once, establishing a seniority system similar to the one accepted by the UAW in Detroit, agreeing to a contract that would run concurrently with the one signed in the United States, and, finally, drawing up individual contracts with the local unions in Windsor and St. Catharines. The key point to the union of course, was the third, which meant that in future American and Canadian contracts would be negotiated at the same time to cover plants on both sides of the border. To further bolster the morale of the strikers, Martin arranged the first conference telephone call in Canadian history in which he spoke to the presidents of all the 45 UAW locals in the United States from San Francisco to Atlanta. The call lasted for twenty minutes and at its conclusion the UAW president announced that the Oshawa local had been promised all the support necessary to win the strike. Immediately after the call, Millard, Thompson, and J.L. Cohen left for Queen's Park to continue negotiations with Hepburn.[41]

The Premier, who had been in discussion with Highfield and Chappell all morning, led Cohen into his secretary's office, where for more than an hour they argued over the status of Millard. Hepburn asked Cohen to sign a statement that "J.L. Cohen and Charles Millard are negotiators for the employees union of the General Motors Company of Oshawa, and are in no way connected or instructed by the CIO."[42] After contacting Martin in Oshawa, Cohen and Millard agreed to sign the document.

The final issue was that of the seniority system. Hepburn presented the company position which Cohen thought acceptable. As he wished to consult with Millard before agreeing, Cohen went out into the corridor and presented Hepburn's proposal to Millard and Thompson. Both agreed that it was reasonable, but Thompson decided to contact Martin before accepting. He was directed by a reporter to a nearby room which contained a phone. Just as he finished dialing, a flustered Hepburn rushed from his office and announced to reporters nearby that the negotiations were finished. "We aren't going to settle this by remote control," he shouted.

The three union men were as bewildered as the newsmen by the sudden change of affairs. Hepburn soon came out of his office and told reporters that it was "nothing but a complete double-cross to have Thompson and Martin try to run this conference by remote control ... Thompson showed great temerity to even appear here, let alone enter my private vault where my personal, valuable and top secret papers are stored." This statement only added to the confusion of the reporters as they had often used the phone in the Premier's vault. Indeed, on Hepburn's orders, tables and chairs had been placed in the room so that reporters, in their spare time, could "sit around, drink tea or play cards." It seemed that Hepburn had used the "phone incident" only as an excuse to break off talks he never had any intention of completing. The three union negotiators then met Martin again at the Royal York Hotel. At this meeting, according to Millard, Martin promised the local the full financial support of the UAW. He also phoned Charles Wilson, the vice-president of General Motors in the United States, and warned him that if the strike were not settled soon the UAW would close down all General Motors plants in the United States.[43]

Perhaps Hepburn's reasons for calling off talks with the union were the ominous secret reports he was receiving from his agents in northern Ontario of increased CIO activity in organizing the gold mines. He was informed that the CIO organizer, George Anderson, had threatened to call a strike if the mine owners refused to meet union terms. It seems that Hepburn was now more than ever convinced that the CIO had to be totally crushed at Oshawa before it succeeded in organizing the mines of Ontario. As the general manager of the Hollinger Mines secretly warned him, "The CIO is only waiting for the Oshawa result, before mobilizing the mines".[44] The Premier therefore issued a statement declaring that his Oshawa stand had "greatly handicapped the CIO's drive to dominate Canadian industry" and that he was "more concerned about the CIO threat in the minefields than in the automobile industry ... for Oshawa is only an attempt by the CIO to pave the way for its real drive against the fundamental wealth of the province and its mine fields." He then issued his battle-cry: "Let me tell Lewis here and now, that he and his gang will never get their greedy paws on the mines of Northern Ontario, as long as I am Prime Minister". He was immediately supported by his mine-owner friends, Joe Wright, Jules Timmins, Jules Bache, and J.P. Bickell who warned that they would "close down the mines before they would negotiate with the CIO." More emphatically Jules Timmins of the Hollinger Mines warned: "Under no circumstances will we recognize the CIO, and should the CIO interfere with our operations we have the assurance of the government that ample protection will be given our men who are desirous of continuing work."[45]

The fears of Hepburn and the mine-owners, whose profits in 1936 in some cases reached 50 per cent on total production, were underscored by a major gold stock collapse on the Toronto Stock Exchange on Monday, 18 April – a collapse due largely to the rumours of CIO activity in the gold fields.[46] On the same day, however, it seemed that the Oshawa strike had been settled. All that day, Mayor Hall had been running between the offices of Highfield and Millard carrying proposals and counter-proposals. By evening the "remote control" negotiations had succeeded with Highfield agreeing to the four points of the "Detroit Agreement" and Millard and Thompson agreeing that the men would return to work before the contract was signed. All that remained was for the strikers to ratify the agreement. That night however, at a large rally, Hall was hooted off the stage by the men who held out in their demand for a signed contract before they returned to work. Tears streaming down his face, Hall attempted to argue with the men. He failed, and the strike continued.[47]

Both Thompson and Millard, however, were now anxious to settle the strike on any reasonable terms because there was absolutely no financial support coming from the American locals. Martin had made promises to the strikers that he had neither the intention nor the ability to fulfil. He had not consulted Lewis or any CIO or UAW executives before promising the Oshawa men full financial support. In fact, the entire strike was carried on without "one cent" of aid from the American unions.[48] Yet on Tuesday, 19 April, Thompson announced that the first instalment of the $100,000 promised by Martin had arrived, and the *Oshawa Times* carried a photograph of Thompson depositing the money at the Bank of Montreal. Unknown to everyone but Thompson and Millard, George Day, the union treasurer, had withdrawn all the local funds from the Royal Bank the preceding afternoon. It was this money that Thompson, with a great deal of publicity and fanfare, had deposited at the Bank of Montreal as "the first instalment from the USA."[49] In this way, the company, Hepburn, and the men on the picket line were led to believe that the strikers were receiving the fullest support from the International.

On that same day, the UAW executive board held a special meeting in Washington to discuss the strike. Martin presented his report, and reneging on his promise to the strikers, stated he was "personally against a sympathy strike" as this would "jeopardize our entire union." Walter Reuther, a UAW vice-president, suggested that the Oshawa local sign a temporary agreement which would be in effect until the termination of the General Motors pact in the United States, so that when a new contract was signed with the company, all Canadian workers would be included. The executive finally decided to leave negotiations to the men in Oshawa. The board also agreed that it would be impossible to support the strike financially as the union's treasury was empty. Nonetheless, for purposes of publicity, Martin wired Thompson that the executive had "unanimously voted necessary financial aid" – a telegram which both Martin and Thompson released to the press.[50]

Hepburn was not completely fooled: he had been informed by his agents in Oshawa that the union was in trouble. When Thompson announced that he was going to Washington "to discuss union matters," J.J. McIntyre, a *Globe and Mail* reporter, wired the Premier that "Thompson is hightailing it to Washington as it is obvious he needs help ... [he] is running out to get his hand strengthened." Previously Hepburn had met a secret delegation of strikers who told him that most of the men wished to return to work. Thus when he was informed by Highfield that the company was anxious to reopen negotiations, a frantic Hepburn took the almost unbelievable step of wiring Colonel McLaughlin, who was vacationing somewhere in the Caribbean on his yacht, to order his men to suspend negotiations with the strikers as he had "confidential reports" that a "total collapse" of the strike was "imminent."[51]

The union negotiating committee however, was ready to sign an agreement on almost any terms, and the General Motors management was anxious to begin producing cars once again. The Ontario Premier correctly feared that, if he were to abort negotiations again, the union and the company would ignore him and settle the strike between themselves. Thus Hepburn made the best of the situation. He ordered Cohen and Millard to sign a document stating that neither of them was "instructed by, or represented a committee known as the CIO." Cohen was also forced to sign a statement that neither Martin nor Thompson "would return to Toronto or Oshawa during the negotiations." When Hepburn got word from his undercover agents that "Claude Kramer, a CIO agent, was in Oshawa agitating the men," and that even if the negotiating committee repudiated the CIO "the men at a mass meeting will take matters out of the hands of the negotiating committee and hold out for recognition of the International Union," the Ontario Premier asked Millard and Cohen to sign a statement that neither knew Kramer or had any intention of discussing the agreement with him.[52]

Later that afternoon, a smiling Hepburn emerged from his office and told newsmen that the strike was over, subject to the ratification of the union. He then arranged with Defence Minister Ian Mackenzie for the strikers to use the Armoury for their vote. On the next day, the strikers, by a count of 2205 to 36, voted to go back to work. After fifteen days, the Oshawa strike was over.

The question of who had won the strike now became as prickly as the issues in the strike themselves. In order to justify his somewhat extraordinary activities on behalf of management, Hepburn strove desperately to prove that he had held the CIO at bay. There is little doubt that Hepburn had won a semantic victory. The CIO had been repudiated in writing by the union negotiators and the agreement was signed between "General Motors Company of Canada and the employees of the Company at Oshawa." Nowhere in the contract was there any mention of the CIO, nor even of Local 222 of the UAW. Millard, in the company's view, was simply "an employee on leave of absence." The *Globe and Mail*, echoing Hepburn, viewed the settlement as a "permanent defeat for Lewisism and Communism in Canada."[53]

In fact, it was anything but a victory for Hepburn and his anti-CIO forces. As the *Daily Clarion* correctly pointed out, the Oshawa strike was "the dawn of a new era ... for the CIO victory in Oshawa ... has broken into the hitherto unorganized and terrorized mass production industry." At a rally of the strikers both Millard and Cohen stated that the settlement was a tremendous victory for the CIO, and that any attempt to claim that the union had not been recognized was, in Millard's words, "just child's play." The strikers then passed a resolution "affirming the alliance with the UAW and the CIO with which our union is affiliated" and sent it to Hepburn.[54]

That the settlement was less than a victory, even Hepburn was ready to admit. In the words of the *Financial Post,* he had hoped to demolish the CIO in one great stand, but had succeeded merely in "holding it at arm's length." Even George McCullagh, editor of the *Globe and Mail* (who later took the credit for Hepburn's anti-CIO stand), admitted that the settlement at Oshawa was not the body-blow to the CIO he had hoped for.[55]

The achievement of the Oshawa strikers in fighting and defeating both the power of big business and government inspired workers throughout the country. It gave the CIO the impetus it so badly needed to begin organization in the mass production industries of the country. Hepburn gave the faltering CIO drive the boost it required to make it the threat he and his mine-owner friends had feared. Just as Roosevelt became the "best organizer" for the CIO in the United States, so, in a negative way, Hepburn became the CIO's most successful organizer north of the border.

2
Expulsion 1937-39

The Oshawa strike, and especially Premier Hepburn's antics during it, suddenly turned the rather limited CIO organizing campaign into a violent crusade. The Oshawa strikers had won a great victory for themselves, but even more important, for the CIO they had created the psychology of success and the enthusiasm needed for a massive organizing effort. What Akron and Flint had done south of the border, Oshawa was to do north of it. It was a landmark in Canadian labour history.

What is perhaps most significant about the Oshawa strike is that it was conducted by Canadians without much assistance from the CIO. Although Hugh Thompson was ostensibly in charge of organization, most of the organizing was in fact done by Canadians. Whatever financial assistance the strikers were given came from churches and neighbours. Not one penny of aid came from the United States. Both the CIO and the UAW concluded that neither had the men or the money to help the strikers. In fact, they even refused to call a sympathy strike of GM workers in the United States to support the strikers in Oshawa. Though the UAW had publicly promised to send $100,000, in the end all it could deliver was its best wishes. Thus what the Oshawa strikers achieved, they achieved on their own.

Indeed, it can be argued that the CIO connection was as harmful as it was helpful. Hepburn and his mine-owning friends were not so much opposed to the creation of a union in Oshawa as they were to the possibility of the CIO gaining a foothold in Ontario. And when reports filtered down to Queen's Park from the north that the CIO was organizing the mines, the determination of Hepburn and his cronies to crush the strike hardened. In fact, the CIO had nothing to do with the increased labour activity in the north. Again, all the organizing was being done by a small corps of dedicated amateurs, few of whom had any official connection with the CIO. The General Motors Company agreed to a settlement in Oshawa, not because of the threats of the CIO, but because it desperately needed cars for the Canadian and Commonwealth markets, and these could only be built in Oshawa. Fear of losing these markets to Ford and Chrysler, rather than fear of John L. Lewis and Hugh Thompson, forced General Motors to recognize the union.

Thus the role of the CIO in the Oshawa Strike seems ambiguous. The strike was conducted, financed and settled by Canadians. The CIO played no actual role, except in the minds of Hepburn, the mine-owners, and perhaps most importantly, in the minds of the strikers themselves. Caught up in the mystique of the CIO, they believed the international connection was essential. Even though just two years before, almost half the organized workers of Canada had belonged to Canadian unions, the workers in Oshawa and across the country seemed to think that only American unions could provide the necessary muscle to protect and forward their interests. It was such an attitude, based, perhaps, more on sentiment than fact, which, more than anything else, has doomed national unions in Canada.

Though the victory at Oshawa was a victory for Canadians, it was immediately hailed across the country as a great CIO triumph. Because Hepburn had defined the enemy at Oshawa as the CIO, the CIO was given full credit for a victory it had done little to win.

The successful conclusion of the strike let loose a flood of pent-up CIO activity. While the strike continued organization was at a standstill. But if the CIO could take on both the largest company in the world and the most anti-labour government in the country and defeat them, then nothing could stop it. At least this was the feeling of the Canadian CIO leaders and press at the time.[1] Most of their efforts had been directed towards assisting the strikers at Oshawa. With victory there, they turned back with renewed vigour to mount an organizing campaign unprecedented to that time in Canadian history. Printing presses began working overtime. Young Communists and CCYM members headed out all over southern Ontario to begin organization. Graham Spry, an Ontario CCF leader, complained to David Lewis, the party's national secretary, that "everywhere there is the demand for union organizers, everywhere there is the cry 'labour party', everywhere there is a new attitude, a new public opinion, and everywhere the CCF is almost totally ineffective."[2] He wrote that places such as Galt, Guelph, Brantford, Hamilton, and Kitchener were "hives of labour activity," but the CCF groups in these cities were "really out of touch with the community", that they were "almost useless" and in some cases the groups were "for practical purposes dead." For these reasons, Spry, who had spent all his funds and efforts for the party and had received no support from the party executive, sadly told Lewis that he was resigning his leadership "just at the time when our greatest opportunity has come."

By default therefore, the well-oiled Communist machine was able to take sole advantage of this newly created opportunity. Long before the CIO had undertaken the organization of the mass-production industries, the Communists had maintained an elaborate framework of unions, both inside and outside the Workers Unity League. Some of these had existed only on paper, but they had been built around a faithful and militant nucleus of experienced party members who knew how to chair meetings, make motions, give speeches, print pamphlets, mimeograph handbills, and organize picket lines – all indispensable when thousands of workers without previous trade union experience flocked to union halls.[3] As Tim Buck put it, "our Party had trained and developed a whole cadre of people who knew about unions and knew how to go about organizing them. And the Party members, even though they didn't work in the industry, would go out distributing leaflets, helping to organize the union."[4]

In 1935, when Moscow ordered the Workers Unity League to disband, the Communist unions had moved directly into the Trades and Labor Congress, and shortly thereafter, many of the WUL organizers began organizing for the CIO. Without their aid CIO efforts in Canada would have been vastly circumscribed and conceivably even aborted. Under the guidance and direction of J.B. Salsberg – "the commissar of the trade unions" – such able young Communists as Harvey Murphy, Dick Steele, Harry Hunter, and Alex Welch took charge of the various CIO organizing efforts in Ontario.

Their first task was to capitalize on the victory at Oshawa. No sooner had the ink dried on the Oshawa agreement, than handbills began rolling off the party's mimeograph machines in Toronto and Hamilton. Workers trudging to their jobs at the huge Westinghouse plant in Hamilton on the early morning shift of Monday 28 April, only two days after the Oshawa strike was settled, were met at the plant gates by a bevy of young party members led by Burt McLure handing out handbills. Under a banner headline reading "Oshawa workers win, Hamilton next," the handbill informed the workers that despite the "greatest odds" the CIO had won at Oshawa, and that with this victory "the CIO has opened the doors for all Canadian workers to organize and better their wages and conditions by collective bargaining."[5] It urged the workers to join Local 504 of the United Electrical Workers, a CIO affiliate, which had just been created. Handbills like these were handed out that morning by party members in front of various plants in Hamilton, Toronto, Oshawa, Cornwall, Peterborough, and other industrial centres in southern Ontario.

The days following the strike were euphoric for the CIO. From everywhere across the province appeals poured into Thompson's office in Oshawa asking him to address workers and launch organizing campaigns. On the day that Local 222 accepted the General Motors offer, the Crow's Nest Coal Company in Alberta signed an agreement with the UMW in which the principal demand – recognition of the union's affiliation with the CIO – was granted. Panic-stricken financial page editors ran a host of articles warning that one million unorganized Canadian workers in five major industries – rubber, textile, auto, steel, and metal mining – were soon to be the object of CIO organization. Success by the CIO would, they warned, "cripple" the Canadian economy. In addition, the *Financial Post* reported that the increase in CIO activities in Canada was being paralleled by an "outcropping of strikes and labour restiveness" in other industries not organized by the CIO.[6]

For the next few weeks at least, the *Financial Post's* clarion rang true. From Timmins it was announced that George Anderson, the Communist party organizer, had succeeded in forming a CIO local in the huge McIntyre and Hollinger operations in the area. Another Communist, Alex Welch, supported by his Young Communist League troops, organized a local of the Textile Workers in the large Silknit plant in Toronto, and within a week the several hundred immigrant girls working in the plant were on strike. Welch was also active in the huge Empire Cotton Mills in Welland as well as in textile plants in Cornwall and Peterborough. C.S. Jackson, a young party supporter, had just quit his job as an auditor at the Thor washing-machine plant, and began organizing for the newly created United Electrical Workers. Dick Steele, Harry Hambergh, and Harry Hunter, all active party members, started organizing steel plants in Toronto, Oshawa, Hespeler, and Hamilton. Other party members, led by Bill Walsh, were organizing in the rubber plants of Kitchener, Toronto, and Hamilton. The UAW extended its Oshawa contract to General Motors employees in Windsor and St. Catharines. The CIO impact was also felt in British Columbia where 400 miners, members of a Mine-Mill local in the Cariboo, went out on strike.[7]

These halcyon days for the CIO did not last very long. The Silknit strike was lost, as was the strike in the Cariboo. The first SWOC strike in Canada, in the small Cuthbert plant in Montreal, was also defeated. A good number of those who had signed up with the CIO in the first flush of enthusiasm after Oshawa drifted away. By August, 1937, CIO organization had come to a standstill. Despite its twelve months of activity SWOC had contracts in only three small plants in Oshawa and Hespeler, and had signed up only a handful of steel workers in Hamilton. The rubber workers had been even less successful; some plants had been partially organized, but even in these the union membership was rapidly declining. The UAW had succeeded in organizing only a few small auto part plants in Oshawa and Windsor, and the UE had nothing to show for its four months of activity. But even more disillusioning was the fact that several textile locals left the CIO and returned to the TLC, largely because the resistance of the employers to the CIO proved too great to be overcome.

The CIO collapse following Oshawa is readily understandable. Canadian CIO organizers were completely on their own. There was absolutely no support from below the border – no money, no organizers, no advice. The CIO hierarchy in the United States was just too involved in its own projects to lend much assistance or thought to Canada. As one relieved hostile observer wrote: "There has been no noticeable repetition in Canada of the CIO system below the border – turning whole squads and battalions of organizers loose on a particular plant, area, or industry, selected for penetration." Indeed, by October, largely because of the worst business recession for several years, CIO organization in Canada had come to a standstill. In addition, the determined opposition of premiers Hepburn and Duplessis as well as their utilization of the provincial police at their disposal, had broken several CIO organizing efforts. Hepburn's landslide election in the fall of 1937 on an anti-CIO ticket further demoralized the CIO, despite a heartening though somewhat imaginative *Globe and Mail* report that CIO agents were planning to kidnap Hepburn's two children.[8]

The antagonism of industrial leaders was also unyielding. A survey of Canadian businessmen conducted by the *Financial Post* revealed that they would resist the CIO to the "very end" and "by all means at their command." The *Post* noted that "companies are revealing themselves prepared to close their plants ... rather than give ground before the CIO advance."[9]

Against this combined offensive from both government and business, the CIO could do little. As it was, it was already finding itself spread much too thinly across a wide front in the United States, and hampered at every turn by its lack of money and personnel. Of even more importance, however, CIO leaders in the United States had made the significant strategic decision that organization in Canada would have to be undertaken by Canadians themselves. For this reason Hugh Thompson was transferred from Oshawa to Buffalo. From there he would look after CIO organization in upstate New York, but would also be close enough to lend advice to the Canadian organizers. As Sidney Hillman, the 'theoretician' of the CIO put it: "Canada must develop its own leaders if it is to have a sound labour movement." Both John L. Lewis and Hillman felt that organization in Canada would have to wait until there was sufficient Canadian personnel to carry out the job.[10]

Both Lewis and Hillman were admitting the obvious: that CIO organization in Canada was almost entirely the work of Canadians; little help had been given in the past, and now even less would be given in the future. Canadian organizers for the CIO would again be on their own, though they could still use the CIO label. But in fact, the advantages of using the CIO name seemed dubious. Whenever and wherever the three magic letters appeared, employer and government resistance stiffened immeasurably. Canadian union organizers perhaps would have been more successful had they dropped the CIO affiliation – an affiliation which at the time provided little of benefit to the Canadian organizers and workingmen.

Significantly, just when the CIO was deciding to respect Canadian autonomy, the AFL was increasing its pressure on the TLC to follow orders and suspend all its CIO affiliates. As early as March 1937, AFL organizers had received instructions to destroy the CIO. John Noble, president of the Toronto and District Labor Council and AFL organizer in Ontario, warned that the CIO would severely damage the Canadian labour movement and must be kept out of Canada. Nonetheless, following the lead of its vice-president, John Buckley, the Toronto Council publicly supported the CIO strike in Oshawa. Bowing to the relentless pressure from the AFL president, William Green, Noble then demanded that the Hamilton Labor Council expel its CIO unions. By a vote of 51 to 22, the Council refused and Noble lifted its charter and suspended it from the TLC – the first suspension of an organization supporting the CIO in Canada. Though the breach was healed through the mediation of TLC president Paddy Draper, the CIO issue continued to bedevil the TLC.[11]

At all costs, the Congress wished to avoid the split that had occurred in its parent organization below the border. At the 1937 TLC convention there were more than 125 delegates from CIO-affiliated unions. A bitter floor fight was avoided only by the last-minute decision of the executive to combine the several dozen resolutions on the CIO issue into one general statement urging all groups to refrain from any "harmful" activity pending negotiations between the CIO and the AFL. Furthermore, the TLC executive offered to act as a mediator between the two hostile camps in the United States. For the time being at least, because of the relative impotence of the CIO and the unwillingness of the TLC to join battle, Canada remained on the sideline of the bloody inter-union strife below the border.

On the whole, however, the year 1937 had not been a total failure for the CIO in Canada. From a reported membership of 46,000 in 1936, the CIO claimed that by the end of 1937 it represented upwards of 65,000 workers in

Canada. Though this number was vastly exaggerated, there was no doubt that the CIO had greatly enlarged its membership in Canada, although most of the increase had taken place in the first six months of the year. As well, CIO regional offices were set up in Toronto, Hamilton, Oshawa, Calgary, and Peterborough, and organizing staffs were greatly expanded. The decision to use only Canadian personnel prompted John L. Lewis to appoint Silby Barrett CIO director and SWOC subregional director in central Canada. There was already a CIO director of organization for Western Canada in Calgary – Bob Livett of the UMW – but it had become quite apparent that the vast membership potential of southern Ontario would require special attention. It was to be Barrett's task to co-ordinate CIO and SWOC activity in this area.[12]

The task proved extremely difficult. In January 1938, under the authority of the infamous Padlock Law, Quebec provincial police raided the Montreal homes of Quebec SWOC organizer Lucien Dufour and several of his aides and confiscated all union records. Using these, the police then raided the homes of members of the union. Within a few short weeks the SWOC lodge in Montreal of approximately one thousand men was officially disbanded. It was rebuilt shortly thereafter on the basis of 'very carefully concealed groups'.[13]

Emboldened by the support of Duplessis and Hepburn, the large steel companies refused to negotiate with SWOC. Indeed, the entire union executive in the huge Dofasco plant in Hamilton was fired, while workers at the Stelco works seen reading the SWOC publication *Steel Shots* were summarily dismissed. So intimidated was the union that SWOC regional secretary, Dick Steele, sadly reported that in March of 1938 only 16 percent of those who had orginally signed up with SWOC in the previous year were still paying dues. Sensibly, the union refused to publish the names of the sixty-one delegates attending the June conference of Ontario SWOC lodges in Toronto "in order to protect members against the danger of discrimination."[14]

The major problem facing CIO unions in Quebec and Ontario was that whatever labour legislation there was worked to the advantage of the employers. In Canada there was nothing comparable to the Wagner Act; companies were not compelled by law to negotiate with their employees' representatives. Only in Nova Scotia – where the UMW was politically powerful – was there such legislation. Thus CIO unions in Canada found it difficult to follow policy decisions arrived at in the United States. For this reason, at a special SWOC policy conference in Pittsburgh on 6 June, 1938, Silby Barrett demanded that the Canadian section of the union be granted autonomy. There was no opposition to this demand and on 1 July, 1938, Canada became the fourth regional district of SWOC. Barrett confidently assumed that this meant that all Canadian dues would be transferred back to the Canadian regional office, and that collective bargaining decisions would be made in Canada rather than in Pitts-burgh. In fact, however, the opposite was true; most of the dues remained in the United States and all important decisions were still made south of the border.[15] Nevertheless, the CIO decision to use only Canadian organizers and the SWOC decision to give its Canadian section autonomy were to prove the twin keystones upon which the CIO was to build its organization in Canada.

SWOC was not the only CIO union with problems; internal disputes seemed to be tearing apart the UAW. Unlike SWOC which had been created and staffed by experienced unionists from the UMW, the UAW was the handiwork of the auto workers themselves. This inexperience, and the bitter rivalry among the leaders of the larger locals, were greater threats to the survival of the union than the hostility of the large automobile companies. The UAW in 1937 resem-bled, in one observer's words, "nothing so much as a feudal kingdom."[16] President Homer Martin was surrounded by a group of self-reliant, independ-ent men whose loyalty was to their own districts and ambitions rather than to their president and their union. And with good cause: Martin had proved a disaster as leader of the UAW. He was an orator – almost a demagogue – an emotional, impulsive, irresponsible man with no administrative ability, no program, and no conception of trade unionism.

The UAW was also beset by a plethora of political groups which had coalesced into two principal caucuses. The "unity" caucus was made up largely of militant socialists and communists, who found a common bond in their violent antipathy for Martin. On the other hand, the "progressive" caucus, led by Martin, was strongly anti-communist, and was guided ideologi-cally by Jay Lovestone, a zealous anti-communist. The schism in the UAW was fanned by Martin's decision to purge many of the more capable "unity" leaders from staff positions. Only the appearance of John L. Lewis at the 1937 UAW convention in Milwaukee prevented the union from dissolving in a morass of recriminations.

To a lesser extent this squabbling was emulated north of the border. Though Millard did his best to stop the turmoil in the UAW at the border, he was no more successful than Hepburn had been in attempting to keep out the CIO. Millard, however, was largely the author of his own misfortunes. As an active proselytizing CCFer, Millard brought the strife between the CCF and the Com-munist party in the union to a head. But even more damaging, in the struggle below the border he aligned himself closely with the Martin group, at a time when the Communist party as well as most rank-and-file Canadian workers were supporting the "unity" caucus. Though Millard was unanimously re-elected president of Local 222 in March of 1938, most of his fellow executive members were supporters of the "unity" caucus. As a result Martin came to

Oshawa, ostensibly to help celebrate the first anniversary of Local 222, but actually to help consolidate his personal support. He did not succeed. In the July election for three representatives to the newly created Ontario regional council of the UAW, the "unity" group captured all three positions. Millard's position became even more untenable when Martin refused to accept the conference's recommendation that the Canadian section be given complete autonomy. He argued that the conference acted merely as an advisory body and did not represent the will of the rank-and-file worker. When Millard accepted this explanation, he was accused by Local 195 in Windsor of being nothing more than "Martin's rubber stamp."[17]

The opposition to Millard was growing. The "unity" forces controlled the executives of all four Canadian locals (222 in Oshawa, 199 in St. Catharines, and 195 and 200 in Windsor). The opposition in Canada, moreover, was largely to Millard rather than to Martin. Many autoworkers felt that Millard was spending too much of his time at UAW offices in Detroit, and too little in Canada helping organize and strengthen the new locals. More significantly, the Communists had finally decided to use their influence to get rid of Millard. A CCF leader in Ontario, E.B. Jolliffe, pointedly warned David Lewis that "the CP is making a big effort to get control in Ontario and oust Millard."[18]

The dominance of the Communist party in the UAW at this time was supreme. In fact, so influential was the party that the international headquarters in Detroit would ship the weekly edition of *The United Automobile Worker* to Communist party headquarters on Adelaide Street in Toronto to be distributed to the various UAW locals in southern Ontario.[19] Much of the early organizing in the auto field had been done by Communists, and though there were few party members in the union, the party had built up a legacy of good will which would allow it to influence the UAW for the next ten years. At the time the party opposed Millard less because he was in Martin's camp than because, as an executive of the CCF, Millard would undoubtedly move the UAW from the Communist into the CCF orbit.

As Martin's position became more precarious so did that of Millard. In June 1938, Martin suspended five of the seven executive officers of the UAW, including secretary-treasurer George Addes. In protest, six members of the 24-member executive board (but significantly not Millard) walked out of the board and refused to attend any further meetings. At this point Sidney Hillman and Phillip Murray, chairman of SWOC, acting as Lewis' special representatives, intervened in an attempt to restore harmony. They convinced Martin to lift the suspensions and to approve a new "peace plan" formulated by the CIO which would "eliminate factionalism and institute a new harmony." Unfortunately any hope for harmony and unity was shattered in January 1939 when

Martin denounced John L. Lewis and the entire CIO organization, suspended fifteen of the twenty-four members of the executive board, and called a special convention for the fourth of March. The suspended members, fully supported by the CIO, constituted themselves the official UAW executive and called their own convention for 27 March in Cleveland.

This time Martin had gone too far even for Millard. He denounced Martin's act as unconstitutional and agreed to attend the insurgent convention on 27 March. The anti-Martin forces gained control of the *United Automobile Worker* by obtaining the union mailing list at a Detroit printing plant. In turn the Martin forces occupied union headquarters and thus gained control of the union's records. The UAW was in shambles. So bad was the situation that Millard was talking out loud of leading the Canadian locals out of the UAW and founding a strictly Canadian auto workers' union. It took some eloquent persuasion by Silby Barrett and Sol Spivak of the Amalgamated Clothing Workers to change Millard's mind. In turn, Millard charged that it was actually the Communist faction in the UAW in Canada "guided by J.L. Cohen and Salsberg" which was trying "to separate the Canadian UAW from the parent organization in order to gain control of the union." Significantly, Millard hinted at his own unhappiness with the American relationship when he warned the "unity" leader George Addes that there were so many "strictly Canadian problems" that the UAW members in Canada "were becoming less interested in even considering the Martin angle." In any event, Millard wired Addes that the Canadian regional conference supported the anti-Martin forces and would attend the Cleveland convention of the pro-CIO elements.[20]

This was to be the last convention Millard attended as leader of the UAW in Canada. At a stormy caucus meeting of the Canadian delegates to the convention, Millard was attacked from all sides. Speaker after speaker pointed out that the sorry record of the UAW in Canada was largely the result of Millard's ineptitude. He was accused of failing to organize the Chrysler and Ford plants in Windsor, and other plants in Peterborough, Chatham, and Brantford. He was charged with introducing factionalism into the Canadian section, of publicly denouncing John L. Lewis and the CIO, of maligning the "unity" group, and of being the "Canadian shadow of Homer Martin."[21] By a vote of 27 to 9 George Burt, the candidate of the "unity" group, defeated Millard for the post of Canadian representative. Burt's election proved to be an inspired gesture since he was acceptable to all factions in the union. Though he was the "unity" candidate Burt was nevertheless not a Communist. For the next ten years, however, he would flirt with strong party elements in the union in an effort to keep out of Canada the disruptive factionalism which would harass the UAW in the United States. He was to prove as flexible in his relations with the extreme left as Millard was unbending. He was to succeed in keeping the UAW in Canada intact, where as Millard could only have failed.

Though Millard was taken aback by the vitriolic attack against him, he was not at all surprised by his defeat. For more than a year he had realized that his days with the UAW were numbered.[22] As an ardent anti-Communist in a union whose Communist element was strong, and as a defender of the discredited Martin forces long after Martin had shown himself to be a "traitor" to the CIO, Millard realized that he no longer controlled the Canadian section of the union. Nonetheless, largely because of the prominent role he played in the Oshawa strike Millard was still identified in the public eye as "Mr. CIO" in Canada or as the "John L. Lewis of the north."

Capitalizing on his reputation, immediately after the Cleveland convention Millard pleaded with Lewis to make him CIO director in central Canada. In a letter to Lewis' assistant, John Brophy, Millard stated that because of his role in Oshawa he was strongly identified in the public mind with the CIO, and would therefore be a valuable addition to the CIO in Canada. He argued that the time had arrived for a fullscale organization campaign in Canada, and since Burt was "very parochial" he was not equipped to speak in any way for the CIO. He added that Burt was "playing into the hands of those who sponsor National Unions," even though Millard agreed that "a national policy for Canada by the CIO body would have a great public appeal because politically the 'Good Neighbour policy' of President Roosevelt is very popular." On the following day, 6 May 1939, Millard was hired as the CIO representative in Ontario to work as Silby Barrett's aide at eight dollars a day.[23]

The position of the Canadian CIO when Millard took over as Barrett's assistant was quite different from what it had been the year before. The year 1938 had failed to bring about any of the great expectations of the CIO organizers. Indeed, membership in CIO unions in Canada had declined drastically from 1937; the UAW was down by over one thousand; both Rubber and Electric had lost half their membership; the Woodworkers were down by a third; SWOC membership declined by two thousand; Textile did not even bother filing a report. In large part, the decline in CIO membership (except for the established UMW and ACW whose membership had actually increased) was attributable to the business recession that had begun at the end of 1937 and had lasted through 1938. Nonetheless, the lack of central organization and the onslaughts from both industry and other labour groups had taken their toll of CIO efforts.

It was further demoralized by the decision of the TLC to oust its CIO unions. The efforts of the TLC leadership to keep the CIO split out of Canada had failed because the AFL leadership south of the border had wished it to fail. Over the heated opposition of president Draper of the Congress, Green and the AFL executive were unyielding in their pressure to force the TLC to suspend the CIO unions. They received support from most Canadian craft unions and from the district labour councils throughout the country which were dominated by these unions. Only the CIO unions and the Communists supported Draper. But the CCF was ambivalent. Most members wished to preserve unity, but not at the cost of alienating the TLC leadership. Jolliffe warned David Lewis that the "whole question of a split was so charged with dynamite that any outsider attempting to take part would get into trouble." The official CCF policy was therefore to call for unity – "but very tactfully."[24]

At the annual convention of the TLC in September 1938 Draper prevailed. For the forty-five resolutions on the CIO issue the Congress executive substituted a resolution calling for unity of the labour movement in Canada, and offering the Congress once again as an arbiter between the two factions in the United States. At the same time it emphasized that any "action taken shall be on terms acceptable to international trade unions thus avoiding any disregard for or defiance of their laws and policies." The resolution, in the words of one of the delegates, "was rushed through before anyone had a chance to speak" and was passed by a vote of 526 to 18. In fact, some delegates did have time to shout at Draper that "the whole matter was being railroaded" through the convention. Significantly, however, the executive council in its annual report specifically pointed out that it had the constitutional power "to disaffiliate unions which encouraged secession or dual unionism." Furthermore, the executive made quite apparent that in the past year "conditions have arisen ... which would have warranted your executive disassociating a number of its affiliated international unions from membership. It was considered however, that the spirit of the resolutions adopted at our last convention would be best served by leaving the decision ... to this convention."[25]

On the whole, the convention was a victory for the forces of unity. SWOC organizer Dick Steele exultantly informed Philip Murray that Green had been thwarted "in his attempt to utilize the Trades and Labor Congress of Canada as a means of stabbing the CIO in the back." In keeping with the Communist line at the time, Steele stressed that since the "unity of the Trades and Labor Congress ... is the first essential for the successful organization of the unorganized workers in Canada," Murray must take a "strong stand in support of the TLC position" at the forthcoming CIO convention in Pittsburgh. Murray's reply was non-committal. Though nothing was said concerning Canada at this convention, three of the Canadian delegates to the convention, Millard, Jackson, and Harold Pritchett of the Woodworkers in British Columbia, met privately and decided that if relations worsened with the TLC, the CIO would set up its own Canadian committee to direct all CIO activities in Canada. The proposal was brought to Murray, who approved it, though he thought it somewhat "academic" until the TLC actually expelled its CIO unions.[26]

Within a month, the proposal was no longer academic. At the AFL convention in November 1938, Green ordered the TLC to expel the CIO affiliates, or the AFL would sever its relationship with its Canadian counterpart. This meant that all TLC affiliates would lose their AFL charters. The following week Draper met with Barrett and informed him that unless the Canadian CIO affiliates cut their ties with the American organization, the TLC would be forced to expel them. In January 1939, while Draper lay gravely ill in an Ottawa hospital, the executive of the Trades and Labor Congress went ahead and suspended the CIO unions. Ironically, despite the suspension order the CIO unions were permitted to keep their positions on most of the local labour councils throughout the country, and D.W. Morrison of the UMW was not removed from the TLC executive.[27]

As soon as the suspension order was issued, Barrett contacted all the CIO representatives in the country. They agreed that no independent congress should be set up as the suspension order "did not basically effect CIO relations with the local AFL unions." Barrett believed that the "rank and file of the AFL in Canada [was] determined to defeat the effort of the small number of road-men of the AFL to provoke a conflict" and that the CIO's strategy should be to bide its time until the rank and file could make its feelings known to the TLC executive. But Barrett was opposed to setting up a separate congress for a more significant reason. At an earlier meeting with Millard he had been apprised of the overriding influence of the Communists within the CIO organizations in central Canada. Millard's views, as he outlined them to several CCF leaders at an informal conference, were that the head office of SWOC in Toronto under Dick Steele had become "the centre of Communist trade union activity in Toronto" and that the Communists were "likely to make a strong attempt to control the CIO in Canada should a separate organization eventually be formed as a result of expulsions from the Trades and Labor Congress."[28]

Another result of the suspension was a most extraordinary correspondence, in the spring of 1939, between AFL president Green and John Buckley, a staunch craft unionist, yet leader of the pro-CIO forces within the TLC.[29] Angered by the Toronto District Labor Council's support of a CIO affiliate, the American Newspaper Guild, in a jurisdictional fight with an AFL local, Green accused Buckley and his council of "deception," of being an affiliate of the AFL and yet always supporting the CIO. In turn, Buckley told Green that his 'imputations' against the Council were "unbecoming the dignity" of his office, that Green had not looked carefully into the situation, and that he must not cloak himself in the "garment of infallibility" in the CIO-AFL dispute. Green, enraged, then accused Buckley of having an "antagonistic attitude towards the AFL," and of "sailing under false colours," supporting the CIO while being an officer of an AFL organization. In conclusion he added: "I am suffering under no illusions, I have watched the recorded action of you and others in Toronto, in which you have reflected your hostility, yes, your antagonism towards the American Federation of Labor. I resent your action. No sophistry in which you indulge and no reference "to unbecoming dignity" as you have indulged in your letter can offset the facts. I know what you are, and have placed you where you belong for that reason."

Finally, Buckley in closing the correspondence wrote: "as reason, truth and logic, seem to have no place in your mental make-up, and as I do not deal in sophistry, our mentalities are as far apart as the poles. In the past, I have remained tolerably passive, under the accusation you have made upon myself, and my associate trade unionists, in which you indulge on every possible occasion ... but I for one do not recognize in you any such vast immeasurable superiority to myself, as to entitle you to pronounce, dictatorially, upon my moral tendencies, my principals or my mentality. Above all I do not discern in you that calmness of judgment, or of temperament, or that impartiality in collecting and weighing evidence, that power of representing to yourself the feelings of others or that accurate knowledge of the minds and motives of men, that are so necessary in carrying out so high a judicial office faithfully ... In the past it has been considered a mark of wisdom to deride all progressive schemes or ideas of human progress as visionary. Yet in the majority of cases posterity has been wiser than the generation that preceded them. To call an individual Communist or pro-CIO is not proof of wisdom or even infantile intelligence. It is what any fool could do, but unfortunately the fools have always had a majority in our democracies, and have created that type of reasoning like the howl of packs, presuming that weight of numbers gives them the reputation of exceptional intelligence ...

'So far as I am concerned this concludes this regrettable interchange of letters that should have had no part in the American Labor movement, but as an Englishman and a Canadian by adoption, I cannot but refuse to concede to any individual no matter how highly placed he may be, or what his authority or personal ego, may entitle him to, to make a personal attack upon myself, as an individual, when I was acting on behalf of, and without the instructions of, a collective body, without giving a vigorous reply, as I am not to be intimidated by threats, misled by premises, or imposed upon by authority.'

Symbolically, Buckley's letter manifested the same pent-up frustrations that prompted John L. Lewis as the representative of the struggling new industrial unions to bloody the nose of "Big Bill" Hutcheson, the 300-pound president of the Carpenters, and staunch opponent of the "new unionists," at the 1935 CIO convention. Buckley's was the last gesture of defiance by those who resented the AFL intrusion into the Canadian labour movement.

But the most significant result of the suspension was the CIO's decision to intensify its organizational campaign. The suspension, in Barrett's opinion, would draw CIO representatives closer together to enable them to launch a broad organization campaign "throughout the country." It was to be Millard's first task as a CIO official to direct this campaign.[30]

At first his appointment had surprised and angered Barrett who had not been consulted beforehand. (Indeed it was almost three weeks after Millard was appointed that Barrett was told.) But Barrett's reaction was mild in contrast to that of other members of the CIO. In response to a request from president R.J. Thomas of the UAW, Barrett ordered Millard to investigate the internal problems of the UAW locals in Windsor. As soon as the local leaders in Windsor got word of this, they immediately complained to Barrett that they had no confidence in Millard and that his past record did not qualify him for any position in the labour movement. George Burt also protested that Millard should no longer "mix into" UAW affairs. Although Millard felt that he could help in "composing the internal situation" in Windsor, he thought it wiser, because of Burt's opposition, not to interfere. Moreover, he believed that the UAW was "washed up here in Canada" and that Burt was "like a blind man leading the blind."[31]

Millard's appointment had also come as a shock to the CIO organizers in Ontario. Naturally the Communists and their supporters – Hunter, Steele and Hambergh of SWOC, Welch of Textile, and Jackson of the UE – who had been directing CIO activities were upset. They believed that a man like Millard, who had been repudiated by his own union, was not the suitable person to take over the CIO in Ontario. More significantly, they feared the intrusion of a dedicated anti-Communist like Millard would undermine both CIO organizing activity and more importantly party strength in the labour movement. Millard's frosty reception at the CIO office at 302 Manning Chambers in Toronto continued for some weeks until the party decided, in Salsberg's words, that "labour unity was more important than one person" and that the party people should co-operate with Millard in the hope that if they "gave him enough rope he would hang himself." Within a week of the party's decision, Millard was able to tell Barrett that "Brother Jackson is doing a good job directing publicity, and Brothers Steele and Hambergh have given of their time and services in many ways."[32]

Late in June, Barrett left the CIO organization in Nova Scotia in the hands of the recently appointed organizer Foreman Way, and headed west to take charge of CIO activities in central Canada. His most important responsibility was to organize the "Coordinating Committee of the CIO Unions in Canada." The strength of the Communists in the CIO may be gauged from the composition of the delegates to the first meeting of this committee on 27 June, 1939. On the Communist side were Jackson, Hambergh, Steele, and Leo Robin of the Fur Workers. There were only two anti-Communists – Millard and Joe Mackenzie of the Rubber Workers. The other delegates (aside from Barrett) – Karl Scott of the Shoe Workers, George Burt, and Roger Irwin of the Newspaper Guild – were "fence-sitters," but usually voted with the Communists. Fortunately, at the time, the policies of the party – which was still in its "united front" phase – coincided with those of the CIO, so that clashes were rare.

In his speech to the committee, Barrett explained that he had called the representatives of the CIO unions together in order "to find ways and means of coordinating the efforts of these unions locally and later nationally." He emphasized that coordination among CIO unions was essential because of the hostile activities of the TLC. The delegates discussed the efforts of their individual unions to organize the unorganized; most concluded that these efforts suffered from lack of concerted action, finances, and publicity, as well as from the "slanderous attack of the manufacturers ... encouraged by AFL official splitters and the Ontario Government." It was decided that a committee headed by Dick Steele and including Millard and Sol Spivak of the ACW would prepare a detailed report on the Canadian situation for John L. Lewis. The question of financing the organizing campaign was also discussed, but after a lengthy debate was referred to the Steele committee for recommendations. As for the CIO attitude towards the TLC, the committee decided that it "must leave no stone unturned to strengthen the pro-unity forces in the AFL by sharpening the exposure of William Green's representatives in Canada who would unscrupulously extend the formal division at the top to the entire rank-and-file membership which had maintained unity." Finally the committee decided to hold a strategy meeting before the TLC convention, and, in the interim, only Barrett, Hunter, and Steele – but significantly not Millard – were authorized to make statements regarding the relationship between the two labour centres.[33]

In July the committee met to approve the report of Steele, Millard, and Spivak. The report pointed out that of the 1,288,000 Canadian workers directly within its jurisdiction, the CIO had organized less than five per cent. Furthermore, the average weekly wage for industrial workers was less than $20, while

84 per cent of Canada's wage earners received less than $10 per week. With the minimum subsistence level set by the government at $21.50 per week, most of Canada's working force was obviously earning well below that figure. The report also pointed out that the two most industrialized and populous provinces – Ontario and Quebec – had the worst labour and social welfare legislation. With regard to organizational activities, it stated that "the greatest contribution which the CIO in Canada can make to genuine trade union unity will be increased membership." To facilitate this, it suggested "the establishment of a central organizing body with adequate financial resources" and the appointment of a publicity director and a legal counsel. Above all, the report concluded that the CIO "must now launch a Canadian crusade for industrial democracy" and warned that an unorganized Canada would "become a menace to the American labour movement." The report was adopted unanimously by the Committee, and Barrett and Steele were delegated to present it to Lewis. In addition, the committee decided that "no effort must be spared in encouraging and supporting the pro-unity element" in the Trades and Labor Congress at its September convention.[34]

This effort was doomed. The CIO had lost a champion in the TLC leading circles with the retirement of Paddy Draper. More importantly, Green had also ordered all unions affiliated with the AFL to vote for the CIO expulsion or have their charters lifted.[35]

Responding to Green's decision, the committee issued a press statement denouncing "the reactionary Tory" John Noble, and his "unscrupulous clique of American Federation of Labor officials" for refusing "to abide by the decision of the Trades and Labor Congress membership which at three consecutive conventions overwhelmingly voted to maintain unity of the AFL and CIO unions with the Trades and Labor Congress of Canada." The Committee accused these men of attempting "to provoke internecine strife" in the Canadian labour movement against the will of the majority of labour councils, unions, and workers. The CIO was particularly enraged with the TLC decision to set up an automobile union in Windsor to siphon off membership from the two established UAW – CIO locals in the area.[36]

With the CIO unions barred from the TLC convention of September 1939 in Niagara Falls, their expulsion from the TLC was assured. Nonetheless the debate on the expulsion issue was long and acrid. The TLC executive admitted that it was compelled to suspend the CIO unions "in order to retain in membership during 1939 those organizations affiliated with the American Federation of Labor." It justified its position by pointing out that at its convention in Pittsburgh, the Committee for Industrial Organization had changed its name to the Congress of Industrial Organizations and had thus "become a dual organization." Buckley strongly fought the resolution on the grounds that in a time of crisis, when Canada was at war, unity was more essential than ever. In turn, the acting president, R.J. Tallon, countered that the TLC had been warned by most international unions that they would no longer remit taxes on their Canadian membership if the CIO unions were to remain in the Congress. The Communists, led by J.L. Salsberg, who was the strategist for all the unity forces at the convention, all spoke forcefully against the resolution. They warned, in the words of C.M. Stewart, that "the employing class are watching and hoping that the split will be made and the movement handed over to reactionaries." A delegate from the Railway Carmen argued that the suspended unions should have been given a chance to present their case to the Congress and urged that the resolution be submitted to a vote of the entire Canadian membership including the suspended CIO unions.[37]

The vote to expel the CIO was carried by 231 to 98, a margin of 133. Significantly, the CIO unions barred from the Convention had been entitled to approximately 160 votes. Because it was not allowed a voice in deciding its future in the Congress, the CIO was forced to set out on its own, and thus begin a new and important chapter in the history of the Canadian labour movement.

3
The merger 1939-40

The CIO's reaction to its expulsion was not long in coming. At a hastily convened meeting in Toronto on 4 October, 1939, the CIO representatives in Canada decided to set up a Canadian Committee for Industrial Organization to "coordinate the work of the CIO unions in Canada in order to initiate and direct a powerful organization drive." The representatives at this meeting had considered forming a new labour congress rather than a committee, but decided that the latter was a more attractive magnet for "other organized bodies [who] might wish to cooperate." It was also decided to hold the founding convention in November in Ottawa so that the CIO unions attending the convention could "present matters of vital concern to the government ... concerning social and labour legislation." Soon after this meeting, Barrett met John L. Lewis at the CIO convention in San Francisco to discuss the Canadian situation. Lewis agreed that the Canadian Committee would serve the dual function of a co-ordinating body for CIO organizing activities in Canada and a lobbying body to meet with government representatives.[1]

This Committee's first meeting took place on 25 October in Ottawa. Present were Barrett as chairman, Millard as secretary, and Spivak, Hunter, Jackson, Burt, Mackenzie, Irwin, Tommy Church of Mine-Mill, Bob Livett of the UMW in the West, and Donald Morrison of the UMW in the East. They decided to call a conference of all CIO affiliates in Canada to discuss how to unite the CIO "forces most effectively in order to organize the unorganized." The Committee also made arrangements to meet with the federal Minister of Labour, Norman McLarty, to present its brief. Later that week the Committee decided to invite the Algoma Steel Workers Union, which was an affiliate of the strongly anti-international All-Canadian Congress of Labour, to attend the national conference of steel workers called by SWOC for the day before the CIO convention.

Though the Committee had only two weeks to plan the conference it was a glorious success. Millard proudly reported to Allan Haywood, the CIO Director of Organization, that "it was the first major move of the Canadian Committee for Industrial Organization ... Though hurried, because it was necessary to place certain matters before the government, nevertheless it was well attended ... received very favourable publicity and undoubtedly constitutes an important step forward."[2] Attending were 105 delegates from 29 locals representing 55,000 workers in nine international unions (Auto, Steel, Rubber, Electric, Mine-Mill, Newspaper Guild, Shoe Workers, Mine Workers, and Fur Workers).

On the day before the convention began, 4 November, delegates of SWOC locals in Hamilton, Sydney and Toronto met with representatives of the Algoma Steel Workers from Sault Ste Marie and discussed common problems such as wages and working conditions. They then drafted a resolution for submission to the federal government calling for a conference of workers, owners, and government officials. The fact that a CIO and an ACCL affiliate could meet and present a common front was a significant harbinger of future developments in the Canadian labour movement.

The CIO conference opened with a short address from Barrett urging the delegates to "take off your coats, roll up your sleeves" and "work like never before ... to organize the unorganized." Millard then read the Committee's report entitled *CIO Autonomous in Canada*. It stated that the main purpose of creating the new Committee was to help the war effort by "coordinating the activities of the CIO unions in Canada" and by launching campaigns to "organize the large number of unorganized workers in Canada." It stressed that, though the CIO in Canada accepted the policies of the CIO in the United States, because the CIO was "founded upon an intimate exchange of ideas, habits, and mutual assistance with the US organization ... nevertheless mutual respect for each other's national problems finds its frank expression in a recognition of each other's autonomy in all matters of policy appertaining to organization and legislation in each other's individual status." The report went on to emphasize the Committee's intention to fight for higher living standards, legal recognition of collective bargaining in all industries, and a reunified Canadian labour movement. Finally it demanded that labour be given representation on all government war boards and agencies, that efforts be made to stop profiteering, that wage levels be adjusted to rising prices, that the war effort not detract attention from "internal economic security," and, finally, that neither labour and social legislation nor democratic rights be curtailed because of the war.[3]

One of the major purposes of the conference according to Millard was for the delegates to "speak their minds" on what the policy of the CIO should be. Some thirty-five delegates took Millard at his word and spoke on subjects ranging from rockbursts in the mines to the necessity for ladies' auxiliaries. The theme of the conference was emphasized in the peroration of Barrett's opening speech. "The front line of the fight for freedom," he said, "is here." Indeed, none of the resolutions adopted said anything about supporting the soldiers overseas; the stress was on the workers at home. A resolution calling for the nationalization of the country's basic industries was unanimously adopted. The sentiments of the delegates were best articulated by Dick Steele. In his report on organization, Steele passionately pleaded that, though Canada was at war, the CIO must "launch a crusade to bring industrial democracy into every Canadian plant." "Our influences, our times, our energies, our devotion to the crusade of labour, everything we have that is possible," he concluded, "must be thrown into this crusade."

The emphasis on the home front indicates how powerful the Communists and their supporters were in the CIO. As a result of the Nazi-Soviet Pact, the policy of the party had suddenly changed from support of all measures against Hitler to denunciation of the war as "another conflict between capitalist countries." That the conference supported this view was not surprising since 82 of the 105 delegates represented six unions – UAW, United Shoe Workers, SWOC, UE, Fur Workers, Mine-Mill – in which the Communist element was strong and, in the latter four unions, in a position to determine policy.

Even in their submission to the government, the delegates emphasized again and again that the war "must not be allowed to detract attention from unemployment and other pressing problems of internal economic security." The theme of the submission was that "the greatest contribution that can be made to the cause of democracy, peace and prosperity is through the building of a progressive labour movement." To achieve this goal, the Department of Labour would have to "re-examine its function and place itself squarely behind organized labour in its service to the Dominion of Canada." On the question of strikes during the war the Committee argued that, until employers were forced to negotiate with their employees and until the government prohibited discrimination against unions and enforced collective bargaining, the unions would have no recourse but to strike. The Minister of Labour replied that the government was "trying to do its duty," but that since it did not "want a war on two fronts," the CIO must at all costs avoid "unnecessary strikes." Though the CIO was not pleased with the government's reception of its brief, Millard reported to Haywood that the submission had received a great deal of "favourable publicity" and would not only cause the cabinet to give the CIO "more serious consideration than ever before," but would "earn the loyalty and support of those now organized, as well as the unorganized."[4]

Much more significant, however, than anything discussed at the convention, had been a secret meeting of Barrett, Millard, and Hunter with Aaron Mosher, M.M. Maclean, and Norman Dowd, leaders of the All-Canadian Congress of Labour to discuss a merger between their organizations. That the ACCL should be contemplating a merger with the CIO, seemed, on the surface at least, the height of fantasy. The ACCL had been established in 1927 by A.R. Mosher. Its entire *raison d'être* was its opposition to international unionism. During the 1920s and 1930s, Mosher, Maclean, and other ACCL leaders had denounced American unions throughout the length and breadth of Canada. They had bitterly fought both the AFL and the Trades and Labor Congress. And from the moment the CIO had appeared on the Canadian scene, the ACCL had been second to none in the malevolence of its attacks. Indeed after the Oshawa strike, Mosher, its autocratic president, had privately written Hepburn thanking him for attempting to "curb domination by foreign agitators and Communists." At the same time, the *Canadian Unionist,* the ACCL's official periodical, commented that Hepburn had "done a great service to Canadian labour."[5]

The ACCL's hostility was understandable. Aside from the obvious rivalry and competition, the CIO was an American union and seemed to be full of Communists. Both were anathema to the ACCL leadership. In his position as president of the ACCL, Mosher had had many dealings with the Communists, all of them unfortunate. He often complained that he had been "doublecrossed every time he dealt with a Communist." But it was the fact that the CIO was an American creation that caused most of the ACCL's animosity. As soon as the Oshawa strike was settled, Mosher's lieutenant, Norman Dowd, the editor of the *Canadian Unionist,* wrote that he could not "concede that there is room for both US and Canadian unions in this country ... the sooner we get rid of US unions in Canada the better it will be for the workers and people of this country." A later editorial stated that American domination was "detrimental to the best interests of the workers and people of Canada ... an obstacle to national culture and national unity ... and ... should be broken as soon as possible."[6]

The ACCL, however, was in no position to compete with the CIO. In fact the arrival of the CIO in Canada had severely weakened it. According to a CIO analysis, the ACCL was "poorly financed and organizationally impotent." Though the report was naturally biased, its conclusion was nevertheless accurate; aside from Mosher's Canadian Brotherhood of Railway Employees and the recently affiliated Algoma Steel union, the ACCL was simply a "nuisance," and at times acted as an agent of companies wanting to keep out CIO or TLC unions. Understandably, the CIO had nothing but contempt for the ACCL. A SWOC conference in Amherst, Nova Scotia, in March 1939 condemned the ACCL for "disruptive activity" and "co-operating with the steel companies to weaken the collective bargaining unity of the men." Barrett also accused the ACCL of "interfering with the jurisdictional rights of the UMW" amongst New Brunswick miners and Toronto gas workers and charged the ACCL with playing "into the hands of the operators."[7]

But by November 1939, the attitude of CIO had altered considerably. Several months earlier, Mosher had promised to co-operate with the CIO unions by ordering a halt to ACCL organization among workers within the jurisdiction of the CIO. He had kept his word. The ACCL was in danger of disintegrating and Mosher knew it. He needed help; so he began co-operating with the CIO.[8] A major change had occurred in the CIO leadership. Coached by Millard, Barrett had at last become fully aware of the "dangers" of the Communist influence within the CIO. For months the anti-Communist element within the CIO had been attempting to warn Barrett of the possible repercussions of working too closely with the Communists. David Lewis wrote to CCF Member of Parliament Harold Winch, who was on a tour of the Maritimes, that Barrett was "naive" on the subject of Communists, and that Winch should "play up to him a little" and do what he could to wean Barrett away from the Communists toward becoming "a really devoted supporter of the CCF as against any other working class party." It was not until John L. Lewis began "weeding all the Communists out of the CIO in the US" towards the end of 1939 that Barrett finally decided that he must do the same in Canada. Barrett, along with Millard and David Lewis, felt that merger with the strongly anti-Communist ACCL would dilute the Communist element which, for three years, had dominated CIO activity in Canada. The ACCL would also provide the respectability that the CIO had coveted since it entered Canada, along with a valuable printing plant owned by the CBRE. Thus, in November 1939, the needs of the ACCL seemed to coincide with the desires of the CIO, to make possible a merger which several months before would have been impossible.[9]

By the end of November the merger seemed complete. On 27 November, Barrett, Hunter, and Millard met again with Mosher, Maclean, and Dowd. They quickly decided that "if the needs of Canadian industrial workers were to be met, a genuine programme of unity, organization and legislation must be followed." At a meeting on 30 November, a seven-point "memorandum of understanding to form the basis for the purposes and constitution of the new

Canadian Congress of Labour" was adopted. The seven points included: "1/ all organizations affiliated with the new Congress 'shall be autonomous with respect to their economic and legislative policies' and 'shall not be subject to control in these matters outside of Canada'; 2/ that the new Congress should 'exercise both economic and legislative functions,' that is to present briefs to governments and to co-ordinate activities to organize the unorganized; 3/ that all ACCL and CIO affiliates be eligible to join the new Congress and no charter be granted to any new group 'in which National or International unions affiliated with the Congress are functioning'; 4/ that the new Congress should "advocate the industrial organization of Canadian workers on the broadest basis" and should not interfere with the right of each affiliated union to organize workers in its own particular field; 5/ that the Congress should establish a fund for the organization of all unorganized workers in Canadian industries and that this fund should be under the control of the Executive board which would "plan organizing campaigns, employ and assign organizers and ... set up organizing committees for each industry"; 6/ that the new Congress should co-operate with other labour centres in other countries, and that if peace is reached in the US between CIO and AFL forces, that "negotiations for unity in Canada shall be conducted wholly in Canada between the TLC ... and the new Congress"; 7/ and finally, that the CIO unions may provisionally affiliate with the ACCL with the understanding that a convention would soon be called for the adoption of a new constitution and the election of officers."[10]

No sooner had agreement been reached, than some serious obstacles appeared. On 6 December, while on an organizing trip to northern Ontario, Millard was arrested for making "statements prejudicial to security in contravention of Section 39 of the Criminal Code." According to a police report Millard had said that "the manufacturers would take advantage of this war just as they did the last, ... that there would be profiteering unless the government did something to prevent it, ... that men were joining the army because that was the only way they could be sure of eating regularly, ... we should have democracy in Canada before we go to Europe to fight for democracy," and finally, that "there was not a great deal of sense in going to Europe to fight Hitlerism, while there was Hitlerism right here in Canada."[11]

On the day following Millard's arrest, the CIO offices in Toronto were raided by RCMP officers who removed files and documents, not only from Millard's SWOC offices, but from the offices of all the unions in the building. It was somewhat ironic that the government had chosen to arrest the man who was its strongest ally in the labour movement in the battle to undermine Communist influence. Barrett called it an "act by the most labour-hating member

[Attorney-General Gordon Conant] of the most labour-hating government [Hepburn's] in Canada," while George Taylor, president of the Algoma Steel Union, and no ally of Millard's, believed that his arrest on "such a flimsy charge" was the work of the "mine interests who, to keep labour organization away from their domain, have weight enough to have organizers jailed." Though he was never brought to trial, Millard's arrest delayed the merger talks because the ACCL received many letters and telegrams from its affiliates who had heard rumours of the merger and who, because of Millard's sudden notoriety, were anxious to avoid any connection with the CIO.[12]

In fact, the ACCL had been anxious to keep the news of the proposed merger as secret as possible. Very few, even of the ACCL executive board, had been informed of the negotiations. When affiliates requested information, Dowd denied that the Congress was even "contemplating" a merger. Mosher's strategy had been to avoid publicity until the merger was completed. He feared that rumours would stir up opposition to the merger, and to inform his ACCL affiliates he felt would "be a bad move just at the moment." Indeed, it was not until the regular meeting of the ACCL executive board on 28 December that Mosher first informed the other board members of the negotiations. The opposition was bitter. Vice-president Beatty of the Railwaymen's union was suspicious of the motive behind the CIO proposal "as it appeared that they are trying to get control of the Canadian Labour Movement." George Taylor of the Algoma Steel Union accused the CIO of "unethical behaviour." Not until Mosher pointed out that the Canadian branches of the CIO had been given "complete autonomy ... in all matters of legislative and economic policy in Canada," did the Board reluctantly agree to the proposed merger.[13]

Opposition to the proposed merger emanated not only from the ACCL; the CIO was also split on the issue. In the early part of January 1940, Millard met with CIO officials in Buffalo to discuss the merger. He was told that many CIO officials were opposed to the merger because they feared that the new Congress would ultimately sever its international connection in favour of the ACCL's policy of national unions. Millard was also warned that before the CIO would give its approval to the merger the ACCL must transfer its "dual" unions to the appropriate CIO jurisdiction.[14]

When Millard relayed this information to Mosher, the ACCL president agreed to "start immediately to have those dual bodies transferred to CIO unions." The ambitious Mosher was extremely anxious for the merger to be completed. He would brook no delay, would override all opposition, and overcome all obstacles; he was determined to become again the president of a large, powerful, nation-wide labour organization. The ACCL was now too small for Mosher's pretensions.

Finally, on 13 January 1940, on behalf of the 50,000 members of the CIO in Canada, Barrett applied "for affiliation with the ACCL for the purpose of implementing the understanding reached." According to the merger agreement the CIO would pay a two-cent per member per month affiliation fee, the constitution of the new Congress would be "based on the same principles as the CIO" and the executive body would be set up like that of the CIO. Five days later, the ACCL finally wrote to its affiliates informing them of the negotiations and of the proposed merger. It assured them that the status of the Congress would not be changed since the CIO in Canada was autonomous and that the new Congress would "carry on its own affairs without dictation or interference of any kind from those outside of Canada."[15]

But the road to the merger was still strewn with obstacles. On 5 February 1940, Mosher was reported to have told an ACCL local in London, Ontario, that the ACCL would not merge with the CIO unions in Canada until the latter severed all connections with their American parent organizations. Though Mosher hurriedly denied this statement and complained that the press reports of his speech were "wholly untrue," opponents of the merger used the statement to stir up opposition in the CIO to the amalgamation. A disheartened Mosher complained that, while the ACCL was anxious to consummate the merger, negotiations had slowed down considerably because the CIO leaders had "found it necessary to do some spade work amongst some of their organizations ... to smooth out all difficulties." Millard assured him that the CIO was paying no attention to the statements attributed to him, though he did not deny some unions were still dubious about the merger. When Mosher heard that Millard had offered to co-operate with TLC unions in Ontario to defeat the Hepburn administration, he anxiously wrote Millard demanding assurance that the delay in negotiations would not result in "overtures being made by officers of the TLC to certain of the CIO unions" to prevent the CIO's affiliation with the ACCL. Millard patiently soothed the harried Mosher and reassured him that the CIO unions would not renege on their agreement.[16]

The greatest threat to the merger, however, was the attitude of Communists. The party's opposition was not difficult to understand. In the CIO it had played the primary role; within the new merger its role promised to be secondary. All the leading forces behind the merger, Mosher, Millard, and Barrett, were active supporters of the CCF and threatened to take the new Congress along political paths alien to the party. Then, too, after the signing of the Nazi-Soviet Pact, the ardour of the party for labour unity had considerably abated. Taking its cue from the May Day editorial of the party newspaper, the *Clarion*, that "any action to merge the two bodies under a bureaucratic set-up from the top without rank and file participation must be fought vigourously," most Communists within the CIO denounced the proposed merger. Millard informed Mosher that the *Clarion* article had made it clear who was causing the delay in the merger. Similarly, Millard told of opposition from the West Coast CIO unions where the Communists were strong, and from George Burt who was strongly influenced by the Communist elements in his union. On the other hand there were some Communists – Salsberg and Jackson among them – who fought bitterly within party circles in support of the merger. Aware of this split within the party, Mosher wrote Millard that it was sad "that our Communistic friends, while accepting the dictates and leadership of Moscow do not want to accept the leadership of those in Canada who have really done something worthwhile for the workers."[17]

The favoured party tactic of opposition was to undermine support for the merger among the CIO leadership in the United States. Karl Scott of the United Shoe Workers, for example, complained to his international president that if the merger were completed the CIO unions in Canada would lose their CIO identity and that the merger arrangements left "entirely too much to chance." On seeing this letter, Haywood warned Millard that "under no circumstances will any members of the CIO be allowed to affiliate with other groups if it in any way severs it from the CIO, its laws, and policies." Millard quickly replied that Scott's letter was "deliberately misrepresented and largely untrue," and pointed out that opposition to the merger "was based purely on political grounds." He also informed Haywood that Scott had his offices in "one of the recognized Communist headquarters here in Toronto" and that Scott's close associations with party members were doing the CIO "a disservice."[18]

In its May Day issue of 1940, *Clarion* also accused Millard and Barrett of acting dictatorially in ordering the CIO unions to affiliate with the ACCL. The Communist-influenced UAW Local 195 in Windsor continued the offensive with a letter to Haywood complaining that Millard was undermining the CIO in Canada. When Haywood replied calmly that the union should "stop attacking and start 'boosting' the CIO in Canada," the local responded coldly that Millard was a "pie-card artist" who had proven disloyal to the CIO in the past and was now leading the CIO into a "prostituted hegemony." In milder tones, Burt complained to UAW president Thomas that there was "considerable unrest" amongst CIO unions in Canada because of the apparent inactivity of the CIO Committee. He stated that the UAW needs had been ignored by the Committee and that before any merger with the ACCL was completed, the CIO should hold a conference to discuss the matter in greater detail. He accused Barrett of ignoring his CIO duties in favour of his own UMW and charged that the CIO Committee had been "lax" in its responsibilities. He also threatened to withdraw the UAW from the Committee and to call a conference of like-minded people within the CIO to counter its "laziness." Informed of Burt's letter, Millard stated that he was "too sore" to reply and that he was "sick of Burt's allegiance to this trouble-making element." "I wish," he added, "somebody would put some stiffening in his spine."[19]

Communist opposition only delayed the creation of the new Congress; it did not abort it. With the affiliation of District 18 of the United Mine Workers to the ACCL on 22 February 1940, it was only a matter of time before the other CIO unions followed suit, for it was still the UMW with its 25,000 members which was keeping the Canadian CIO alive and its treasury solvent. None the less, the CIO leaders in Washington were still somewhat dubious. In late July, Millard complained to Barrett that, even though he had gone to Washington to argue for the merger, Haywood had not been convinced. He was now becoming very impatient over Haywood's perversity and inactivity.[20]

The final CIO decision was made at a conference between Canadian and American CIO leaders on 18 August 1940. The meeting was in Millard's words, "fairly warm in spots chiefly because of one or two Communists who made a great deal of wind and very little sense ... and who played upon the ignorance and cupidity of one or two others." After six hours of heated debate, with Millard and Barrett leading the pro-merger forces, the Communists at last agreed to endorse the merger. Though still doubtful, Haywood gave official CIO approval and agreed to ask every CIO union in Canada to affiliate. Within a week all the CIO affiliates in Canada, except for the Amalgamated Clothing Workers, had joined, and a founding convention had been arranged in Toronto for the week of 9 September. To prove that it indeed intended to submerge itself in the new Congress, the CIO asked all delegates to the founding convention to avoid any "caucus or grouping" since the purpose of the CIO was "to build, not to dominate or seek positions" within the new Congress.[21]

The final problem was the drafting of a constitution. From the start this had proved a tortuous task. On behalf of the ACCL, in December 1939, Dowd had drafted a "preamble and declaration of purposes" for the new Congress which J.L. Cohen, for the CIO, turned down as it lacked "sufficient tone or body." In Cohen's words, "I do not want merely to tell the Canadian worker that it would be *better* if they united. I want to say to them that it is *essential* for their proper protection. Similarly, I do not want only to *invite* them to come in under one roof, but to *call* them." In turn, Cohen's draft, which he had turned out with the help of Hunter and Jackson over a boisterous Christmas dinner (and which contained the "blood and guts" missing from Dowd's), was rejected by Mosher as totally "unacceptable" without extensive alteration.[22]

The final draft of the constitution was largely the work of Cohen. In fact, however, without the knowledge of the ACCL or CIO leaders, Cohen had worked closely with J.B. Salsberg in drafting the document. The major conflict between the CIO and ACCL was naturally enough the question of jurisdiction and the position in the new Congress of the local chartered unions of the ACCL. After several tumultuous meetings, the ACCL at last agreed to the CIO position that all chartered unions within the CIO's jurisdiction would automatically join the appropriate CIO union. With that agreement, all CIO opposition collapsed, though some Communists still continued their sniping from the sidelines and some ACCL leaders remained dubious. Indeed at the final meeting of the executive board of the ACCL, vice-president Beatty stated that he "still had doubts in his mind" concerning the wisdom of the merger.[23]

The convention met in Toronto on 9 September 1940. For the anti-Communist and pro-merger forces at least, it was a complete success, but only because of the last minute affiliation of the Amalgamated Clothing Workers. With its forty delegates, the ACW – which had previously barred all members of the Communist party from union positions – swung the Congress balance against the Communists. As Sol Spivak, the ACW director, later reported to his board, only the ACW affiliation "made it possible for the Congress to go in the 'right' direction."[24]

Spivak's evaluation was largely accurate. It was only by a vote of 111 to 81, and after several hours of heated debate, that the Congress approved a resolution condemning communism (as well as nazism and fascism) and urging all affiliated unions to refuse membership to members of "such subversive groups." A resolution supported by the extreme left denouncing the statement in Mosher's presidential address that "the primary consideration which should be in our minds at this time is winning of the war" was narrowly defeated. Another left-wing resolution urging affiliates of the Congress to support "progressive" candidates "on a non-partisan basis," was barely defeated when it was pointed out that District 26 of the UMW had already affiliated with the CCF. Throughout the convention the Communist delegates and their supporters were extremely vocal, speaking on almost every resolution and opposing the Congress executive on most issues. This prompted some anti-Communist delegates to complain of the "shocking tactics ... and long-winded declarations and obstruction speeches" of party members and supporters.[25]

As the Communists had feared, the CCF replaced them in the leadership of the new Congress. David Lewis had been paid by the ACCL leaders to spend the week at the convention "to assist them in whatever way necessary in getting the thing properly launched." An ecstatic Lewis claimed that this "establishes the relation between our office and their work on a much more direct basis ... and [shows] the need [of the new Congress] for working together with the CCF." The success of the convention was partly the result of Lewis' activities. At a meeting with the ACCL leaders in early September, Lewis succeeded in persuading them "of the need to sound at the convention a note of unity of the two bodies and the creation of a new central labour body rather than that of the continuation of their old Congress." He convinced them that to please the CIO unions it was necessary "to avoid any suggestion that what is happening is that the CIO unions are being absorbed in the ACCL," but rather to stress "that the ACCL unions and the CIO unions are joining together for the creation of a new central labour body."[26]

Lewis had succeeded beyond his wildest expectations. In the elections of officers, the entire CCF slate was easily elected. Of the six executive offices, four – Mosher, Barrett, Millard, and Spivak – were active supporters of the CCF and the other two – Pat Conroy of the UMW and M.M. Maclean of the CBRE – seemed sympathetic. The left-wing slate led by Jackson, Hunter, and Nigel Morgan of the IWA was shut out. Morgan lost to Mosher in the presidential election by 148 votes to 76, and Hunter failed by 47 votes in his bid for a position on the executive committee.

For the CIO unions, the convention was an even greater triumph. The new Congress constitution called for the same centralized organizing fund and authority which characterized the CIO structure south of the border. Though the Congress consisted of unions with jurisdictions in the same industrial fields, a resolution was adopted which would "apply the principle of one union in one industry" and would "avoid duplication of unions in any given industry." This, Mosher declared, must be done without the use of "force." Rather the Congress would use its "persuasive powers" and educational facilities to promote the policy of having all workers in one industry in one organization. As in the CIO, the Congress executive was given the authority to launch organizing campaigns and to form organizing committees in all unorganized fields.

The opposition of ACCL delegates to the affiliation of the CIO was sporadic and inconsequential. Some delegates felt that the CIO unions should not be allowed representation at the convention until after ACCL delegates had been allowed to vote on the merger. Others claimed that the CIO was an international union and therefore not eligible for membership. However, when Mosher emphasized that the CIO did not exist in Canada but that the CIO "delegates were representatives of organized Canadian workers, members of autonomous Canadian locals which the Executive Board of the Congress had accepted into affiliation," most ACCL members resignedly voted to seat them.

Aside from the Communists, the other major victim of the convention seemed to be the federal government. Resolutions were passed demanding that the government enforce conscription of wealth, condemning its anti-labour attitude, and reaffirming labour's right to strike during the war. Yet, in a sense, the government could claim at least one victory; the merger assured a less radical leadership and a more responsible attitude than could have been expected had the CIO continued to go it alone. Indeed, the convention confirmed the hegemony of the three oldest, largest, richest, and therefore most conservative unions, the CBRE, the ACW, and UMW, over the new labour Congress. Only Millard, of the executive members, represented the "new unionism" of the CIO. In the views of one observer, with the new Congress, the ACW and UMW had found "release from the importunities of their headstrong young brethren in the CIO" who would forge ahead into new areas of organization which would draw largely from the treasury of these two established and wealthy unions and which would require of them "a vision to recognize long-range gain" in return for their "present sacrifices." [27]

The triumvirate of CBRE, ACW, and UMW, would dominate the Congress for the next few years until the new unions, most particularly the Steel Workers, had finally resolved their internal conflicts, and could concentrate their attention and their large memberships and treasuries on the problems of the new Congress.

4

The Steelworkers' Organizing Committee

In the United States, the Steelworkers' Organizing Committee met with immediate success; in Canada, it was dogged from the beginning with defeat and failure. Only nine months after it was created in June 1936, SWOC had signed an agreement with the largest American steel company, United States Steel. It took the Canadian section of SWOC ten years to force United States Steel's equivalent in Canada, Stelco, into a contract. That Canada had no Wagner Act to compel management to enter into collective bargaining may explain SWOC's sorry Canadian record. In few places south of the border did SWOC meet with more forceful opposition than it did from the governments of Ontario and Quebec. But even if the environment had been congenial and circumstances ideal, it is questionable whether SWOC could have much improved on its poor performance. During its first few years too much time was spent resolving family quarrels to allow for a concentrated organizing campaign.

The organizing of steel workers first began in Canada in 1881 with the arrival of the Knights of Labor. Before they disintegrated in the 1890s the Knights had organized several hundred workers in three locals in Hamilton, Brockville, and Gananoque.[1] Some thirty years later, another attempt was made by an AFL affiliate, the Amalgamated Association of Iron, Steel and Tin Workers of America; by 1919 it claimed to have an organization in Canada of 21 locals and 8000 members. By 1930, because of the depression, and the union's craft emphasis, there was nothing left of the Amalgamated in Canada. It was to fill this void that in the fall of 1936 CIO president John L. Lewis appointed Silby Barrett, the director of the UMW in Nova Scotia, to organize Canadian steel workers into SWOC.

Within two months Barrett had succeeded in enrolling into Local 1064 of
SWOC at Dosco in Sydney, 2600 of the plant's 2900 workers.[2] Though the
Nova Scotia Trade Union Act compelled the company to recognize the union,
it did not force it to sign a contract. On the other hand, Dosco was prohibited
from dismissing any worker for union activity, and was forced to deduct the
union's dues from its workers' wages.[3] This monthly "check-off" of approximately four thousand dollars provided the funds with which SWOC would
organize other steel workers in Canada. More significantly, on many occasions
these dues from Nova Scotia made it possible for the international in Pittsburgh to meet its financial obligations. For some time the Sydney check-off
"paid the freight" for SWOC in the United States. Without the life-saving dues
from Sydney, the history of the steel workers' union in the United States might
have been considerably different.[4]

In central Canada, however, where most of the Canadian steel workers were
situated, SWOC was almost routed. In 1936, Lewis sent an ex-miner, Ernest
Curtis, to Hamilton to organize Stelco. When Curtis died a few months later,
Barrett was appointed to direct all SWOC activity in Canada. To help in this
task Barrett hired three men, Milton Montgomery, a long time steel worker
who had been Curtis' assistant, and two former organizers for the Workers
Unity League, Harry Hunter and Dick Steele. Their achievements were
meagre. By 1939, after almost three years of effort, SWOC in Ontario had fewer
than one thousand dues-paying members, and most of these were in small
plants in Toronto, Oshawa, and Hespeler.[5]

Their most singular accomplishment, however, was to make the SWOC-CIO
headquarters in Toronto a centre of Communist activity. When Millard was
appointed CIO regional director, he found himself surrounded by party members. Only on Saturday morning, when the party held its weekly meeting, was
the office empty, and even then, Jack Douglas, a party member, and Steele's
secretary, stayed behind "to keep his eye on things." There was a direct
"pipeline" from the CIO offices to Communist headquarters; decisions made at
the latter would shortly thereafter be made at the former, while those made
at the former, would instantly be known at the latter.[6]

Millard's appointment, however, threatened the Communist domination.
He provided the day-to-day surveillance of CIO activity which Barrett, who
rarely left the Maritimes, was unable to give. His reports of Communist
influence in the Canadian CIO soon alarmed the American leadership. But it
was the Communists themselves who unwittingly set the stage for their own
defeat. In response to appeals from Harry Hunter and Burt McLure, SWOC
president Philip Murray agreed to address a huge Labour Day rally in Hamilton in 1939. Both Hunter and McLure – a party supporter and SWOC organizer

in the huge Stelco plant – believed that Murray's presence would stimulate organizing activity in the Hamilton area where SWOC had achieved nothing. After addressing the rally, Murray spoke with Hunter, Steele, and other SWOC members. From these conversations Murray concluded that "all [was] not well with SWOC in Canada."[7] Soon after the meeting he warned Millard that unless the Communists were "cleared out" of the union he would abolish the Canadian district and start SWOC all over again in Canada. Murray subsequently appointed Tom Murray and Howard Hague, both capable SWOC organizers in the United States, to inquire into the Canadian situation.

In early November 1939, the two men spent several days in Canada investigating the SWOC organization and talking with CIO and SWOC organizers. On the final day of their mission they met with Millard in Hamilton. Out of this meeting came the decision to launch a concentrated campaign to rid SWOC of its Communist leaders.[8]

For the next few months, however, Murray refused to act. An impatient Millard pleaded with him to honour his "offer of assistance." "I am now," he admitted, "in a situation with which I frankly feel unable to deal effectively." "CIO forces in central Canada," he warned, "are suffering from an overdose of Communist interference." Millard noted that he would probably "again be dubbed a 'red-baiter,' " but added that "the matter is so important organizationally that what I'm called is immaterial." The cautious Murray replied that he had decided to wait for the SWOC convention in Chicago at the end of May before taking action.[9] Meanwhile, Murray harshly reprimanded Hunter and Steele for calling strikes in Canadian plants without the knowledge of the international office, and warned them that they should keep the international office informed of all SWOC activity in Canada. In response, Steele warned that because of the war the international office must no longer "interfere in our national affairs" nor should it continue to determine organizational and wage policy for Canada. Steele added that "the restriction of democratic rights and civil liberties because of the war, and the attempts of many Canadian employers to take advantage of the nation's crisis to speed up industrial production while keeping wages down" made it essential that important decisions affecting the Canadian membership be made in Canada.[10]

At long last, Murray made his decision to oust the Communists. At the 1940 SWOC convention, the Canadian caucus was informed that Murray's personal representative, Phillip Clowes, would make a thorough investigation of the SWOC situation in Canada to recommend "such action as might be necessary to promote the best interests of the organization." Within a week Clowes was on the job; one week later Steele lost his.

On 4 June, Clowes confronted a surprised Steele and after a furious discussion fired him. Though Steele denied that he was a member of the Communist party, Clowes stated that his "political opinions were responsible for the slow growth" of SWOC and that the strikes he had called "were not in accordance with the policy of the international office and had been unnecessary." Clowes also intimated that the Federal Department of Labour had promised to cooperate "in seeking to influence employers to deal with SWOC" if Steele were removed. And so, with Barrett's approval, Clowes ordered Steele to resign from SWOC. On 7 June 1940 Millard gleefully confided to David Lewis that he had now been "placed in full charge of SWOC," replacing Steele. He added that "other members of the staff have been plainly informed that they are to take their instructions from me and that any connections (they have all flatly denied membership) with the party will mean immediate and summary dismissal."[12]

Steele, however, did not submit without a struggle. After a series of strategy meetings with Salsberg and other party and SWOC members, he wrote a long bitter letter to Murray, and sent mimeographed copies of it to all SWOC lodges in Canada. In this five-page letter Steele protested against his dismissal, and demanded that Murray put him back on staff. He charged that SWOC leadership in Canada was "bankrupt," that the Sydney local, the largest in Canada, had not paid its dues for two months in order to call attention to its demands that Barrett be removed because he was "incapable of providing the leadership and direction needed for the task in Canada." As for Millard, Steele complained, "he has nothing, absolutely nothing to his credit"; he had already displayed his "incompetency and irresponsibility" in the UAW, and his appointment "without even asking the opinions of the SWOC staff" demonstrated "that my removal was the result of partisan political trickery." "Barrett's union policy today," he went on, "is being determined by political considerations of the Cooperative Commonwealth Federation." He charged that Barrett and Millard had capitulated "to the vested interests of the nation" and he warned that his dismissal struck "at the very heart of union democracy," and would signal employees "to launch a witch hunt among the executive and rank and file membership of our unions." This, he added, would "transform the democratic trade union movement into a 'national labour front' very similar to that in Nazi Germany." Finally, he outlined "the years of unstinting service" he had given SWOC and cautioned Murray that Canadian Steelworkers "will not for long tolerate any element of dictatorship in their organization." In a covering letter to the SWOC lodges, Steele warned that the policies of Barrett and Millard would "greatly weaken and endanger the CIO organizing efforts in Canada" and accused them of ignoring the desires and needs of SWOC.[13]

These letters had the intended effect. Within a week Millard was complaining to Murray that some of the lodges "were quite influenced by the letters and were even considering withdrawal from the SWOC" and that Norman Mackenzie of the large SWOC local in Sydney had even asked the Algoma Steelworkers' union "not to go in the CIO." Murray replied that all Millard could do was to "frustrate any attempt" by Steele "to interfere with the regular operations" of SWOC. He promised that he would send a letter to the SWOC lodges in Canada ordering them to ignore all letters from Steele.[14]

But the damage had been done. On 23 June delegates of four locals in southern Ontario, 1039, 1005, 1817 and 1111, met in Toronto, in the words of one delegate, because of the "general indignation raised at membership meetings following the news of the shake-up in SWOC." After a three-hour conference two resolutions were passed and sent to Murray and John L. Lewis. The first condemned the dismissal of Steele as "a very grave violation of the principles of justice with which the SWOC is supposed to be connected." It further praised Steele's "long and faithful service" and warned that his dismissal suggested "political discrimination." The second condemned the appointment of Millard and urged that he be fired since he was "a man in whom the workers can have no confidence." The delegates also asked Murray to call an immediate convention of SWOC in Canada and warned that "without Brother Steele's capable and first-hand direction, it would be very difficult to maintain our present membership."[15]

SWOC strategy was to ignore the protests. As Millard put it, "I feel that the reaction which is taking place is to be expected and that the matter will soon adjust itself." On 3 July, Barrett firmly informed SWOC members that Millard had been appointed subregional director for Quebec and Ontario and that all questions, problems, and negotiations must be cleared through his office. To members who were unhappy over Steele's dismissal, Millard coldly replied that, though the SWOC executive had "not felt it in the best interests of the organization" to divulge the reasons for Steele's dismissal, the decision had been taken "only ... after a very thorough investigation was made." At the same time, a relieved Millard reported to Murray that the police had come to the SWOC office looking for Steele and thus "embarrassment to SWOC was narrowly averted." Millard was also pleased when Vince Sweeney, editor of *Steel Labor,* the international's newspaper, congratulated him for the "fine copy" now being submitted for the Canadian edition. As Sweeney put it, "previously we had to read every bit of copy with infinite care, looking for any sly 'bugs.' And even after that we never felt secure. Now, with you at the helm, I feel like a great load has been lifted from my shoulders." On the other hand, Millard was angered when George Burt publicly denounced the dismissal of

Steele and promised "that if he could put another man on, he would certainly choose Dick Steele."[16]

More significantly, Millard reported to Murray that Steele "had succeeded in building up quite a personal following in local [SWOC] unions and in other CIO unions" and that "his admirers were not altogether party people, but in many cases uninformed union members who believed that his first interest was the welfare of the union movement." Sadly, Millard added that "some of these people continue to sing his praises and show their resentment for the one they feel is responsible for his removal" but that "this will soon be overcome." He pointed out unhappily that organization was at a standstill since Steele's firing and he blamed "staff members [who] have not shown the responsibility for the business of the international which would mark them as good organizers." He warned that "if they do not measure up" they would soon be dismissed.[17]

Two weeks later, on 17 September, immediately following the founding convention of the Canadian Congress of Labour, Murray fired Hunter and Harry Hambergh. It seemed that Millard's campaign to clean the Communists out of SWOC had at last succeeded. But within days, Lodge 1111 had sent out circulars to other lodges in southern Ontario complaining that the dismissals were the "last straw" because SWOC had now "been swept clean of its only organizers." In order "to establish some form of democracy" within SWOC, all SWOC lodges were urged to send delegates to a special conference in Toronto.[18]

Four lodges, 1111, 1039, 1817 and 2000, responded and met on 29 September, to discuss the situation. They unanimously adopted a resolution stating that they had no confidence in the Canadian leadership of SWOC and were appalled by its 'autocratic' behaviour in dismissing Steele, Hunter, and Hambergh without consulting the Canadian membership and "thereby displaying a complete lack of understanding of the temper of Canadian workers." They therefore decided to set up their own "Ontario Executive" of SWOC with Hunter as chairman and Hambergh as secretary – Steele by this time had gone "underground" to avoid arrest* – and no longer to recognize Barrett, Millard, and Montgomery as SWOC officers with any authority over them. Further, they requested other SWOC lodges in Canada to join them in a conference of all Canadian steel workers "to formulate a policy for Canadian Steel Workers." More significantly they voted to pay their dues to the new Ontario Executive

---

* The federal government had begun interning Communists and other "enemies of the war effort." As one of the most capable and active Communists in the country, Steele was one of the first to be interned. After the Nazi invasion of Russia, Steele was released and joined the Canadian army. Ironically, he became a war hero and was killed in action.

rather than to SWOC. Murray was assured however, that the locals' "highest ideal" was "the development of the SWOC" in Canada; but because of "inefficient and short-sighted Canadian officialdom" they had reluctantly decided to set up their own organization.

If the Ontario Executive hoped to attract other steel locals, it was soon disappointed. Not only did no other lodge join with it, but the Algoma Steel union, reassured at last that SWOC was "cleaning out" its Communists, finally agreed to affiliate its 2700 members with SWOC.

Discussions between SWOC and the Algoma union had been initiated in 1938, but it was not until the CIO conference in Ottawa in November 1939 that both unions agreed to co-operate in presenting a common front against the government. Even then, a majority of the Algoma union were opposed to affiliation because, in the words of their president, George Taylor, "the CIO have a reputation for trouble." On the other hand, two influential members of the union, Erie Dalrymple and Ivan Campbell, led the movement in favour of affiliation. Both were soon appointed to the SWOC staff. By June 1940, after a discussion with Algoma leaders, Barrett was convinced that the executive was "solidly in favour of coming over to SWOC." At the Congress founding convention, Millard and Barrett met with Campbell and other Algoma executives to complete arrangements. On 19 September, after a spirited "pep talk" by president Campbell, the union unanimously agreed to hold a referendum on the subject. With 94 per cent of the ballots cast in favour, on 28 September the Algoma Steel Union voted itself out of existence and became Local 2251 of SWOC.[20]

The affiliation of Algoma doomed whatever hopes the Ontario Executive had of building a successful alternative to SWOC. With the large "check-off" from the Dosco local in Sydney and another now from Algoma, SWOC in Canada was at last on a solid financial footing. It could now, in Millard's opinion, adopt a policy of "going ahead with [its] own work" without paying too much attention to the Ontario Executive.[21]

The vigour of the Ontario Executive's attack on SWOC leaders, however, was not diminished by the Algoma affiliation. In a series of stinging letters to SWOC lodges, the Ontario Executive assailed Millard and Barrett as "big puffed-up labour leaders," "obstructionists ... whispering old hooey to a worker here and there in poison-tongue fashion." They were accused of hiring as organizers Milton Montgomery's 17-year-old son who had "never before held a job," Murray Cotterill, "not a steelworker" but "Millard's personal friend," and two or three others whose only qualifications were that they were "friends" of Millard. It was charged that Barrett and Millard were attempting to "bring about a fusion of the CIO and the CCF" in which the former would merely be "an adjunct" of the latter, by ousting "every leader who was not a CCF man." Hundreds of workers in various plants in the Toronto area, the circulars proudly – but wrongly – claimed, were leaving "the bankrupt, impotent and unscrupulous" leadership of SWOC for the Ontario Executive and were being provided with benefits received under SWOC. The Ontario Executive, the SWOC lodges were informed, "was set up in self defence" and "speaks as the only truly representative body of organized and unorganized steelworkers" in Ontario. It consisted of one elected member from each local and four elected members "at large." The chairman and secretary were elected by referendum vote. The Ontario Executive's circulars further emphasized that it had not seceded from SWOC. "We want the CIO. *We,* and not they, are the SWOC." The Executive further warned, "We will not permit the CIO to be destroyed by self-seeking autocrats, by clique control, by political domination." Its purpose was to give the rank and file a voice in policy decisions, and it resolved to "fight for a Canadian policy developed by Canadian steelworkers" and to "safeguard and maintain the principles and aims of the CIO in Canada." Finally, it urged all steelworkers and all CIO members to support it in its fight for a "solid, militant and progressive union."[22]

Some support was forthcoming. The Ontario Regional Conference of the UAW endorsed the Ontario Executive, as did various locals of the UE and the Fur Workers. Norman Mackenzie, president of the large Sydney local, offered his personal support and complained to John L. Lewis that the "voice of the rank and file" at SWOC had been stifled by Millard and Barrett. But on the whole, the response to the Ontario Executive was something less than overwhelming. None of the other steel lodges in the area took up the cause, although in several (particularly Local 1005 in Hamilton, which Burt McLure helped organize) the Executive had much support.[23]

To make sure that the steel workers remained "loyal," Millard decided that it was time for SWOC to "start swinging the big stick." He suggested a three-pronged attack; first, that SWOC devote all its energy to "*new* work"; secondly, that the members of the Ontario Executive locals be "fed propaganda as to their undesirable union connections"; and thirdly, that necessary steps should be taken "to stop these disrupters from using and soiling the good name of SWOC ... and from spreading their dirty tactics ... into other unions." He also suggested that Murray should write James Carey, president of the UE, and R.J. Thomas, president of the UAW, asking them to order their Canadian representatives "to stop giving aid and comfort to these people."[24]

At a special strategy meeting in Pittsburgh on 3 February 1941, attended by Barrett, Millard, Murray, Clowes, Hague and David McDonald, the union's secretary-treasurer, Millard's suggestions were adopted. Both Carey and Thomas were soon informed that their representatives were supporting a dual union in Canada and it would be in the best interests of the CIO if they were ordered to co-operate fully with SWOC. A harsh letter was sent by McDonald to all SWOC members in Canada denouncing Hunter, Hambergh, and the Ontario Executive. Members were told that the two men had been dismissed since they were "negligent and had failed to carry out the policies of SWOC." "They are trying to deceive you," McDonald warned. "Their presence and suggestions should be completely ignored ... They speak for no one; they can be of no service to you and they are acting in an illegal manner. They are illegally using the name 'Steel Workers' Organizing committee' ... The 'Ontario Executive' is in no way connected with SWOC ... It is simply a tool of the men named above." SWOC members were ordered to co-operate with the SWOC organizers in Canada and to "disregard the false representations" being made by the Ontario Executive.[25]

Hunter and Hambergh immediately complained to McDonald that his statements were "totally out of line with the facts of the case" and both wondered out loud "from where and from whom such misleading information" was received. They reaffirmed their intentions to reach an understanding "that would place all of our efforts in one channel and thus build a powerful steelworkers' union in Canada." They were joined in their remonstrations by many of the local members of the Ontario Executive who grumbled that McDonald was "sadly misinformed of the true nature of affairs in Canada" and that Hunter and Hambergh represented the "militant CIO policy" and the "true labour tradition" in Canada. To these complaints, McDonald coldly replied that Hambergh and Hunter had set themselves up as a "dual organization" to SWOC and therefore could expect no sympathy from the international office.[26]

At the same time George Burt protested to McDonald that SWOC had no right to "relay information" to Thomas of the UAW about his attitude toward the Ontario Executive. He blamed the entire situation on the "clumsy policy adopted by the SWOC" and stated that he could not support the international union because in so doing he "would have to fight a great portion" of the UAW membership in Canada who supported the Ontario Executive. He accused the SWOC people of using an "underhanded route" in maligning him and he warned McDonald that SWOC must make thorough investigation of the situation "before it ruins the International CIO movement in Canada." In response, McDonald countered that SWOC had not been "clumsy"; on the contrary, as a result of its recent actions, it was "now well on the road to building a splendid steelworkers' union in the entire Dominion."[27]

Indeed, it seemed that at long last the corner had been turned in SWOC's dismal record in Canada. Millard crowed to Haywood that "in the Hamilton area, which is the Birmingham of Canada, we are breaking through at last." "As far as the dual movement is concerned," he wrote McDonald, "the principals are definitely on the defensive, and ... some rank-and-file members ... are demanding the removal of Hunter and Hambergh and a return to SWOC." He attributed this to the success of the organizing campaign in Hamilton, which was in stark contrast to the failures of Hunter and Hambergh in the same area. SWOC had succeeded in organizing the large National Steel Car plant in Hamilton and the Peck Rolling Mills, a Dosco subsidiary, in Montreal.[28]

To capitalize on this new spirit, Millard recommended to McDonald that a Canadian conference be held in Montreal on 19 April 1941, and he begged Murray to attend. To ensure that some others would also attend, Norman Mackenzie, president of Local 1064 in Sydney, sent a circular to all SWOC locals urging them to send delegates to create "a united front" to fight for "complete autonomy for the Canadian region" and for "a democratic organization." He urged that the other locals communicate with him and with each other so that the views of the rank and file would be represented. Members of the Ontario Executive he pointed out, would be on hand to assist the rank and file in expressing their unhappiness "with the national set-up, the failure to organize the unorganized, the lack of democracy and the absence of a clear-cut policy."[29]

If this is what Mackenzie actually expected, he was sorely disappointed. By a vote of 19 to 12, the delegates to the conference refused to seat the representatives of the Ontario Executive. Millard stated that "the door was open for the 'Ontario Executive', but at the present time they had no official connection with SWOC." On the other hand, a suggestion by Howard Hague, that they be allowed to sit in as observers, was accepted.[30]

Ironically, unity was the theme of the conference. Speeches by David McDonald, Walter Burke, and Howard Hague, all officers of the international, called, in McDonald's words, for the "forces of the organized steelworkers in Canada to unite solidly and follow a militant policy of organization." In his report to the conference, Millard stated that in September of 1940 when Hambergh and Hunter were dismissed, SWOC – outside of the Maritimes – was in a "defeated state of mind" with only one small functioning local in Hespeler, and only twenty-five dues-paying members in all of Hamilton. Since then membership had increased drastically and though the "dual organization had impeded progress," SWOC was now "making rapid progress."[31]

As the conference was ending, Hunter dramatically announced that the Ontario Executive had voted to support the policies of SWOC, and would therefore like to be readmitted. Barrett assured them that "the front door was wide open" and SWOC would "welcome them back as soon as the necessary arrangements could be made." These were soon completed. On 7 June 1941, the Ontario Executive formally dissolved, and its four locals once again became part of SWOC.[32] And shortly afterwards Mackenzie and MacEachern – the left-wingers in Local 1064 in Sydney – were defeated in executive elections.

Whatever the Communists had hoped to achieve in forming the Ontario Executive they failed dismally. As they were to prove again and again, so certain were they of the justice and infallibility of their program and ideology, that they often took actions which proved disastrous for their goals. What possessed them to start a dual organization to SWOC, whether it was frustration, sincerity, or a desire to disrupt, is debatable; that they failed, is not. Understandably, Steele, Hunter, and Hambergh were angered by their dismissal from an organization they did much to create. With strong pockets of support in many of the lodges, they were hopeful that their dual organization would triumph over the SWOC apparatus. It failed because the latter had access to funds the former did not. Within weeks of the dismissals, Millard had hired five more organizers, most of them paid out of the dues from Algoma and Sydney. SWOC was consequently able to mount large organization campaigns and to reap the concomitant publicity.

The Ontario Executive could do little but look after its own locals, though it did vainly attempt to organize several plants in Toronto. In the end its total failure was obvious, even to its most committed supporters. By March 1941, it had become clear that the party could achieve more by working within SWOC than by attempting to attack it from without. For this reason Hunter was ordered by the party to reaffiliate his organization.[33] His dramatic announcement at the SWOC conference was simply the humble admission of the Communist party that one of its policies had gone terribly awry. With the impending Nazi invasion of Russia the party was rapidly retreating to its old cry of "labour unity."

Even in the eyes of many non-Communists, the dismissals of Steele, Hunter, and Hambergh seemed dictatorial, unfair, and simply the perpetuation of the vendetta between Millard and his CCF supporters with the Communists. That the three men played a significant role in creating and building the CIO in Canada is beyond question. But with the onset of the war their usefulness to the CIO was indeed questionable. Party policy and CIO policy no longer coincided.

Whenever there was a major change in the "party line," a courier from the American Communist party headquarters would arrive at the party office in Toronto and announce the new policy. Then, the party theorists in Canada, – men like Tim Buck and Joe Salsberg, – would adapt the new policy to the Canadian situation.[34] Since the Nazi-Soviet Pact and the waning party desires for labour unity, party policy was often at odds with that of the CIO. As long as the party opposed the war and the CIO in Canada supported it, the loyalty of Communists in the CIO was severely tested. In the end most supported their party over their union. Strikes were called – and lost – without CIO approval. Decisions were made which ran counter to SWOC and CIO policy. Denunciations of SWOC leadership, particularly of Millard and Barrett, became more violent. It was little wonder then that Millard should demand of Murray that the Communists be removed from SWOC.

The key to Millard's policy then, and for the remainder of his career, was that "loyalty was more important than ability." Steele, Hambergh, and Hunter were all men of great ability but, to Millard at least, their loyalty was to the party and not to SWOC. There was no doubt in Millard's mind, from the day he was appointed CIO representative that these men would have to be removed.[35]

In just over a year, he had succeeded. To replace them, Millard reached into the ranks of the CCF and its youth section, the CCYM, on whose loyalty he had no doubts. Fortunately for the CIO as well as for Millard, these people, including Fred Dowling, Murray Cotterill, Eamon Park, Margaret Sedgewick, and Eileen Tallman, proved to be amongst the most capable in the labour movement. In the long run, the expulsion of the Communists proved a benefit for SWOC. In exchange for men with great ability and little loyalty it soon acquired people with an abundance of both. With its Communist element weakened, though by no means destroyed, and with the Ontario Executive disbanded, SWOC was at last prepared to give its full attention to the dangers confronting it from without – from industry, from government, and from other unions – rather than from within.

5

The CCL, the CCF and the Communist Party 1940-46

Like most new organizations, the Canadian Congress of Labour suffered a period of growing pains. For the Congress it was longer than most. Undoubtedly the most serious problem confronting it in these early years was the strength of the Communists and their supporters. At the very first meeting of its executive committee in September 1940, the Congress took steps to counteract the party's influence. Millard suggested that the constitution be changed so that representation on the executive council would be granted only to unions that "have at least three locals and aggregate membership of at least 500 members." He suggested this, he told Haywood, because most of the smaller international unions – the UE, the Newspaper Guild, the Shoe Workers, and Packinghouse Workers – were sending Communist delegates to Congress meetings. Millard felt that before these unions should be allowed representation they must "clean up their Canadian woodsheds," because now they were nothing but a "fire hazard" to the Congress. To help remove the danger, Mosher invited Haywood to attend the first meeting of the executive council. He hoped that at this meeting Haywood would order a change in the policies of those CIO unions "who do not appear to be giving their full co-operation to the Congress and who are inclined to carry on subversive activities."[1]

According to the new constitution, the council was to be the "supreme authoritative body of the Congress" between conventions. In order to dilute the influence of the left-wing unions, the Congress leadership decided to adopt Millard's proposal and limit council membership to the larger unions. The leader of the left-wing forces, C.S. Jackson of the UE, hotly disputed the committee's decision, not only because this would undermine the potential strength of the left, but also because Mike Fenwick, then an active Communist and representative of the only Packinghouse Workers' local in Canada, was outside the council meeting waiting to be admitted. Jackson's complaint that the Congress action was unconstitutional was easily overridden. More significantly, the executive committee decided to ignore the new constitution and to transfer to itself all the vast powers of the council – to enforce the constitution, carry out the policies and programs of the Congress between conventions, create committees, make appointments, and select organizers. This prompted Jackson to charge – quite correctly – that the committee was "riding roughshod over the constitution" and that the council had been reduced from an authoritative body to a "useless appendage."[2] In its battle against communism, obviously everything was fair to the CCL leadership.

The effect of the executive committee's decision, as was intended and as Jackson foresaw, was to ensure that the left-wing unions would never be in a position of authority within the Congress administration. Since each Congress affiliate was entitled to a place on the executive council, Communists and their supporters would certainly be represented on the council, but since membership on the executive committee was restricted to six men elected by the Congress convention, it was hardly likely that any Communist would ever be chosen. The decision gave the committee, in Jackson's words, "the right to carry on any policies it sees fit, freely and without check or restraint." Because of its fear of the Communists, the Congress had taken all the powers given to the council and transferred them to the executive committee. Though the CCL would now be less democratic, it would be safe against possible Communist domination.

Over the opposition of Jackson, the council also approved the executive committee's decisions that "a picket line did not necessarily mean a strike" and that only the committee could decide when a strike was legal. This would permit the Congress to decide which strikes to support and allow it to disavow strikes called by Communist unions which were aimed, in the eyes of the Congress at least, at disrupting the war effort. Again over Jackson's opposition the committee recommended that the CIO not charter any new locals in Canada without Congress approval. This would give the Congress the right to make certain that the prospective locals would not be "disruptive." To prevent the left-wing unions from communicating their ideas to other unions, the council prohibited unions from circularizing each other without Congress approval. Despite Jackson's strenuous objections the council also decided not to send the minutes of executive meetings to Congress affiliates nor to allow any council member to discuss meetings because "divulging the plans and activities of the Executive was not in the best interests of the Congress." Through these dubious, though legal manoeuvres the Congress felt that it had defused the "Communist threat." At the cost of some of its democratic rights, the Congress was now securely in the hands of its non-Communist majority.

This setback at the hands of the executive council spurred the left to greater activity. Despite the council's decision, immediately following the meeting Jackson forwarded his own version of the minutes to various "friendly" unions – the IWA locals in British Columbia, the Sydney local of SWOC, some Auto locals, and his own UE locals. These minutes were, in Mosher's words, "one-sided and inaccurate," though in fairness to Jackson, they were more informative – and of course more colourful and partisan – than the official minutes issued by the Congress. Explicitly against the council's orders, Jackson also publicly criticized the federal government's attempt, by order-in-council 7440, to control wages. This prompted Dowd to recommend that the Congress ought to take action against a man as "dangerous" to their interests as Jackson. Two weeks later, addressing the Kirkland Lake local of Mine-Mill, Jackson harshly criticized the "anti-democratic tendencies" of the Congress and singled out Mosher, Dowd, and Millard for specific "ridicule."[3]

More seriously, however, under Communist auspices – and particularly under that of the Ontario Executive of SWOC – in early 1941, a new organization, the Shop Stewards' Councils, was created. Its aim, according to Jackson, was "to unify labour in order to organize the unorganized" by bringing together rank-and-file workers from different plants and unions, including AFL unions, to discuss common problems. The Councils met regularly and the minutes of the meetings were published and distributed to "serve both as a medium for reporting developments within various shops ... and ... to give encouragement to workers to move in concert with fellow workers in other shops." In the members' own words, the Councils were formed because workers were "denied the right of criticism within their own union meetings and councils, hoodwinked ... by their leadership, tied to acceptance of legislation which is detrimental to the interests of the workers ... and stifled in their demands by the leadership of the main union centres in the country." The Councils provided, according to Jackson, "the means whereby the workers could exchange experiences and ideas in the common interest." Referring to the recent behaviour of the Congress executive, the Councils complained that "reactionary elements have always sought support for their throttling moves in the constitutions of their organizations," and since "democracy had been almost completely eliminated from the meetings of such bodies, it was necessary for the workers to establish separate apparati through which they could freely discuss and arrive at decisions on every problem confronting them."[4]

To the Congress there was no question that the Councils were a "dual" movement, and as such, dangerous to Congress interests. The treasurer of UAW Local 222, Arthur Schultz, complained to David Lewis that his union was "gradually coming under CP control" and great pressure was being exerted on it to support the Councils, withdraw from the Congress, and set up an independent organization. At the same time, Millard warned David McDonald that the Communists, using the Stewards' Councils, were intent on forming "an independent movement which they could control." They had already approached the UAW, he added, to withdraw from the Congress and support them in their efforts "to pursue a militant trade union policy" by means of a new labour centre.[5]

When Millard protested to Jackson about the policies of the Councils, Jackson sent him a three-page reply, documenting Millard's history of "subversions" within the Canadian labour movement, accusing him of "Hitlerism" and of being an "agent of the monied interests" and charging that he and his CCF colleagues in the Congress had stifled democracy and local autonomy in the union movement. The Congress also sent a circular to all unions charging that the Stewards' Councils were "controlled by the Communist Party, [were] opposed to the policy of the Congress and [were] ... detrimental to it." The Congress also ordered all affiliated unions to "have nothing to do" with such Councils. Jackson replied that these attacks were "motivated by fear of rank and file discussion of policies and legislation affecting the working people, and by a fear that the existence of such Councils threatened attempted dictatorship by some leaders within the labour movement."[6]

It was apparent that the Congress would have to take even more dramatic action to curb the left-wing opposition group that had centred around Jackson and the UE. Jackson rebuffed the first Congress effort ordering him to retract his statements in Kirkland Lake and on order-in-council 7440. Instead he accused the Congress of denying him "the right" to express his opinions "on matters of concern to the workers." Dowd then wrote Bob Carlin of the Kirkland Lake local requesting a full report on Jackson's "objectionable statements" as the Congress had decided "to put a stop to his attacks upon the organization."[7]

On 12 May 1941, the executive committee recommended that Jackson be suspended from membership on the executive council. On the following day, the suspension was heatedly debated in the executive council meeting. Jackson was accused of circulating minutes of the council meetings of 5 November, of attacking the Congress publicly in his Kirkland Lake speech, of supporting the Stewards' Council despite official Congress opposition, and of sending circulars to other Congress unions. In addition, Mosher charged that Jackson was in the Congress "entirely for the purpose of wrecking it ... and had no right to sit on the Council." Conroy accused Jackson of "disrupting" the Congress and of making "wildly untrue statements," and Millard added that Jackson was "supporting the Communist attempt to destroy the Congress."

Undaunted, Jackson replied that no specific allegations had been made concerning his statements in Kirkland Lake, that he was not alone in his opposition to order-in-council 7440, that the Stewards' Councils were not detrimental to the Congress, and that he had written a report of the council meeting only for the information of his own members. But only Prince of the UAW and Nigel Morgan of the IWA defended Jackson; both argued that the constitution did not allow for the suspension of council members. When the resolution of suspension was approved, Jackson refused to leave the room because he felt it was a violation of his "constitutional right." Only when Mosher threatened to phone the police did Jackson leave, warning that he would appeal his suspension to the next convention. The suspension shortly became irrelevant. On 24 June, Jackson was arrested by the RCMP and "interned" for his "anti-war" activities.[8]

On 22 June, 1941, the Nazis began their campaign against Russia. On the same day, the Communists called off theirs against the Congress. More correctly, the Communists continued to attack the Congress, but no longer for co-operating with the government and with industry to help win the war; rather, the Congress was now accused of not doing enough to aid the war effort.

Astounded by this sudden and startling change in party policy, Conroy warned Mosher that he feared that the Communists within the Congress would "become too patriotic ... so that those of us who have assumed that our country needs our services will be portrayed in the light of traitors because we are not pushing the war on a "proletarian" basis sufficient enough to save Russian Christianity and Russian Democracy." The Communists, he warned, "may develop into such ardent patriots that we shall pale into fifth columnists by comparison."[9]

Conroy was right. Those labour leaders who were being excoriated by the party for supporting the war effort found themselves, after June 23, being attacked for not supporting the war more strenuously. A Millard editorial in the August 1940 issue of *Steel Labor,* urging workers to unite behind the government to fight the war, had been denounced by the party as "one of the most disgusting articles ever printed in an organ which supposedly represents labour."[10] In April 1941, Hunter had warned Murray that if SWOC continued working "hand in hand" with the government and the "industrialists" on the pretext of "winning the war," the union movement would be destroyed. But just two months later – and after the Nazi invasion – Hunter urged SWOC members to support the war effort and to increase production.[11] At a SWOC conference in September, Hunter and Norman Mackenzie introduced resolutions pledging full SWOC support for the war, repudiating all "illegal" strikes, urging workers to increase steel production, asking the government to create a committee of employees and management to plan ways to step up production, and ordering all union officials and members to improve the quality of production and eliminate waste. Then, after a fiery address by Hunter, by a vote of 64 to 19, the delegates also censured Barrett and Millard for their part in conducting a strike at the Peck Rolling Mills in Montreal. Barrett shrugged off the censure as simply an attempt of the "Communists and their tools to gain control of the leadership of SWOC in Canada" though he bitingly pointed out that those who before June were urging peace with Hitler and were criticizing the war effort were now suddenly in the forefront "urging workers to support the war effort by all possible means."[12]

At the Congress convention in September 1941, the left-wing forces were less fractious than usual. This was partly attributable to a determined effort by Mosher to exclude all Communist delegates. In a letter to Silby Barrett, for example, Mosher had requested that he make certain that the UMW delegates to the convention were "of the same turn of mind upon whom we can depend for support against those who will undoubtedly be there for the purpose of seeking control of the Congress," and that he make it "difficult or impossible" for "troublemakers" to attend. In turn Barrett warned that there were a number of UMW delegates who could "not be trusted" and that Mosher should make sure that he got as many "good delegates" as he could from the CBRE to counter them. In desperation, Mosher urged Barrett to ask the international office of the UMW in Washington to declare delegates from the "disgruntled groups" (that is, the left-wingers) in District 26 "outlaws and not eligible to become delegates."[13]

Though Mosher did not succeed with the miners, he had made similar requests of other unions to send only "reliable" delegates. And in some unions his efforts met with success. In any case, the left-wing delegates at the convention were surprisingly tolerant of the Congress policies. They did complain, however, that the Congress had not done enough to "give leadership" to the workers in order to "spur them on to increase production," and that the Congress had not been forceful enough in clamouring for Jackson's release from prison. (He was set free before the end of 1941.) But on most issues they sided with the executive. Most ironically, they even joined with the Congress executive in condemning District 26 of the UMW for conducting an "illegal strike."[14]

To compound its difficulties with the left wing, despite sincere efforts to co-operate the Congress found itself continually at odds with the federal government. At the beginning of the war, Mosher promised his "whole-hearted support and co-operation" in whatever action the government took "in the defence of Canada." One year later, Mosher "gladly confirmed" the Congress' commitment to support government policy and denounced those who criticized the government and the Prime Minister.[15] As a defender of Mackenzie King and his policies, however, Mosher found himself almost alone amongst Congress leaders. For the duration of the war, the Congress would pass resolutions at every convention severely critical of the government's labour policies.

These resolutions forced Mosher to attack the government publicly. Privately, he still supported the King administration. At the very first executive committee meeting he dissuaded Millard from resigning from the National Labour Supply Council, as he felt that the Council was valuable as a link between labour and government. Undeterred, Millard soon resigned from the Council charging that it had become "openly partial to ownership," and he repudiated Mosher for continuing to co-operate with a government which was anti-labour. He argued that only when the Congress was strong enough to exert sufficient political pressure to "counterbalance" the other influences on the government, could it expect favourable legislation. Mosher also resigned from the Council, but at the urging of the Minister of Labour he decided to stay on. "Otherwise, " he explained, the Congress "would be playing into the hands of the AFL representative as well as the employers."[16]

Mosher's major complaint against the federal government was that it was "giving undue recognition to the TLC" and ignoring the "status" of the Congress. Yet when Millard urged the Congress to protest the appointment of Humphrey Mitchell as minister of labour, Mosher demurred on the grounds that this would serve no purpose other than to alienate the government. Despite Mosher's argument, Millard publicly condemned the appointment. However, when the director of the National Selective Service Commission, Elliot Little, resigned because of the government's and especially Mitchell's "hostile attitude towards labour," the Congress belatedly decided to press for the dismissal of the labour minister.[17]

But Mosher's attempts to influence government labour policy met with little success. Orders-in-council were passed freezing wage levels, facilitating the use of troops in labour disputes, and limiting the right to strike. The government also refused to force employers to negotiate with their workers and continued to appoint men whom the Congress considered "anti-labour" to government boards. Its abolition of the Unemployment Insurance Commission, the only independent body on which labour was represented and its refusal to give the Congress representation on government bodies, saddled Mosher with too many debits for even that ambitious labour politician to overcome. Disappointed with the attitude and actions of the Liberal government, the Congress sought redress by entering into political activity of its own.

It would be inaccurate however, to describe the policies of the King administration as anti-union. The government was under constant pressure from industry to adopt even harsher measures against labour, particularly against the CIO. At a secret meeting in May 1941 of the Cabinet War Committee, a delegation from the Canadian Manufacturers Association warned the government that the CIO was a "foreign-dominated," "Communist" union. The cabinet was told that CIO unions were "disrupting" the war effort, "holding up production" in vital war industries, and fomenting unrest throughout the nation. The CMA delegates urged the government to outlaw industrial unions since they "were an excellent method of spreading subversive activities." These industrialists longed for a return "to the good old days" before the CIO arrived, "when there was little trouble with labour." Canadian workers, the delegation added, "would be loyal if left alone," and since "labour unrest in Canada was 90 per cent imported" from the United States, they demanded that the government take immediate action againt the CIO.[18]

The cabinet vigorously rejected the CMA's arguments. Indeed, C.D. Howe, the Minister at Munitions and Supply, and certainly no friend of the CIO, charged that the "manufacturers had been guilty of the most flagrant disregard of labour laws so far encountered." Labour Minister McLarty joined Howe in denouncing the CMA for its wild and insupportable allegations and accused business of being as much at fault as labour in causing industrial unrest in Canada. Finally, before dismissing the delegation, the Prime Minister said that while his government "held no brief for the CIO," it could not accept the sweeping charges made by the CMA. He demanded that the delegation withdraw them and flatly stated that his government would not interfere with the CIO nor would it change any of its labour policies. The chastened CMA delegation was then ushered out of the room – sadder and somewhat wiser. Obviously the King government was not as anti-labour as they had hoped – or as the Congress had feared.

From the outset the attitude of the Congress towards political action had been ambivalent. Though many of its leaders were partisans of the CCF, they wished, if at all possible, to avoid committing the Congress to any political activity. Only Millard of the executive members, urged a positive program in support of the CCF. This, most executive members feared, would further divide an already splintered Congress. Led by Conroy, the Congress succeeded in keeping the CCF proponents at arm's length, at least until the apparent anti-labour attitude of the government became too unpalatable to ignore. Until 1943, therefore, the Congress did what it could to discourage CCF pretensions.

Because of Conroy's complaints about his close connections with the CCF, Millard resigned as chairman of the party's Ontario council and from its national committee. When Mosher recommended to Conroy that William Irvine, the CCF leader in Alberta, be hired as an organizer, Conroy demurred on the grounds that this would identify the CCF too closely with the Congress. Mosher accepted Conroy's argument that it was "undesirable to combine political and labour activities," and so he urged Irvine to "give up his political activities completely." This Irvine would not do. Needless to say, he was not hired. In addition, Conroy refused to allow Alex McAuslane, the Congress organizer in British Columbia, to stand as a CCF candidate in the provincial election as he did not wish Congress organizers "to be implicated with any particular political group." When David Lewis protested this decision at a meeting with Conroy, Dowd, and Mosher, he came away convinced that they were "ready to give the CCF support if they can do so without any publicity, [but] they are not yet ready to take even one definite step in the direction of independent political action."[19]

Following this meeting, Conroy sent a circular to all Congress organizers warning them not to participate in political campaigns or to become identified with any political party. Millard protested vehemently that the CCF represented the real interests of the worker. He pointedly asked Conroy "how an organizer who is unpolitical is ever going to succeed in shaping our unions for constructive political action after sufficient progress had been made on the economic front." Conroy replied that Congress organizers must be "extremely circumspect about their political activities" because the Congress had "to do business with employers" who may be "blinded by the particular colour of political attachment which may restrict the chance of our trade union getting established."[20]

Despite the Congress attitude, Millard was not dissuaded. Without the knowledge of either the Congress or his international, he had "concocted" a scheme whereby SWOC contributed one hundred dollars monthly to the CCF in return for "lobbying" for labour legislation by the CCF members of Parliament. Similarly he put only CCF partisans on the staff of the USW and he publicly urged all Steel locals to affiliate with the CCF. Attempts by Millard to introduce resolutions at Congress conventions urging the CCL to affiliate with the CCF were successfully countered by Conroy.[21]

By 1943, however, largely because of the intolerable labour policy of the government and the surprising successes of the CCF in the Ontario elections and the public opinion polls, the Congress executive swallowed hard and urged the Congress convention to pass a resolution recognizing the CCF as the "political arm of labour in Canada" and urging all locals to affiliate with it.

The debate was hot and furious, the Communists and their supporters desperately fighting against the resolution. David Lewis who had helped word the resolution and had "worked hard for two days" organizing CCF forces to support it, was present during the debate to keep the CCF "people supplied with information to answer CP distortions." After powerful speeches by Millard, Clairie Gillis, the CCF member for Cape Breton South, and Conroy in support of the resolution – the latter admitting to the delegates that he was "sick and tired of going cap in hand to Mackenzie King" – it was carried by a large margin.[22]

But the resolution did not resolve the problem. In fact, for the next year the Congress leaders, especially Conroy, seemed intent only on repudiating it. At a special executive committee meeting in February 1944 called to implement the resolution, Mosher informed David Lewis that it was "unwise" for labour leaders to act as "spearheads" in political action because they were required to deal with government. In any case, the executive adopted Lewis' suggestion to set up a Political Action Committee along the lines of the CIO Political Action Committee "for the purpose of educating the workers of Canada regarding the necessity of action in the political field." But at the next committee meeting Conroy made it known that Congress organizers still could not accept political nominations because "they were paid by the Congress to work in the economic field and if they must go into politics, they should withdraw from the work of the Congress." It was also decided that the request of the new Political Action Committee, headed by Millard, to be allowed to circularize unions soliciting financial support would be tabled until Conroy could meet with the committee to discuss the relationship between it and the Congress.[23]

The relations between PAC and the Congress was exacerbated by the personal conflict between Conroy and Millard. Conroy was first and foremost the trade unionist, Millard, who had just been elected to the Ontario legislature, more the politician. Millard felt that Conroy should be doing more to further the cause of both the CCF and international unionism within the Congress. Conroy, on the other hand, feared that Millard was willing to sacrifice the interests of the Congress for these two less important concerns. He felt that the CCF element in the Congress was every bit as contemptible as the Communist faction. He distrusted Millard and his allies and saw little difference between them and the Communists. Both, he felt, wished to "capture" the Congress and make it their "subject instrument."

Conroy had no confidence in the trade union ability of these men. "Building unions," he wrote, "was hard objective work. It was no job for a romantic, for an irresponsible." Millard and his supporters had "no practical experience in trades unionism. In great measure they were by-products more of the political process, with the fights with Hepburn over the CIO being the level of their trades union background." "Politicians," he added, could not build a strong union movement.

The Congress when Conroy was appointed secretary-treasurer, was, in his own description, "nothing ... an empty shell ... a ludicrous assortment ... which was given by some objective observers roughly a year to survive before it splintered into fragments and disappeared as just another strange phenomenon." In his mind there was no time for politics. The CCL's only priorities were to "build a national Congress ... to organize the unorganized into unions ... and to have a free independent centre for Canadians workers." Affiliating with the CCF, he believed, would compromise this independence and divert the Congress' energies from organizing and other union acitivty. He therefore fought the CCF forces in the Congress as strenuously as he campaigned against the Communists.

Furthermore, he feared that the attempt to "affiliate" with the CCF would split the Congress and possibly destroy it. Those urging affiliation were in Conroy's opinion "persons of warped priorities ... and juveniles" who were out simply to make the CCL "a mere appendage of the CCF." "Political parties," he wrote, "must be instruments of the trades union movement, not masters." If Millard's campaign to affiliate were to succeed, it would lead, warned Conroy, to the Congress "handing decision making over to groups of political individuals whose knowledge of the trade unions is a fragmentary thing."

To Conroy, the entire concept of a Political Action Committee was therefore also wrong. Not only was it a "borrowed title," it was, as well, a "borrowed instrument negatively successful in the United States." As he put it: "It has an alien connotation of US pressure in Canada, where such pressures rebound against the users more often than they are successful. Steady plugging, instead of the glamorous medium, is, as I see it, the medium for Canada. Borrowed instruments start off with a strike against them." He was opposed to donating money to the CCF because the Congress was already desperately short of funds. Instead, he suggested that PAC be reorganized "with a new name, the Political Education Committee, and a new function, purely as an educational medium." He complained to Mosher that PAC was too closely identified with the CCF and it should be "made definitely clear that the Committee is a Congress one and responsible to the Congress."[24]

In his battle to move the Congress away from its endorsement of the CCF, Conroy was naturally opposed by Millard. Sensing the probable repercussions of the dispute, David Lewis wrote Conroy that he was worried about the PAC for only one reason, "the obvious difficulties between yourself and Charlie Millard, and the undoubted fact of your serious distrust of Charlie's motives." He warned Conroy that it "would be a tremendous disservice ... if personal differences were allowed to create obstacles in the way of PAC," and asked him to ignore some of Millard's "foolish" actions which were "never motivated by insincerity or dishonesty" but stemmed from his "fanatical ... sincerity with regard to certain basic principles."[25]

Support for the CCF was also undermined by the hostile attitudes of various Congress unions. The left-wing unions – UE, IWA, Mine-Mill, and the Fur Workers – naturally wished to broaden the PAC so that it was "more representative ... of the main divisions of thought within the Congress and not merely the instrument of one political group." District 18 of the UMW refused to support PAC because its director, Bob Livett, felt that it would further divide union members of various political affiliations at a time when unity was necessary. District 26 followed suit. George Burt announced that the UAW would have nothing to do with PAC until it withdrew its support from the CCF and supported "non-partisan labour political action."[26]

As a result, most of the 32 resolutions submitted to the 1944 Congress convention called for the repudiation of the previous year's endorsement of the CCF. Largely because of this opposition, but also because of his own personal doubts, Conroy backed away from his support of the CCF at the 1943 convention and recommended that no union should affiliate with the CCF unless "a large majority of the members were in favour of such action." By a vote of 272 to 115, the convention adopted a resolution merely endorsing the 29-point program of PAC which did not specifically mention the CCF, and recommending that it be submitted to all political parties for their acceptance or rejection.

This, was not nearly enough for the left-wing unions. At the UE convention following the CCL convention, a resolution was passed condemning the Congress for ignoring the sentiments against partisan politics expressed in almost all the 32 resolutions, and for following the "dangerous and one-party position of being the appendage of the CCF." The delegates also attacked Millard for his "blind partisanship" which "damaged the interests of Canadian workers" and risked "throwing the country and the people's future into the hands of the Tories." The Congress was also condemned for not accepting the UE proposal for a coalition in Ontario of CCF, Liberal, and Labour Progressive parties "to oust Premier Drew ... and to clear the decks for great provincial and national reforms."[27]

These accusations brought a prompt retort from the USW which accused the UE of "following the Communist line of using smear tactics," and a warning from Conroy that the UE was attempting "to sabotage" the Congress and would therefore be liable to suspension. Jackson protested that his union had done nothing wrong; rather, it had contributed greatly to fostering "the greatest possible unity within the CCL." Conroy retorted that any attempt to criticize convention decisions in public must be interpreted as "derogatory to the Congress and as holding its Convention in complete contempt." Because Communist policy at the time called for unity of the labour movement to help win the war, Jackson promised to publicly retract the statements made by the UE and to apologize to the Congress.[28] This, however, did not end Communist opposition to PAC.

At the PAC meeting held on 16 November, 1944, the left-wing led by George Harris of the UE, once again demanded that PAC become a non-partisan political instrument of all unions and not merely an "agent" of the CCF. The motion was defeated. But because of the strong opposition from the left, Millard introduced a motion – unanimously adopted – stating that PAC was "wholly independent of any political party" and would join with other democractic organizations "to defeat reaction and to ensure the election of a representative and responsible government of the people federally and provincially."[29]

But at the very next meeting of the PAC Millard announced that only the CCF had promised to support fully PAC's 29-point legislative program. He therefore introduced a resolution endorsing the CCF and calling for the election of a CCF government. When this resolution was passed, Nigel Morgan and Harris announced that they could no longer remain on the committee and resigned. After consulting his district council, Burt also resigned from PAC on the grounds that it was being "dictated to by a political party" and because the decision to endorse the CCF would "render the forces of this Union partially impotent" and split the UAW. He warned that the Congress could not afford "to put all of [its] eggs into one basket" and gamble with the future of unionism in Canada in such a way. With the departure of these men from PAC, its internal difficulties, at least, were resolved. But with such large and important sections of the Congress boycotting it, PAC's prestige and influence suffered a crippling blow.[30]

On the whole, its first year of operation – 1945 – was an unmitigated disaster for PAC. Its efforts in the Grey North by-election, as well as in the federal and Ontario elections, were total failures. The CCF, which in 1943 and 1944 had scored such emphatic successes in Ontario and Saskatchewan, was badly mauled in all three elections, despite the efforts of PAC. The IWA, UE, and the

UAW kept sniping away at PAC's policy throughout the year, particularly the UAW, whose paper, according to the PAC director, Eamon Park, was completely "subservient to the Communist party." In addition, the Mine-Mill president, Reid Robinson, on receiving David Lewis' complaint that the union's representative in British Columbia, Harvey Murphy, was interfering with the work of PAC in that province and supporting the Communist party, coldly responded that Mine-Mill would "resist any effort to make the labour movement an adjunct of any political party." He added that he himself would vigourously and firmly oppose any attempt to affiliate any Mine-Mill local with the CCF.[31]

In his year-end review of PAC's activities, Millard analysed the reasons for its failures. He attributed these to the "vocal political elements in the unions" who refused to accept Congress decisions and who with the "willing co-operation of reactionary interests through the press" were able to confuse both Congress members and the public. Further, he noted that "PAC American techniques were not altogether adaptable to Canada," and that "Canada's political system required a Canadian approach to problems." Conroy agreed that PAC had not "caught on" largely because it was a foreign import on the Candian political scene. He again urged that, instead of supporting the CCF, PAC should reorganize itself as an educational committee to "analyse, from time to time, current problems as they affect the Congress and its whole membership." Because of PAC's dismal showing, Millard offered to resign as its director. He was dissuaded by Mosher who thought it better to wait until the Congress could discuss the matter further.[32]

Opposition to PAC, however, reached its peak at the 1946 convention. In what proved to be the longest debate in Congress history – more than eight hours – the issue of political action was thoroughly aired in an atmosphere of bitter acrimony. The Communists and their left-wing allies demanded that a resolution calling for non-partisan political action be submitted in place of the resolution supporting the CCF. In an unforgivable tactical blunder one of the Communists, George Harris, stated that what was at stake was the struggle between the CCF and the Labour Progressive party. The supporters of the CCF pounced on this admission and argued that if their resolution was defeated the Congress would become a tool of the Communists. Finally, in his most vigorous and passionate attack yet against the Communists, Conroy accused them of attempting to subvert the free democratic institutions of both the Congress and of the country. He warned that "the issue in this convention is whether the Labour Progressive Party will dominate the Canadian Congress of Labour or whether the Canadian Congress of Labour shall remain in the hands of its membership." By a large majority the convention decided for the latter and voted for the resolution to support the CCF.[33] Though the question of the CCF affiliation would be discussed at future conventions, never again would its opponents provide such vigorous resistance. Their defeat marked the beginning of the end of the strong Communist element in the Congress.

Compared to their other activities within the Congress, however, the Communist opposition to PAC pales into insignificance. A good part of the party's energy during the war years had been expended in attempting to persuade the Congress to adopt a no-strike policy, and to support the war effort with all the vigour it could muster. Undoubtedly, however, the Communists made their greatest impact in British Columbia. Almost the entire Congress operation on the West Coast was controlled by the Communists. As Conroy complained to Millard, "it seems the Communist party is more or less overrunning both trade unions and political organizations in the Pacific Coast province, and is at the present time enjoying a sort of Roman holiday."[34] The leadership of the IWA, Mine-Mill, the Vancouver Labour Council, the Dock and Shipyard Workers, and the Boilermakers and Iron Shipbuilders Union, which represented the vast majority of Congress membership in the province, was largely Communist.

It was the case of the Boilermakers and Iron Shipbuilders Union, since 1942 the largest in the Congress, which best illustrated the problems faced by the Congress in dealing with its Communist minority. At the beginning of the war this union was a struggling organization of about 200 men; only two years later, with the ever-increasing demands of the war for ships, membership had passed 13,000. Most of these new members had little knowledge of either politics or unionism. It was therefore possible for a small group of politically oriented persons to capture the leadership of the union. It was the manner by which they succeeded, however, that raised the ire of the Congress.

The Boilermakers' union was the CCL's most important affiliate. Not only did it have the largest membership of any Congress union, but its financial contribution in 1942 was more than the combined total of all the international unions.[35] It followed, therefore, that the Congress would react violently should this union, and especially its funds, be threatened. Naturally enough, at least in the eyes of the Congress executive, such a threat came from the Communist party.

To the Communists, the Boilermakers' union was a prime target. With its large treasury and growing membership inexperienced in unionism, the union was ripe for a Communist coup. Starting off with one member, a shop steward named Malcolm MacLeod, the party was soon sending in other organizers –

Stewart of the IWA, McPeake of Mine-Mill, and even veteran BC Communist leader Tom Ewen, amongst many others – to infiltrate the union. Their success was later described by the Congress commission set up to investigate the situation: "By a process of strategy, relative terror, and with a definite organized campaign, these adventurers sought to discredit the builders of the union by slander and ridicule, and union meetings became a nightmare where order disappeared and disorder took its place. Political generals placed themselves strategically in the meetings of the unions, and on an organized basis were able to disorganize them to such an extent that the sincere trade unionists became disgusted and invariably left, thereby leaving the business of the union in the control of these political strategists ...

'Owing to this unhealthy, chaotic state of affairs, many members became thoroughly disgusted, and desisted from attending the meetings of the local union. This was responsible for the development of apathy among a large section of the membership, and as time went on the attendance at meetings of the union decreased to such an extent that those whose main purpose was to secure political control were enabled to take virtual possession of it ...

'The most interested group represents what is commonly known as the Communist Party. It is well organized and has been successful in burrowing its way into the councils of the union and a number of positions of authority ... Many individuals from all parts of the country and from various industries who were regarded as outstanding Communists ... have apparently concentrated their numbers and strategy inside practically all shipyard workers' unions in Vancouver, and in the Boilermakers' Union more than any other organization. Certain individuals who were regarded as members of their political organization left salaried positions with other unions to obtain employment in the shipyard, evidently for the purpose of securing membership in the Boilermakers' Union and concentrating their political forces in it.

'Their first step seems to have been to obtain minor positions in the union and to use such position to secure employment for more members of this Party in the shipyards. Their next step was to place their members in the more influential positions in the union, with the object of securing control of its treasury ...

'The evidence indicates that the next step in their program was designed to assure election of large delegations to conventions of the Canadian Congress of Labour, with the ultimate object of acquiring control of the Congress itself.'[36]

Because of this situation, when a Communist-supported slate overturned the union executive in the elections of December 1942, the Congress representative in British Columbia, Alex McAuslane, recommended to Mosher that the union be placed under a Congress administration and that the election be nullified on the grounds that only a small percentage of the workers had voted. Perhaps too precipitately, Mosher concurred, and without informing the newly elected Boilermakers' executive, he appointed McAuslane to administer the union for one year and to set up a board to assist him. Equally rash, McAuslane chose a board made up entirely of the defeated candidates in the election, completely ignoring the new executive members.

The elected executive ignored Mosher's order and on 1 January, 1943, in a ceremony attended by Harold Pritchett and Nigel Morgan of the IWA, and president Leary of the Vancouver Labour Council, they were installed in their offices. At once, the defeated secretary-treasurer, Robert Stephen, secured an injunction from the Supreme Court of British Columbia restraining the new executive from taking office and freezing the union's treasury of approximately $60,000. In turn Stephen and the old executive were barred from the union offices by a phalanx of 120 shop stewards who had taken possession of the office. They also formed a committee to take over administration of the union. The newly elected executive and the shop stewards were supported, predictably enough, by the IWA, the Ship and Dockyard Workers Union, Mine-Mill, the Vancouver Labour Council, and other Communist-influenced organizations in British Columbia. Surprisingly, however, many non-Communist organizations were equally appalled by the dictatorial behaviour of the Congress.[37]

Not only did the Congress action appear autocratic, but there was doubt whether it was even legal. Because the election vote had been by referendum, Mosher claimed that, according to article 14, section 9, of the Congress constitution which provided that officers of local unions can be elected only at a meeting, the Boilermakers' election was unconstitutional. To support his position, Mosher secretly consulted a large legal firm in Ottawa. Their reply shocked the Congress president. It was their opinion, they informed him, that his actions were "illegal, totally unwarranted and unconstitutional." Neither the executive committee nor council which met to consider the situation were apprised of this legal opinion. In fact, the only versions of the BC situation they heard were from Alex McAuslane and Aaron Mosher.[38] The committee and council therefore approved Mosher's and McAuslane's actions, recommended the suspension of the IWA for supporting the new executive, and set up a committee of Conroy, J.E. McGuire, and Millard to investigate the situation, but Millard resigned before the investigation began.

The Congress investigating committee held its first session in Vancouver on 18 January 1943. The Shop Stewards' Working Committee, which, by this time, exercised total control over the Boilermakers, protested that the Congress commission was "one-sided" and merely a "kangaroo court," and consequently, it refused to permit any member of the union to testify before it.[39] Therefore, aside from the testimony of the IWA leadership, the committee only heard from such Congress supporters as Stephen and McAuslane. And with such biased evidence, the committee predictably came to a rather one-sided conclusion. It denounced the Shop Stewards' Working Committee as "an outlaw body, a species of union dual to the Congress." For the previous two years, it reported, the "well-meaning but ineffectual" executive of the union had been undermined by the "slander and deceit" of certain groups "who were trying to secure political control of the union." The union's structure, it stated, was "cumbersome and impracticable" and made the task of the Communists in capturing the union easier; the union thus became "a relative menace to itself and the community." The election, it declared, was justifiably declared illegal by Mosher because "a substantial number of members were disenfranchised from voting"; "only 22% of the membership had voted and only 10.95% had supported the new executive." Because of these "chaotic conditions" the committee saw no merit in holding new elections and recommended that the charter of the union be suspended and the workers in the shipbuilding industry be reorganized into smaller locals in each yard or plant. As well, it recommended that the Congress suspend the British Columbia District Council of the IWA which continued to support the Shop Stewards Working Committee "in defiance of the commission."

In British Columbia, the report was greeted with unusual resistance and violent disapproval. Pritchett protested that the committee had no right to ask for the suspension of his union as neither he nor his organization had done "anything wrong." The Shop Stewards' Council of the Boilermakers also condemned the decision. Under its auspices, new elections were held and the same executive to which the Congress objected was re-elected. Immediately, the union declared itself independent from the Congress. Unfortunately for the Boilermakers, Conroy had made arrangements with the manager of the bank containing the union's funds to transfer all its assets to the Congress.[40]

The report was naturally acceptable to the Congress executive council which approved the recommendation to suspend the Boilermakers' and Woodworkers' unions, and agreed that action be taken at once to set up a British Columbia federation of shipyard workers. Party policy still called for labour unity in order to aid the war effort and at the executive committee meeting in June, Nigel Morgan pleaded unsuccessfully for the reinstatement of the two suspended unions. At a special executive committee meeting held during the Congress convention in September 1943 the representative of the Boilermakers, Jack Stewart, was informed that if the Boilermakers would agree to follow

Congress laws and policy, the union would be welcomed back into affiliation and its funds returned. At the request of the committee, and because of their own desire to reaffiliate, the Boilermakers did not appeal their suspension to the Congress. Instead they agreed to submit a seven-point executive proposal to a union referendum. At the same time, the IWA, on orders from its international president, also withdrew its appeal to the convention, and agreed to abide by the committee's decision.

Once back in British Columbia, however, Stewart repudiated the agreement. He did so on the advice of the union's lawyer, Nathan Nemetz, who informed him that the British Columbia Supreme Court would likely rule that the Congress injunction freezing the funds of the union was illegal. At a mass meeting of the Boilermakers, Stewart stated that there would be no further discussion concerning reaffiliation until the Court announced its decision. If the Court ruled in favour of the union, it would regain control of its sizable treasury and would then be in a position to dictate terms to the Congress. Realizing this, Mosher issued an ultimatum to Stewart to accept the Congress proposals at once; if he refused, Mosher threatened to place the union under a permanent administration and to hold on to all the union's assets.[41]

The Congress had proposed that the Boilermakers reaffiliate as a charter local subject to Congress control. Stewart now maintained that the union would return to the Congress only as an affiliate or as a national union with the autonomous powers concomitant with the new arrangement. (This would lower the union's payment to the Congress from twenty-five cents per member per month to three cents.) According to the Congress representative in British Columbia, Danny O'Brien, the union's membership supported Stewart. "Most of the officials and almost all the membership," he wrote Mosher, "are unanimously against a union with a membership of fifteen thousand being considered a local union subject to all of the summary powers given to the Congress." With this support Stewart felt safe in ignoring Mosher's ultimatum. Infuriated, Mosher ordered O'Brien to take over administration of the union and take control of its funds. Astutely, O'Brien persuaded Mosher to "soft-pedal" the situation, arguing that if the Congress acted too rashly and tactlessly, the Boilermakers would likely set up, outside the Congress, their own Communist-controlled shipyard workers' federation with more than 20,000 members.[42]

On 3 November 1943, the Court set aside the injunction obtained by the Congress and ruled that the Boilermakers' executive was "legally elected ... with complete control over union property and funds." A chastened Mosher resignedly accepted all Stewart's terms and agreed to lift the suspension of the union, to recognize its new executive, and to set up a federation of shipyard workers. The proposals were accepted by the Boilermakers, and on 15 January

1944, the Boilermakers, the Dockyard Workers, and the smaller Congress shipbuilding locals in British Columbia met in Vancouver to create, as a Congress affiliate, the British Columbia Federation of Shipyard Workers.[43]

Though the situation was far from resolved – the Federation and the Steelworkers would become involved in several acrimonious jurisdictional disputes requiring the personal mediation of Conroy and Mosher – temporarily at least, the Congress had reached an accommodation with its largest union. From the start, the Congress had badly mishandled the affair. Mosher had reacted too rashly in accepting McAuslane's advice and had aggravated the problem by refusing to back down from his position once he was informed it was illegal, unconstitutional, and self-defeating.

For the left it was a major tactical victory. The Congress, to supporters and opponents alike, had appeared anti-democratic, rigid, vengeful, and wrong, while the Communists seemed democratic and flexible. The Communists now controlled the new Federation and its huge treasury, ignored Congress policy when it suited them, and made decisions which affected the entire Pacific coast shipping industry in Canada. With the end of the war, however, and the dramatic decline of the ship-building trade, the Federation lost most of its membership, and with them went its power and influence. After 1945 the Federation would no longer cause the Congress much concern.

6

The International Union of the Mine, Mill and Smelter Workers 1936-48

The history of no union within the Congress is more dramatic or more puzzling than that of the Mine, Mill and Smelter Workers.[1] No union had greater potential and failed so miserably, or secured larger gains and suffered larger losses in so short a time than did Mine-Mill. From 1916 to 1919 Mine-Mill made prodigious gains in Canada. In 1920 it was extinct. Between 1936 and 1941, Local 240 in Kirkland Lake claimed that its over-5000 membership made it the largest in Canada; One year later with fewer than 150, it was amongst the smallest. Local 239 in Sudbury was founded with a flurry of excitement and organization in 1936; two years later it was defunct. In 1946 Local 241 in Timmins reported 5000 members; and in 1950, 25. In 1938, Mine-Mill reported a membership of 4000 in Canada; in 1940, 176. These bizarre fluctuations had one basic cause – the remarkable internal disruptions that were a hallmark of the history of Mine-Mill in Canada.

Internal feuding and inexperienced leadership brought about the demise of Mine-Mill in the 1920s; this same factionalism, compounded by the imposition of a militant left-wing leadership on an essentially apolitical membership, led to the rapid deterioration of Mine-Mill a generation later. To blame the left-wing leadership for this decline seems, at first glance, a much too simplistic explanation. Unlike the situation in most party-influenced unions, however, the Communists in Mine-Mill, with the possible exception of Harvey Murphy, seemed more concerned with the interests of their party than their union. Even more significant, because of its leftist orientation, other unions often refused to advance the co-operation and assistance to which Mine-Mill should have been entitled as a Congress affiliate. And the CCL itself did all in its power to undermine Mine-Mill's leadership. This external hostility, coupled with the internal disruptions, hastened the demise of Mine-Mill.

Organization amongst miners in northern Ontario had begun at the turn of the century with the Western Federation of Miners. But it was not until the 1930s with the emergence of, first, the Workers Unity League, and then the CIO, that a serious attempt was made to organize the miners of northern Ontario into one union. A zealous Communist and erstwhile organizer for the WUL, George Anderson, directed the Mine-Mill campaign. Under his guidance locals were established in Sudbury, Timmins, Kirkland Lake, and other mining centres.

The union's future seemed bright. As one enthusiastic organizer informed the Mine-Mill president, Reid Robinson, in 1937, "within a fifteen mile radius of Sudbury alone there is a work force of over 11,000 waiting to be organized." Frantic requests for aid went out from these overworked organizers to both the CIO and the Mine-Mill head offices. Significantly the Canadian leadership of the union wanted "financial aid rather than organizational assistance." Their reasoning, according to one organizer, was that "the Canadian press ... is quite reactionary [and] has taken a very hostile stand against the CIO and has labelled the organizers who have been sent here as 'foreign agitators' ... in view of the situation we deem it advisable and diplomatic to further our cause by placing our own local organizers on the job." Predictably, they received neither financial nor organizational assistance. Instead, as a sop, Canada became a full district of the union and thereby entitled to a position on the Mine-Mill executive board.[2]

The first Canadian representative on the board was another Communist, Tommy Church, whose interests lay more in the area of politics than labour. Consequently, a large proportion of the revenues of the various locals, most of which were also controlled by the party, were diverted from union activities to Church's personal political campaigns. Concerned over this situation, Robinson sent his personal "trouble-shooter," Alex Cashin, to investigate. On Cashin's advice, he dissolved the Canadian district in 1939 and removed Church from his executive position.

Many of the Mine-Mill executive also felt that the union's operations in Canada should be terminated. With only one local, in Kirkland Lake, still functioning, they feared that it would require more funds than the union had to mount an organizing campaign in Canada. Largely because of Robinson's insistence, their arguments were rejected and Thomas McGuire was appointed the union's administrator in Canada. At the same time, Bob Carlin, who had joined the Western Federation of Miners in 1916, and had since worked in the mining camps of northern Ontario, was appointed organizer. To help Mine-Mill maintain its foothold in Canada the UMW loaned it an experienced organizer, Alex Susnar, while the Canadian Congress of Labour contributed $250, although Mosher pointedly warned that this "must not be regarded as a precedent." Ironically, one year later, in support of Mine-Mill, the Congress would be driven to the brink of bankruptcy.

Obviously, the Congress was dubious about supporting Mine-Mill. At the executive committee meeting in March 1941, the Congress informed the Mine-Mill representative that, because his union was financially incapable of mounting an organizing campaign in Northern Ontario, the United Mine Workers should take over Mine-Mill's jurisdiction and undertake a large-scale organizing campaign. But John L. Lewis, on behalf of the UMW, declined the Congress invitation. At the same time, Reid Robinson informed the Congress that Mine-Mill would organize northern Ontario on its own.[3]

Concerned over the strength of the mine-owners and the hostility of the Ontario government, Mosher and Conroy had toured northern Ontario in 1940 and warned the miners against taking any strike action. They privately pleaded with the Mine-Mill leaders to settle "any existing difficulties ... by an energetic but peaceful policy." Their pleas were in vain. When the mine-owners refused to negotiate, as they were required to by law, Local 240 in Kirkland Lake demanded a federal conciliation board. The board held hearings in September and October of 1941 and unanimously recommended that the union be recognized and that the mine-owners be compelled to negotiate. The latter refused. Even then, the Congress urged Mine-Mill not to strike. Conroy begged Robinson "to play down [a] possible strike and [to] capitalize with [the] proper publicity" on the intransigence of the mine owners. None the less, the successful defiance of the law by the mine-owners, backed, of course, by Hepburn and the Ontario government, forced the Congress reluctantly to support Mine-Mill, and to order all its affiliates to do the same.

In asking the CIO for assistance, Conroy warned Haywood that Kirkland Lake would "be the battle-field over the question of collective bargaining for the entire Dominion ... and [would] affect for good or bad all of our organizations in Canada on the question of collective bargaining." And at a Congress executive meeting Millard added that "the situation was an international one, and would be watched all over the world." Finally, on 8 November 1941, the miners in Kirkland Lake voted to strike. Three days later, Bob Carlin and Tom McGuire met with the federal labour minister, Norman McLarty, and urged him to make collective bargaining compulsory. When he refused, Congress officials contacted Lewis for permission to call a strike. Once this was given, a strike was inevitable. Two days later, on 18 November, 1941, the Kirkland Lake strike began.[4]

It was perhaps the most disastrous strike in Congress history. Both Mine-Mill and the Congress had been manoeuvred by the mine-owners into a position in which a strike was unavoidable. To back away would have been catastrophic for their prestige; but neither Mine-Mill nor the CCL was strong enough to combat the entrenched mine-owners. Only the interference of the government on behalf of the miners could have saved the situation. Mackenzie King refused to act, even though the mine-owners had obviously ignored government regulations and had rejected the unanimous recommendation of a government conciliation board. In responding to pleas from the CCF leader, M.J. Coldwell, and others to invervene "on behalf of the democratic rights" of Canadian workers and to order the mine-owners "to conform to the declared policy of the government with respect to freedom of organization and collective bargaining," King said that his "intervention" would only "further complicate the situation." He therefore refused even to meet with union representatives to discuss the problem. Not to be outdone, Premier Hepburn sent in provincial police to "protect the mines" and spoke warmly of his friendship with the mine-owners.[5]

Despite the hostility of both levels of government and of most of the nation's press, public opinion as expressed through various city councils and church groups was sympathetic to the strikers who trudged around the closed mines for twelve bitterly cold and lonely weeks. The labour movement also responded generously. Though many union officials openly questioned the tactics of Mine-Mill – some thought it more advisable to strike such an essential war industry as International Nickel – several hundred thousand dollars were raised to help the strikers. But the opposition of the mine-owners and the government was unrelenting. The former filled the press and the air waves with anti-union propaganda. Many of their leaflets and advertisements were blatantly racist, emphasizing the fact that of the men who had walked out nearly half were foreign-born while of those who remained at work "93% were of British or of Canadian origin."

The mine operators reiterated again and again that they would never recognize the union. Indeed in February 1942 they ignored the request of the new federal labour minister, Humphrey Mitchell, to submit the issue to the binding arbitration of the War Labour Board; and, though he had the power, Mitchell refused to compel the mine-owners to do so. In the face of such insurmountable opposition, the union called off the strike with the rather unlikely explanation that "to stay out longer would have harmed the war effort." In one last, frustrated gesture it issued a leaflet condemning "the vicious coalition of mine management, Canadian vested capital, the Government which is not the people's and a police army of occupation [which] have starved out a union of

Canadian workers and maintained a feudal open-shop. Once again the boot-heel has descended on democracy." With that, the men returned to work, realizing full well that they had lost the strike.[6]

For the next decade the gold mine operators in Kirkland Lake would not be overly troubled by union organizers. The Congress and Mine-Mill, both on the brink of insolvency, had received a devastating blow. But the strike, if nothing else, did serve as a training ground for future labour leaders – Larry Sefton and Eamon Park amongst others – and did draw public attention to the hardships faced by the miners and to the anti-labour policies of the government. Nevertheless, it was an exorbitant price for the union movement to pay.

With the failure at Kirkland Lake, in Bob Carlin's words, "the bottom fell out of Mine-Mill organization in Timmins." Even more serious, the plans for an organizing campaign in Sudbury were abandoned, largely because a "goon squad" of a dozen men raided the Mine-Mill office there on the night of 24 February, 1942, wrecked it, and severely beat up two organizers, one of whom, Forrest Emerson, was an international representative. Two of the attackers candidly admitted they were hired for the job by an official of the International Nickel Company, but no charges were ever laid.[7]

The raid was an ostensible success. Mine-Mill publicly announced the withdrawal of all its organizers from Sudbury and closed its offices. Secretly, however, it ordered them to begin organization "from out of town." Unfortunately, the CCL had had its fill of Mine-Mill. At a special executive meeting, Conroy stated that Mine-Mill was "causing the Congress a lot of trouble," that Emerson should have gone back to the United States instead of going to Sudbury, and that since Mine-Mill was making no progress it should withdraw from Canada. He urged the CIO to study "the entire situation affecting Mine-Mill in Canada" before any more organization was attempted. Because Sudbury, he warned, was "owned, lock, stock and barrel by the Company," and its authorities were "controlled by the Company as well," any attempt to organize INCO was doomed. Indeed, Mine-Mill in Canada also seemed doomed. By March 1942, Canadian membership in Mine-Mill had fallen to 500 and its debt had risen to $35,000.[8]

Cowed though by no means beaten, Mine-Mill, for the third time in less than six years, revamped its organization and started anew. Under the leadership of Bob Carlin a vast organizational drive was again begun in Sudbury. Within months, with little assistance from the international office, Local 598 at INCO in Sudbury organized so many workers that it became the largest local in the entire international organization. As a reward, at the 1942 Mine-Mill convention, Canada was given back its district status on the executive board and Bob Carlin was chosen the Canadian representative. For the next two years considerable progress was made in the Sudbury area and in other parts of northern Ontario, Quebec, and especially British Columbia; fifteen new locals were also chartered in 1943, thirteen in British Columbia alone. By this time the Ontario government had passed a Trade Union Act. Under its regulations, in 1944 INCO was compelled to sign a contract with Local 598, which gave Mine-Mill the check-off it needed so badly. In the previous year the local had swamped a company union in the largest election in Mine-Mill history by a vote of 6913 to 1187.[9] Capitalizing on this resurgence of unionism, Carlin was elected as a CCF member to the Ontario legislature in 1943.

Though gratified with Mine-Mill's success, the Congress was uneasy about the union's flirtation with the Communist party. The international executive board was evenly split between the leftist faction led by Robinson and a strong conservative group. What most troubled the Congress was that Carlin consistently sided with the Robinson faction. Though he claimed that the Mine-Mill organization was completely autonomous in Canada, it seemed that Carlin maintained this autonomy only by supporting the Robinson group. Indeed, it was often Carlin's vote which swung the balance in favour of Robinson at the executive board meetings. At the 1943 convention it was only the support of the strong Canadian delegation led by Carlin which allowed Robinson to continue as president. Undoubtedly, it was Carlin's intention to use this support to force Robinson to increase the international's contributions to the Canadian organizing effort, and to achieve for himself a position in Mine-Mill comparable to that of Millard in Steel – full control and authority over all the union's activities in Canada. If this was his intention, he failed, defeated by the very forces he had done the most to keep in power, that is, Robinson and his party supporters.

By 1943, Mine-Mill seemed well on its way to becoming an adjunct of the Communist party. One of the leading party members in the country, Harvey Murphy, took charge of Mine-Mill activities in British Columbia. At the same time, against the advice of both Carlin and the CCL, Robinson persuaded Mine-Mill in Canada to go along with the "no strike" pledge of other party-dominated unions. The Congress also complained that the union paper, the *Sudbury Beacon,* was carrying "Communist propaganda." This Carlin readily admitted, but he explained to Conroy that he was forced to hire a devoted Communist as editor of the paper because he could find no one else "with his experience and qualifications" for the job.[10]

To keep his eye on Carlin and to help him direct Mine-Mill organization, in early 1944, Robinson sent Thomas McGuire to Sudbury. But according to Ralph Carlin, Bob's younger brother and himself a Mine-Mill organizer, McGuire had been sent to Canada to "balance" the Mine-Mill staff by appointing Communists. According to the younger Carlin, "Robinson's election hinged entirely on the stand that would be taken by the Canadian delegates" at the next convention. It was therefore important that he be able to appoint his supporters to staff positions. This analysis was supported by Jim Kidd, a prominent CCFer in Sudbury and a one-time president of the Sudbury local, who urged David Lewis to convince Bob Carlin to lead a delegation to the convention which would vote against Robinson. Similarly Conroy asked Millard to speak to the elder Carlin and point out to him that McGuire had been sent to Canada simply to create "a machine for Robinson." Millard did in fact speak with Carlin but was hardly reassured: while Carlin felt that he could "handle the party people," Millard remained convinced that he could not.[11]

Millard was right. Though Carlin fervently believed he could control the Communist element in the union, he was eventually betrayed. He faithfully supported the Robinson faction, and even on decisions with which he personally disagreed he provided the Robinson forces with the deciding vote on the union's executive. When Robinson was charged with secretly attempting to "shake down" $5000 from the president of a company with which Mine-Mill had a contract, Carlin voted, though he knew the accusation was true, against asking for the president's resignation and even against setting up a fact-finding commission; his vote was decisive in defeating both measures. In return for his unquestioning loyalty, Robinson promised Carlin that the international would not interfere in Canadian affairs. Yet, despite Carlin's request that the British Columbia area be allocated to his district, it was given to Harvey Murphy who was a much more reliable person for party purposes. In most cases, however, Robinson kept his word: throughout 1944 and 1945 the international rarely interfered in the affairs of the Canadian district.[12]

Unfortunately, this situation was dramatically changed in 1946. Maurice Travis, a Communist, who had been expelled from the Steelworkers for "communistic disruption," was appointed Robinson's personal assistant, even though he had never before been a member of Mine-Mill. His appointment seemed to indicate to anti-Communists in the union that their leadership was now totally under party control. They therefore made a desperate attempt at the 1946 convention to bar all Communists from holding office in the union. This resolution would have passed had the Canadian delegation either abstained or voted for it. Instead, led by Carlin, they overwhelmingly voted against it, and it was defeated by the narrow margin of 23 votes. At the same time, in a hotly disputed election, Robinson was again re-elected and Travis was voted in as vice-president. But so obviously "rigged" had this election been that many locals complained to the union's executive board and presented evidence of the "dishonest manipulations ... of the Robinson machine which

[had] prevented honest elections." When the party-dominated executive board dismissed these allegations, though there is no doubt that they were valid, many of these locals announced that they would secede from Mine-Mill. As a result, Robinson suddenly announced that he would resign his position, and that Travis would be the new president of Mine-Mill.[13]

Startled by these dramatic events, the CIO set up its own investigating committee to inquire into the turmoil in Mine-Mill. After a lengthy investigation the committee condemned the secession movement but blamed it on the Communists. It demanded that Travis resign because he was "continuously dealing with representatives of the Communist Party in shaping the policy of the union." Travis did in fact resign, but not from the executive. He simply appointed himself to the powerful post of secretary-treasurer, promoted the pliable and weak John Clark to the presidency, and made Reid Robinson a vice-president. Thus, by 1947, Mine-Mill seemed more securely than ever under the control of the Communist Party.

Throughout this unhappy period, Carlin faithfully supported Robinson and Travis against both the CIO and the strong anti-Communist element in his own union. He was unshaken in his belief that with this loyalty he could buy the autonomy he so desperately wished for his Canadian district.[14] Travis and Robinson, however, saw things somewhat differently. Unnerved by the growing opposition to their leadership in the United States, and gratified by Carlin's dogged loyalty, they decided to concentrate most of their efforts in Canada where the atmosphere seemed more congenial. From 1945 to 1947 Mine-Mill held policy conferences in Sudbury under the personal direction of Travis. The upshot of each was the drawing up of a brief on wages and working conditions which, in the opinion of Congress officials, was "totally unrealistic." But even more harmful, according to the Congress, before the briefs were submitted to the government they were all "checked over" by the "Communist or pro-Communist labour dignitaries" such as Joe Salsberg and Drummond Wren of the Workers Education Association.[15]

Carlin's concurrence in this arrangement and his support of party policies in general were causing great concern in both the Congress and the CCF. Doc Ames, a CCF organizer in northern Ontario, complained to David Lewis that Carlin was "completely under the influence of Reid Robinson," that Mine-Mill policy invariably coincided with that of the Communist party, that Joe Salsberg was playing an increasingly important role in shaping union policy, that Carlin rarely consulted Congress leaders, and that, under Carlin, Mine-Mill "plods its solitary and lonely way and to hell with the rest of the Canadian Labour Movement." Similarly, Millard warned the CIO headquarters in Washington that Mine-Mill in Canada was coming increasingly under Communist control, and that many of its locals, complaining over the "lack of coordinating policy and direction in Canada," were threatening to secede unless "party control" was terminated. He added that although Carlin was a "very nice fellow" he was weak and allowed Robinson and Travis to "make policy and strategy in Canada that would best suit their own personal positions." Even Carlin's brother, Ralph, lamented that "poor Bob hasn't got the strength to offer any opposition to the constant manoeuvring, intrigue and attacks against any and all trade union leaders who dare to offer any criticism against the devilish action of Communist strategy" within Mine-Mill.[16]

How deeply enmeshed Carlin had become in the Communist net became apparent at the 1947 Congress convention. There, on two "gut" issues – condemnation of both "Soviet imperialism" and "Communist totalitarianism" – Carlin sided with the extreme left against his erstwhile allies in the CCF and the Congress. Upset by Carlin's behaviour, twenty-six stewards of Local 598 in Sudbury placed an advertisement in the Sudbury newspaper condemning Carlin and demanding that he oust the Communists from Mine-Mill.

But much more alarming for both the Congress and Carlin was the fact that Travis and Robinson had decided that the time was at hand for a concentrated organizing effort in Canada.

At a meeting of the Kirkland Lake local a resolution was adopted inviting Reid Robinson to Canada "to coordinate the organizational drive in the gold industry." The secretary of the local complained to Conroy that the meeting had been "carefully staged" with only the Communists and their supporters in attendance. Nevertheless, Travis accepted the "invitation" and announced that because of the "organizational difficulties [in the United States] imposed by the Taft-Hartley Law, it seems logical that we shift our organization concentration to Canada."[17]

When the anti-Communists in Mine-Mill got wind of this move, they immediately informed the Congress that "Robinson's mission to Canada [was not] to consolidate the workers" but rather "to keep the worker in a disorganized order, with the aim of keeping a little group of Communists in control." "The aim of the Communist party," they went on, was "to be in a position to paralyse the production of nickel and copper" in Canada. Finally, they urged that the Congress use its influence with the Minister of Immigration to prohibit Robinson from entering Canada. In response to a personal plea from Ralph Carlin for assistance to help rid Mine-Mill of its Communists, Millard said that he had warned his brother four years earlier that "if he pursued an appeasement policy toward Communist tactics, he would sooner or later find himself completely subject to their dictates." He added that he found no satisfaction that his prediction had proven sound, but he warned that the

members of Mine-Mill must defeat the Communists themselves without outside interference from other unions. Any such intervention, he warned,
"would play more advantageously into the hands of the Communist Party
tacticians."[18]

Party policy, it seemed, had already been settled. On 16 November, 1947,
at a Mine-Mill conference in Kirkland Lake, it was decided that Robinson
would take up residence there to conduct a "massive" gold mine organization
campaign. As if to underscore the Communist character of the new campaign,
two American Mine-Mill organizers, Rudy Hanson and Harlow Wildman,
both closely identified with the Communist party, had already been sent to
northern Ontario to replace two acknowledged anti-Communist organizers.
Other Mine-Mill organizers such as Harry Horowitz and William Kennedy,
both party activists, were soon to follow.

The first results of this invasion were, for party interests, disastrous. At the
December elections of Local 241 in Timmins, the non-Communist slate led by
Ralph Carlin won nine of the eleven executive positions. Pleased, Ralph Carlin
wrote to Conroy that the miners were determined to get rid of the Communists
who had been "destroying" their union for the past ten years and were coming
from the United States in ever-increasing numbers. He warned that, unless
Mine-Mill's policy changed, his local would secede.

On 16 December, an angry Conroy informed Robinson and Bob Carlin that
he was aware that Mine-Mill was sending in organizers "to head up Communist party developments within the union," and that the Congress had finally
reached a "parting of the ways" with the party. The Congress, in Conroy's
words, was "not going to play around with it any longer." He warned Ralph
Carlin, however, that to defeat the party, it would be necessary for the non-
Communist element to adopt a "positive programme" for the union. It was not
enough merely to be anti-Communist, he warned.[19]

The attitude of Bob Carlin toward these unhappy events was puzzling. His
major objective in supporting the Communists – to maintain for the Canadian
section its autonomy – had obviously failed. In fact, the Canadian section now
had less autonomy than ever before. By the beginning of 1948 it appeared that,
on the pretext of launching a massive organizing campaign, the entire Communist apparatus in Mine-Mill had been sent north across the border to escape
the restrictions of the Taft-Hartley Act in the United States. Carlin was no
longer even master of his own district. Decisions for the district were being
made by Robinson and his coterie of imported organizers and then being
transmitted to Carlin. His brother drolly compared Carlin's position to that
of a man "with a foot on two horses each going in opposite directions."[20]

In a private meeting with Conroy, Bob Carlin revealed that the Communists were an "insignificant faction" within the union and that he was having much more trouble with the CCFers who had "a wholly negative attitude" and were trying to take his job. Conroy sadly concluded that Carlin had unwillingly become "a good fellow traveller to the Communist Party" and as such should be expelled from the CCF. This opinion was shared by the leader of the CCF forces in Mine-Mill, Jim Kidd, who stated that Bob Carlin and his supporters in the union were "consorting with and carrying out the policies of the Communists and thus creating so much apathy in the union that there was "virtually no opposition" any longer to the Communists. The feeling in CCF circles, however, was that if any attempt was made to "disown" Carlin, his seat would likely be lost; for this reason, nothing was done for the time being.[21]

More distressing to Carlin than the possible actions of the CCF, however, were the developments within his own union. Paralleling the situation in the United States there were already signs that some Mine-Mill locals were ready to secede rather than submit to Communist leadership. The Congress organizer in Ontario, Henry Rhodes, met with executive members of Local 241 representing miners in the Timmins, Schumacher, and Porcupine area. They demanded that the Congress grant them the status of a chartered local and "take them out" of Mine-Mill. The president of Local 637 in Port Colborne also invited Conroy to speak to his union on the possibility of leaving Mine-Mill and becoming a Congress-chartered local.[22]

Finally, in March 1948, the Congress declared "full-scale war" on Mine-Mill. The *casus belli*, understandably enough, was Mine-Mill's unyielding determination to bring in organizers from the United States, all of whom seemed to be members of the Communist party. The CCL had been embarrassed by a speech made by US Senator Robert Taft in February. To indicate to his fellow Americans the success of the Taft-Hartley labour bill he had co-sponsored, Taft revealed that American labour leaders connected with the Communist party were 'hurrying out' of the United States to Canada. This observation was confirmed by Mackenzie King who told the Commons that his government was exploring ways to restrict such immigration. Though these accusations were heatedly denied by Mine-Mill, they were endorsed by Millard who issued a press release corroborating that Communist leaders were moving into Canada to take over Mine-Mill activities.[23]

In response, Mine-Mill president Clark demanded that the Congress "object strenuously" to any change in the immigration policy of the Canadian government. He also wrote to all CIO unions in Canada warning that any change in Canadian immigration policy towards labour organizers would place serious restrictions on all international unions, and he demanded that the CIO force the Congress to take a firm stand on this issue. Reluctantly, Philip Murray urged Conroy to uphold the position of Mine-Mill. Support for Mine-Mill also came from such anti-Communist unions as the United Rubber Workers, the Amalgamated Clothing Workers, and the IWA, all of whom demanded "vigorous opposition to any change in existing immigration regulations as they apply to representatives of international unions" since this would "seriously hamper" the activities of international unions in Canada.[24]

Reassured by the unanimity of the CIO support for the Mine-Mill position, Carlin demanded that the Congress executive make representations to the government not to change the immigration laws concerning American labour organizers. His request met with a hostile reception. Anxious to underscore the autonomy of the Congress, Mosher and Conroy, pointedly ignored the CIO's views, rejected Carlin's demands on the grounds that Mine-Mill had sent in to Canada not labour organizers but "well-known Communists." Mosher also warned that Canada "must not become a playground for communism" and stated that the Congress would not ask the government to protect these men or even to permit them to stay in Canada. "Communists camouflaged as labour organizers," he said, should not be brought into Canada. Similarly, Conroy condemned the "stupidity" of Mine-Mill importing Communist organizers. This action, he argued, not only alienated the mine-owners, the government, and the public, but it also brought "under suspicion all labour organizers sent from the United States." He offered the Congress' support for the union's gold mine organizing campaign, but only if Mine-Mill sent its Communists back home. The CCL executive rejected Carlin's recommendation that the Congress intervene with the government on behalf of the Mine-Mill organizers. In its place, the council adopted Conroy's suggestion that the Congress not assist Mine-Mill until its American organizers had left the country.[25]

Disturbed, Reid Robinson wrote Mosher and Murray informing them that the Congress decision was "prejudicial and inimical to the interests of the membership" of Mine-Mill. In addition, he contemptuously rejected Congress support for the union's organizational campaign as long as the "independence" of Mine-Mill was under attack. More important to the Congress, however, would be the response of the CIO. Therefore for several days after the Council meeting, Conroy, Millard, and Mosher met together to discuss the contents of the letter of explanation to Murray. Finally on March 9, almost a full week after the decision was taken, Conroy's draft was accepted and sent, not only to Murray but to all international presidents.[26]

The letter began with an outline of the sorry record of Mine-Mill in Canada, with specific reference to the Kirkland Lake strike which, in Conroy's words, had come "close to bankrupting every union" in the Congress and which had brought no appreciable gains to the workers. Claiming that the union had learned nothing from this failure, Conroy charged that once again Mine-Mill was beginning a campaign without consulting the Congress. The influx of Communist organizers he said, had "provided the reactionary interests dominating the gold industry with all the arguments necessary to sabotage an organizational campaign." It had "deliberately irritated public opinion" and was "an unexampled demonstration of sheer ineptitude." The executive committee and council of the Congress had not supported the Mine-Mill position, Conroy explained, because the Congress convention had condemned Communism. The council could therefore not sanction "the importation of foreign Communists" into Canada "especially when their ultimate aim [was] the restriction or abolition of the legitimate function of the trade union movement itself." The Congress would, Conroy stated, fight with all its energy against the prohibition of "legitimate trade union representatives" coming into Canada. But it would not become "an umbrella ... to protect the importation of Communists ... whose first and final objective is control of our trade union movement." Conroy also pointed out that Mine-Mill had rejected the "generous" proposal of the Congress to provide all necessary organizational assistance if the union withdrew its Communist organizers. Finally, he bluntly told Murray that the Congress had had enough of the Communists. Though the Congress action might "not be the smart or politically expedient thing to do," Conroy declared, "the time for smartness or political expediency in regard to communism is now at an end." He warned that "the developments in recent weeks have demonstrated in a sufficiently clear and definite fashion that if the trade union movement is to remain as a force for freedom for itself and for all the people, then it can have no truck with – let alone give approval to – the Communist movement."

The CIO's reaction to this declaration of war on the Communists was mixed. Some unions, mostly on the right, supported the Congress; others, on the left, did not. Officially the CIO said nothing; unofficially Murray gave Conroy the green light to root out the Communists. Reaction to the Congress position when it was made public was greeted in some Mine-Mill circles with delight, in others with scorn. Ralph Carlin commended the Congress for beginning the "de-lousing" process, but most Mine-Mill locals were in bitter opposition and protested loudly to both the Congress and the press.[27]

Taking its cue from the Congress position, the federal government arrested Robinson and held him for deportation on a charge that he advocated the violent overthrow of the Canadian government. He was released on bail only after signing a bond that he would "refrain from engaging in any union activities while at liberty."[28]

The arrest was obviously very embarrassing to the Congress. In E.B. Jolliffe's words, "for pure unadulterated stupidity this certainly takes first prize. The conditions of the bond are all that could have been asked for by anyone seeking to make a martyr out of Robinson." Much against its will, the Congress was now forced to support Robinson because of the "indefensibly stupid" action of the government. In the eyes of even the militant anti-Communists in the Congress, Robinson had been transformed overnight, as Jolliffe suspected, into a hero. Through the efforts of Conroy, the wording of Robinson's bond was changed from "union" to "subversive." The fact remained, however, that the arrest put the Congress on the defensive and gave the initiative back to Mine-Mill. In a furious attack on the Congress, Robinson blamed the CCL for his arrest, charging it with ignoring the advice of the CIO "to place trade union considerations above and beyond political considerations of its individual leaders" and with supporting a "governmental union-busting witch-hunt against foreign-born union leaders." [29] *213 881*

But it was not too long before the Congress regained the initiative. At the beginning of April 1948, thirty-two delegates walked out of a Mine-Mill conference in Sudbury, ostensibly because of their opposition to the union's policies. Actually, the walk-out had been pre-arranged at a secret meeting with Congress officials in Toronto and had been approved by Conroy. Quickly forming a provisional committee, the insurgents met with Congress officers and were informed that the "Congress offer of organizational assistance still stood." Both the Timmins and Port Colborne locals accepted the offer, and expressed their disgust with their international representatives. With the Mine-Mill local in Niagara Falls they formed a Provisional Committee of District 8 and refused to pay their per capita taxes to the international. [30]

In retaliation, Robinson fired Ralph Carlin, the leader of the insurgents, as business agent of the Timmins local. Local members countered by voting overwhelmingly to reinstate Carlin and to censure Robinson. Robinson then suspended the entire executive of the Timmins local. Shortly thereafter, against the advice of Conroy, the local voted to withdraw from Mine-Mill – but not from the Congress – and to form a Timmins Mine Workers Organizing Committee. [31]

The secession once again put the Congress in an untenable position. To support the secessionists while Mine-Mill was still a Congress affiliate would be impossible. But to denounce them when the Congress had been in the forefront of the opposition to Mine-Mill's leadership was equally impossible. Nevertheless, in reply to a reminder from Clark that the Congress was "obliged to condemn all dual or secession movements," Mosher declared that, though the Congress discouraged such movements, Mine-Mill itself was largely to blame "in view of the type of personnel brought into Canada to carry on organizing activities."[32]

At an executive meeting called to discuss the situation, the Congress passed a resolution deploring the "principle of secession," and offered to meet with officers of Mine-Mill to "stabilize the situation." Clark accepted the Congress proposal and on 4 July, 1948, he and several Mine-Mill officials met with Conroy. Before this meeting, the Congress had been secretly informed that Silby Barrett on his own, had offered to take the secessionist Mine-Mill locals into the United Mine Workers. Conroy also had been advised that these locals, which had stopped paying dues to their international were now anxious to become chartered locals of the Congress and to leave Mine-Mill.[33]

At the meeting with Clark, Conroy renewed the Congress offer to assist in the organization of the northern Ontario gold mines. After some discussion it was decided that the union would set up a national office in Canada and Conroy promised to mediate all the disputes which were disrupting the union's efforts. For Mine-Mill, Clark promised to discuss the Congress offer with his executive board colleagues in the United States. But the offer was never accepted. Much more serious crises soon arose which threatened to damage severely both organizations.

Carlin's unswerving loyalty to his union's leadership was as embarrassing to the Congress as to the CCF, but it was the latter organization which acted first. In 1943 he had received more votes than any other CCF candidate in the province. In 1945, when CCF members all over the province were crushed by the Conservative steamroller, Carlin easily held his seat. Then, suddenly, in 1948, he was expelled from the party.

For several years David Lewis, Ontario CCF leader E.B. Jolliffe, Millard, and others had begged Carlin to oppose the Communist leadership of his union; to each in turn Carlin insisted that his "appeasement policies" would build a stronger union. But by 1948, it was obvious to all that Carlin had "appeased" too many times. Complaints were pouring into the CCF office from all over the province, from CCF members of Parliament as well as from local organizers, that Carlin's pro-Communist policies were "harmful and confusing." On 8 April, 1948, Carlin was ordered to attend a provincial executive meeting of the CCF to discuss "serious charges" that had been preferred against him. These charges, Carlin discovered, were that "his loyalty" to the Communist group in his union had "become incompatible with his position as a CCF member of the legislature." He was asked by the CCF executive not to run again in the forthcoming provincial election. Just before the meeting he was also informed by Millard that if he were now willing to accept the Congress offer and "stand four-square on the pledge which the CCF has made to the Canadian people," he was assured the full support of both the Congress and the CCF in ousting the Communists from his union. Carlin rejected this offer because, in Millard's words, he had "become so hopelessly involved that he hasn't the moral courage to turn back." To Carlin, however, the offer was unacceptable because "of the deep principle involved – the whole matter of deportation of labour organizers."[34]

When Mine-Mill was informed of the CCF's executive decision that "under no circumstances" would Carlin be endorsed as a CCF candidate in the next election, Reid Robinson warned Andrew Brewin, Ontario CCF president, that if the CCF did not reconsider its decision his union "would have to fight the CCF" not only in Sudbury but throughout the country. Carlin, he said, would run again even without CCF support. Thus when the CCF nominating convention in Sudbury chose another candidate in May 1948, Carlin immediately announced his intention of running as an independent. Despite the frenetic efforts of the CCF, Carlin finished well ahead of the official CCF candidate and only a handful of votes behind the Conservative winner. But he had violated the CCF constitution by running against the party candidate. The executive of the CCF, with a collective sigh of relief, expelled Carlin from the party.[36]

For the Congress the matter was not quite so simple. It would not suffice merely to oust Carlin; a way had to be found to expel the entire union. Because of Mine-Mill's tactlessness it soon was.

The 19 June, 1948, edition of *The Union*, the official newspaper of Mine-Mill, carried an article severely castigating Mosher for his "attempt to water down the workers' demands" by agreeing to settle a wage dispute with the railways for considerably less than the 28-cents-an-hour increase demanded by his own union. The charge was basically accurate, but what Mine-Mill hoped to gain out of printing it is inexplicable. It did provide the Congress, however, with the excuse it had long been seeking to expel the troublesome Mine-Mill affiliate.

To set the Congress machinery into motion Millard sent Mosher a copy of the article and remarked that it was time for the Congress to act against such unions as Mine-Mill which were continuously attacking Congress leaders and policies. Mosher was enraged and agreed that it was indeed time for "a showdown." More significantly, he indicated to Millard that the Congress was at last prepared to expel Mine-Mill "and to take similar action against every other Communist-led union affiliated with the Congress as the opportunity presents itself."[37] This was the logical outcome of the policies the Congress had followed since the end of the war. Whatever the explanation given publicly, Mine-Mill, UE, and other left-wing unions would be expelled for no other reason than that they supported Communist policies.

On 10 August, 1948, Mosher initiated charges with the executive committee against Mine-Mill for "publication of a false, misleading and obviously malicious statement." A concerned John Clark promptly and humbly apologized on behalf of Mine-Mill and sent along copies of the union's inner-office memoranda which indicated without question that the editor of *The Union,* Morris Wright, was away "during the entire period when the 19 July issue of *The Union* was being prepared," and that the article had been inserted by "a relatively new and inexperienced assistant who had since been severely reprimanded." Bob Carlin also informed Mosher that he had immediately fired the editor of Mine-Mill's local paper in Timmins in which the charge against Mosher had first been printed and from where it was "picked up" and reprinted in full by the international newspaper. [38]

As should have been expected, these apologies did not suffice. On 24 August, the executive council of the Congress, though not without some opposition, suspended Mine-Mill "as an example to others" that Congress affiliates could not forever "defame Congress officials without risking severe penalties." At this same meeting, though for different reasons (see chapter 7), Harvey Murphy was barred from taking part in any Congress activities for two years.

Justly, Mine-Mill complained that the reason given by the Congress for the suspension seemed "patently inadequate and flimsy." The union shrewdly concluded "that other motives may have influenced the decision." About these "other motives" there was never any doubt. In explaining the drastic penalty to his international office, Millard claimed that, under Carlin, Travis, and Robinson, Mine-Mill had for some years been attempting "to bolster waning Communist fortunes in the Canadian trade union movement and in our Canadian Congress of Labour." The attack on Mosher was, in Millard's words, merely "the straw that broke the camel's back." [39]

But Mine-Mill had no intention of surrendering without a fight. It promptly launched its own offensive. In a series of letters to all Congress affiliates, Bob Carlin accused Millard of "raiding" his union and of leading the opposition to Mine-Mill so that Steel could more easily take over the Mine-Mill jurisdiction in Canada. He also accused the Congress of "stabbing at the very heart of inner union democracy, freedom of the labour press and the long established democratic process of the rights of criticism" and urged all unions to support Mine-Mill's demand for reinstatement by sending "resolutions, letters and telegrams" to Congress officials. The British Columbia district of the union sent out similar appeals urging support for their crusade to save the "trade union movement from disruption." [40]

Mosher also circularized all Congress affiliates rebutting Carlin's charges and adding that the "falsehoods and innuendos" contained in Carlin's letter would not be "particularly helpful" to his union. For the next few weeks, however, the Congress office was inundated by a flood of resolutions, letters, and telegrams from various affiliates and locals, almost all demanding that the Congress reinstate Mine-Mill. If anything, these stiffened the Congress resolve. In response to a critical letter from B.T. Doherty, a Mine-Mill organizer, Mosher coldly replied that the "kind of material appearing in ... *The Union* plus the definitely false statements in the circular letter sent out by Brother Carlin, plus the kind of insults to the intelligence of the Congress Executive members in letters being received from some unions ... leave very definite impressions with me adverse to your organization, and it is quite possible they have the same effect on many others."[41]

The barrage of protests, however, did indicate to Congress officials that the actions they had taken against Mine-Mill were not acceptable to many Congress locals. More seriously, many locals – particularly smaller ones – were concerned over the apparently well-founded claim by Carlin that Steel was anxious to take over Mine-Mill's jurisdiction. Already one Mine-Mill plant in Niagara Falls had voted to join Steel; others were threatening to do the same. Mine-Mill locals in Port Colborne, New Toronto, and Timmins were imploring the Congress to permit them to affiliate with Steel. Millard had indicated many times that his union would be more than receptive to any offer to organize within Mine-Mill's jurisdiction. The Congress also received a request from Steel organizer Bill Sefton that his union be permitted to take over the jurisdiction of the large INCO plant at Port Colborne and other Mine-Mill plants in southern Ontario whose locals were threatening to disband or to join AFL unions. Mosher demurred on the grounds that it was better that action should be taken "on a broad scale" rather than confined to one or two locals, and that, in any case, the Congress was probably more "capable" than Steel of "handling" any new "set-up." Instead, he called a conference of all Mine-Mill locals in Ontario and Quebec to discuss the problem.[42]

Clark demanded that this conference "should be called off." In addition, he accused the Congress of "unprecedented and arbitrary action in violating basic CIO and CCL policy" and ordered all Mine-Mill locals "to refuse to participate in any discussions dealing with the question of jurisdiction of this union or its relationship to [the] CCL." On the instructions of Clark, most of the delegates who attended Mosher's conference refused to recognize the right of the Congress to intervene in Mine-Mill affairs, and, as a result, no policy decisions were made. After the meeting, however, Mosher and Conroy met with delegates of the "unhappy" locals and assured them that, if their locals voted to leave Mine-Mill, the Congress would issue them charters.[43]

Also left undecided was the future policy of the Congress towards Mine-Mill. It was probable that the suspension would be lifted as soon as Mine-Mill formulated an acceptable apology; but it was the Congress' intention to keep the suspension in force at least until after the 1948 convention in October, and Clark angrily rejected Mosher's request not to appeal the suspension to the convention. Clark's appeal to the convention was, on the orders of Mosher, not subject to debate, much to the disgust of many delegates. Clark presented his case simply and briefly. The reason for the suspension, he said, was an editorial in *The Union.* Mine-Mill had before, as it was doing now, offered a "sincere apology and unqualified retraction." As far as he was concerned the issue was closed and there was no reason for the suspension to continue.

Presenting the Congress case, Conroy argued that the basic issue was whether "law and order" would prevail in the Congress "so that member unions will be free from lying attacks, slander, and wanton character defamation." These attacks, Conroy believed, all "emanated from the same quarter with one thing in mind – to so undermine, discredit, and hogtie the leadership of these unions that the individuals who dreamed up the charges could walk in and take over control of those great organizations for their own purpose." Not surprisingly, by a huge margin, the convention endorsed the Congress position.[44]

Shortly thereafter, Clark met with Mosher and other Congress officers and successfully "worked out ... the retraction and apology" that would appear in the next issue of *The Union,* and in fact, it did appear on page nine of the issue of 11 October. Unfortunately, this issue was not published until the following week. Thus, when the executive committee of the Congress met on 16 October, all they had before them was a proof copy of the apology. To most members of the committee – especially Conroy – this was not sufficient as it did not "constitute publication."

That the Congress intended to make Mine-Mill's reinstatement difficult was clear; but how to do so, and keep within the bounds of the Congress constitution was a problem. Sam Baron of the Textile Workers argued that it would be a "serious mistake" to expel Mine-Mill after it had tendered an apology. "If Communism was to be met," he felt the issue should be "strong and clear cut." J.E. McGuire of the CBRE claimed that Mine-Mill "had not shown good faith ... since it was under an obligation to clear out the Communists in its leadership." Finally, the committee decided to lift the suspension when the retraction was published. But, intent on humiliating Mine-Mill, the committee also decided to grant a Congress charter to the Port Colborne local of Mine-Mill "as a temporary holding measure until a satisfactory undertaking can be worked out with the International Union."[45]

On 28 October, Conroy informed Clark that the Congress had finally received the 11 October issue of *The Union* and that the executive committee had voted to reinstate Mine-Mill. At the same time Clark was told that the Committee had voted to meet with officials of Mine-Mill to discuss the problems of local unions which had applied for Congress charters. Though the Congress had refused the request of the Timmins local, it had accepted the application from the Port Colborne local "because of the very unsatisfactory situation" and the threat that it "might go over to the AFL." Clark naturally protested the decision. Mosher replied that the Congress had acted "reluctantly" but warned that because of the deteriorating situation of Mine-Mill in Canada "there may be other localities where similar action will be justified, though the Congress, of course, had no wish to enter a campaign" against Mine-Mill.[46] Whatever Mosher's disclaimer, there was no doubt that, if not the Congress, then at least one of its affiliates – Steel – had begun a campaign against Mine-Mill.

Assured of Congress support, on 22 October, the Port Colborne local by a vote of 624 to 457 decided to break away from Mine-Mill. Three days later Conroy informed the local that the "time was not yet ripe" for the Congress to grant a charter. After a series of frantic telephone calls and telegrams from Port Colborne, Conroy agreed to poll the executive committee. On 28 October Mosher informed the local that the executive had decided to grant it a "provisional" charter but would not help it in any way nor allow it to affiliate with Steel. Ignoring these conditions the local executive, on the advice of Steel organizer Bill Sefton and with the encouragement of Millard, decided to affiliate with the Steelworkers.

Mine-Mill naturally protested against Steel's raid on one of its locals. Conroy denied that he had any knowledge of Steel's decision to issue a charter to the Port Colborne local, and added that he had urged Steel not to do so. He did offer the opinion, however, that "members of any local were free to go into any organization they so desire." To a similar query from George Burt, Conroy replied that he had requested the Steelworkers to desist, but that it was "clear that this Mine-Mill situation had to be cleared up sooner or later."[47]

Clearly, the Congress was in a dilemma. It wished to clean the Communists out of Mine-Mill, but this was obviously impossible. It therefore wished to rid itself of Mine-Mill, but did not know how. It also wished to grant charters to the various Mine-Mill locals which requested them, but could not while Mine-Mill was still an affiliate.[48] Finally it wished to do all these things without weakening the Congress, disrupting the labour movement, and strengthening the hand of its opposition – both within the Congress and without.

The Mine-Mill issue was the subject of heated discussion at the Congress executive council meeting on 14 December. Millard defended the action of his union on the grounds that Steel had jurisdiction over workers in the metal industry, and if the workers at Port Colborne wished to be represented by Steel, then there was nothing he could do. As a concession to the Congress, however, Millard agreed to withhold the charter, and turn over all application cards and records to the Congress until the matter was resolved. The council also decided that the Congress, Mine-Mill, and the CIO should hold a joint conference "with a view to bringing about some improvement in the organizing activities of the union and its relationship with the Congress." Informing Clark of this decision, Conroy explained that the conference was necessary because the Congress considered the relationship with Mine-Mill "unsatisfactory both to the Congress ... and to substantial groups of members" in Mine-Mill.[49]

Clark complained to the CIO president, Phillip Murray, that he was "getting fed up and disgusted with the activities against Mine-Mill in Canada" which were "working right into the hands of the mining corporations." He attributed all of his union problems to a "psycho-maniacal opposition" using "the usual nauseating diatribe of red baiting ... [and] disgruntled, power seeking and malicious people telling diabolical lies [whose] personal vindictiveness displaced whatever slight union principles they had ever held."[50]

Perhaps more biting and undoubtedly more troubling was a letter to Conroy from Bill Sefton. Angered by the Congress refusal to allow Steel to organize in Timmins and Port Colborne, Sefton called the decision "utter nonsense" and the "most completely unrealistic analysis" he had ever heard. He accused the Congress of throwing loyal members "to the wolves" and reminded Conroy that the fight against the Communists was "not a tea party." Until the Congress was ready to supply the services and organization promised the workers by Steel, Sefton was adamant that his union would not withdraw from either Timmins or Port Colborne for fear that the Communists could take over again. And so, ignoring the Congress decision, Steel began an organizing campaign in Timmins.[51]

Once again, in January 1949, the Mine-Mill situation was discussed by the Congress executive council. This time the council ordered both Mine-Mill and Steel to vacate the Port Colborne and Timmins areas so that the Congress would issue its own charters. When the "situation became stabilized, the Council would determine the final disposition of the local or locals concerned." The order to Steel and Mine-Mill to vacate and "cease all activities in Port Colborne and Timmins" was issued on 14 January, 1949. Publicly, the Congress decision was applauded and obeyed by Steel. Privately, Sefton wrote Millard a bitter letter complaining that in the Timmins area, at least, Steel had been dealt a "severe blow" by the Congress decision.[52]

Understandably, Mine-Mill reacted much more belligerently. At a conference of the union's Canadian locals attended by Clark and international vice-president Larsen, resolutions to redouble the union's activities in Timmins and Port Colborne were unanimously adopted. Clark termed the Congress action "arbitrary" and called the Congress decision "cannibalism within the labour movement." Referring to the Congress ultimatum, Larsen stated that "no arrogant telegram will drive us out of our backyard." The union charged that the Congress had joined with Steel in an "unedifying" effort to destroy their union, and it urged all Congress affiliates to join with them in their battle against the "dictatorial" policies of the Congress.[53]

To see that they did so, for the next few weeks, Carlin and other Mine-Mill leaders spoke at local meetings of various Congress affiliates, attacking the Congress decisions and announcing Mine-Mill's intention of defying them. Similarly the newspapers of most Mine-Mill locals in Canada joined in the denunciation of the Congress and Steel.

On 22 January the Congress executive issued a statement accusing Mine-Mill of making "vicious" attacks against it and of refusing to comply with its orders. Conroy promised that charges would be laid against the union with the recommendation that the union "be suspended indefinitely, probably permanently from the Congress." A grateful Millard praised Conroy for his "first-class" statement and contrasted the Congress action against Mine-Mill with the "pussy-footing" attitude of other union leaders.

To offset the propaganda of Mine-Mill, Conroy sent a circular to all Congress affiliates and locals describing the sad history of Mine-Mill, the "courageous" attempts of the Congress to assist it, and the rebuffs Congress officials had received from its leaders culminating most recently with the "chief spokesmen" of Mine-Mill "parading up and down the country, attacking, abusing and vilifying the officers of the Congress." Finally on 14 February, Mosher and Conroy issued a formal charge against Mine-Mill recommending that it be indefinitely suspended at the next executive meeting.[54]

At the Ontario Federation of Labour convention in Toronto on 18 February, Carlin presented an eight-page brief to the delegates which pointed out the failures of both Steel and the Congress in organizing workers within their jurisdictions. It also defended Mine-Mill from these same charges and harshly condemned the officers of Congress and of Steel for "a betrayal of the very principles" upon which the CIO and the CCL were founded by "raiding and encroaching upon" the jurisdiction of Mine-Mill. One week later, in a speech on the local radio station in Timmins, Carlin denounced the "devilishly un-principled Congress-Steel campaign," called Millard a "sanctimonious, psalm-singing hypocrite" and reiterated: "We will not move out of our jurisdiction

... we will not be pushed out of our jurisdiction, we shall not be kicked out of it, as some state we will ... Here we are and here we will remain."[55]

Whether Mine-Mill would remain in Timmins and Port Colborne was still open to question; that it would not remain in the Congress no longer was. On 24 March, the executive council of the Congress heard Carlin present the case for his union and emphasize that Mine-Mill had "no intention of relinquishing its jurisdiction at Port Colborne and Timmins." He received little support. Most of the council felt that the Communist party was "dictating the policy" of Mine-Mill and, therefore, that the union was not adequately representing the will of its membership. By an overwhelming vote the council decided to suspend Mine-Mill and to recommend to the next Congress convention that the suspension be made permanent.[56]

The decision triggered an unprecedented attack on the Congress from the left. From the UE, the Fur Workers, the British Columbia Shipyard Workers, Mine-Mill, and some locals in Steel and Auto came press releases, telegrams, resolutions, handbills, and pamphlets objecting violently to the Congress action. Mosher, Conroy, Millard, and other Congress leaders were accused, among other things, of "union busting," "red baiting," and being "front men" for the corporations.

More significantly, the Congress move against a Communist union seemed to have given some impetus to the CIO decision to do the same below the border. At an international board meeting of the United Steelworkers, Millard was told that the CIO was waiting to see the results of the Congress expulsion before it acted against its own Communist unions. According to Conroy most CCL leaders were "a little impatient at the seeming dilatory methods of the CIO in handling this problem," but the CIO looked on them as "outsiders." As Conroy explained, "they take the position that we are handling the situation in our way, and that they intend to handle theirs to suit their position."[57]

The Congress "method" was effective, if ruthless. Because Mine-Mill did not file a formal appeal with the executive before the 1949 convention, Mosher rejected Carlin's personal request that Mine-Mill be allowed to present its case to the delegates. Instead, copies of a letter Clark had sent to Congress officials the week before, protesting against the "arbitrary, unethical and dictatorial" actions of the Congress, were handed out to all delegates to the convention by Mine-Mill supporters. In addition, according to Millard, Mine-Mill representatives sat "in the gallery at the convention and made an attempt with the aid of the few Communists seated to appear as badly abused martyrs."[58]

To many in the convention, however, it did in fact appear that Mine-Mill had been unfairly treated. Many delegates felt that, at the very least, the union should have been given the right of a personal appeal. But because Jackson,

Harris, and Russell of the UE (see chapter 8) had been barred from attending the convention, there was little vocal support for the Mine-Mill position.

On the last day of the convention the delegates were asked to accept the report of the executive council. When one of the delegates asked if acceptance of the report would confirm the permanent suspension of Mine-Mill from the Congress, Mosher responded affirmatively. Two delegates rose to protest but were silenced by shouts from other delegates for a vote. By an overwhelming margin the report was adopted. In this way, ignominious and anti-climactic, with no debate, the Congress rid itself of the troublesome International Union of Mine, Mill and Smelter Workers of America.

In fact, however, Mine-Mill was no less troublesome outside the Congress than inside. Deciding which union would take over Mine-Mill's jurisdiction led to bitter disputes within Congress ruling circles. Silby Barrett who had been in the forefront of much of the opposition to Mine-Mill, maintained that Mine-Mill was obviously in the jurisdiction of the United Mine Workers. Millard argued that Steel was already organizing in the metal mining industry. And Mosher felt that the Congress should do the job itself. Only after pressure was exerted from CIO officers in Washington on international presidents to order their Canadian representatives to support the Steel claim, was the issue resolved. But even several months after this decision was made in favour of Steel, Millard was still complaining that "some of those who should be battling on our side have ... failed to speak or lift a finger in our support," and that "a lot of mud" was being thrown at Steel by people like Burt, thus "helping the Communists and making more difficult" the Steel struggle against Mine-Mill.[59]

It soon became obvious that members of Mine-Mill in Canada were more loyal to their union than the Congress had anticipated. Steel was badly humiliated in its attempts to win the support of the huge Mine-Mill locals in Sudbury and Trail. Even in Port Colborne, the workers voted to remain with Mine-Mill. Steel's attempts to organize the gold mines of Northern Ontario, highlighted by long and expensive strikes in 1951, and again in 1953, were only slightly more successful and much more costly than similar attempts by Mine-Mill. Through bitter experience both Steel and the Congress soon learned that Mine-Mill's failures in the North were perhaps less the result of its own internal disruption, as both Steel and the Congress believed, than the intractable anti-union position of the powerfully entrenched mine-owners. And Mine-Mill's ability to oppose successfully Steel and the Congress over the next two decades in the face of the combined hostility of a united Canadian trade union movement seems to indicate that the union was still capable of managing its own affairs and servicing its own members.[60]

In its treatment of Mine-Mill the Congress was remarkably clumsy. That Mine-Mill was dominated by the Communists, there is little doubt.[61] That Mine-Mill invariably disagreed with and strenuously opposed Congress policy is also not in doubt. But that Mine-Mill was a threat to the Congress, that outside the Congress it was somehow less dangerous than inside, is very much in doubt. Caught up in the frenzy of the Cold War, the Congress sought to cleanse itself by ousting its left-wing unions. Aided by the greed of some unions anxious to take over Mine-Mill's jurisdiction and by the desire of some partisans of the CCF to exorcise their left-wing opposition, the Congress had little difficulty in expelling Mine-Mill.

On the other hand, reluctant to polarize its opposition, the Congress stubbornly refused to state candidly and publicly the real reason for the Mine-Mill expulsion. Rather, by suspending Mine-Mill on such spurious and ingenuous grounds as the union's publication of an article critical of Mosher, by further exacerbating the situation by refusing to accept the union's apologies and retractions, and finally by expelling the union without allowing it to defend itself at a convention, the Congress merely added credence to the charges of its opponents that it was "dictatorial and anti-democratic."

Even worse, the reason given for the expulsion of Mine-Mill, that the union did not follow Congress policy, was fatuous. No union could possibly have accepted the Congress demand to give up two of its functioning locals and withdraw its organization from the areas in which these locals were situated, without suffering a grievous – and likely fatal – blow to its prestige and credibility. In any event, many of the workers in these two areas, Port Colborne and Timmins, the overwhelming majority of them non-Communists, opted for Mine-Mill over both the Congress and Steel. Perhaps recognizing the untenable position of the CCL, when the CIO expelled Mine-Mill in the United States, it did so openly and without any doubt as to the reason. Mine-Mill was expelled, in the CIO's words because its "policies and activities ... are consistently directed toward the achievement of the programme and purposes of the Communist Party rather than the objectives and policies set forth in the CIO constitution."[62]

The Canadian Congress of Labour had neither the foresight nor the courage to pursue this direct approach. In its haste to be rid of its left-wing unions the Congress sacrificed both justice and truth, and succeeded in neither destroying Mine-Mill nor strengthening the Congress.

7

The International Woodworkers
of America 1940-48

Separated from the rest of Canada physically by the Rocky Mountains, and psychologically by much more, British Columbia has often gone its own way oblivious of developments east of its mountain barrier. Its labour movement has proven to be one of the more independent and irrepressible of the province's institutions. In other provinces, non-Communist unions were in a distinct majority; in British Columbia, they were so few as to be almost exotic.

The British Columbia labour movement was, at least until 1948, almost a personal fiefdom of the Communist party. The province's three largest unions – the IWA, Mine-Mill, and the Shipyard Workers – were all controlled by the party; their leaders were all party members or supporters. And even the party, no doubt subject to the same influences as the rest of the province, often went its own merry way, ignoring, much to the consternation of the national office, party policy and strategy whenever it saw fit.[1] Many times, J.B. Salsberg would stoically phone party headquarters in Vancouver to order it not to undertake one of its schemes, only to be told to his chagrin that it had already been carried out. Because of the party's total domination of the union movement, there was little chance for the province to produce, as did Ontario, a Millard, whose major task would be to clean out the Communists. Indeed not until 1948, and then only with the help of the Congress and Millard's right-hand man, Bill Mahoney, did the native unionists in the province successfully repulse the Communist tide, and even then, only a grievous miscalculation by the party made this success possible.

The history of both the labour movement and the Communist party in British Columbia from 1936 to 1948 is largely the history of the International Woodworkers of America. As the largest and most influential union in the province, the IWA played the paramount role in the development of policies of the various labour councils in the province. With its large force of organizers and its relatively sizable treasury it provided both the personnel and funds for many of the Communist activities in the province. In addition to its financial contributions to the party it also contributed its secretary-treasurer, Nigel Morgan, who became party leader in the province. IWA organizers also actively promoted party interests amongst the shipbuilders on the coast and the miners in the interior. Masterminding all these activities was the union's first president, Harold Pritchett.

A one-time organizer for the Workers' Unity League, Pritchett was the first Canadian to be elected president of an international union. For a time he even sat on the executive board of the CIO. When the Workers' Unity League was disbanded in 1935, Pritchett led his Lumber and Sawmill Workers union into the AFL. Unfortunately, in the same year the executive council of the AFL gave to the United Brotherhood of Carpenters and Joiners complete jurisdiction over all workers in the lumber industry. Totally obsessed by their craft consciousness, the haughty Carpenters refused to accept the lumber workers as equals, and granted them instead a non-beneficiary or second-class status, i.e. the lumber workers paid dues but received no benefits and had no vote at conventions. Provoked by this treatment and by the Carpenters' attempt to break up their union into crafts, representatives of the various locals in the Northwest met in Portland in September 1936 and created the Federation of Woodworkers with Pritchett as president.[2]

Later that year delegates from these locals attended the Carpenters' convention in Lakeland, Florida. Not only were their protests and complaints ignored and their right to vote denied, but most demeaning, they were forced to sit at the back of the convention hall with the wives of the Carpenter delegates. Following this humiliation, Pritchett travelled to Washington where he discussed the Woodworkers' problems with John L. Lewis. The CIO leader promised to give the Woodworkers whatever assistance they required in their struggle with the Carpenters. But because the CIO was fully occupied elsewhere, Lewis urged Pritchett to be patient. Encouraged, Pritchett told the Woodworkers Federation of his talk with Lewis and of his disgraceful treatment at the Carpenters' convention. He urged the lumber workers, however, to bide their time and not to alienate the Carpenters.[3]

But with the rising tide of CIO sentiment in the United States and the spectacular victories of the CIO in the spring of 1937, the patience of the lumber workers ran out. A conference of district leaders was hurriedly called for 7 June, 1937. After listening to speeches from Lewis' aide, John Brophy, and from Harry Bridges, left-wing leader of the CIO longshoremen, and after receiving promises that the CIO would provide a $50,000 organizing fund, the delegates decided to hold a referendum on CIO affiliation.

The CIO immediately sent a cheque for $5000 and Pritchett, and his vice-president, O.M. Orton, met with Lewis to discuss future plans. At the Federation's convention in July, it was announced that the membership had approved the CIO affiliation by 16,354 to 5306. After five days of heated discussion most of the delegates voted to accept the results of the referendum and affiliate; those who did not, left the convention. On July 20 the convention reconvened as the International Woodworkers of America and elected Pritchett as president. All the executive positions were captured by Pritchett's left-wing allies.[4]

Thus began one of the most bitter labour struggles in American history as the Woodworkers struggled desperately to survive the brutal attacks of the Carpenters from without and of the various opposition groups from within. The Carpenters had immediately declared war on the new union and with the help of other AFL unions picketed IWA-organized plants, refused to handle IWA-produced lumber, instituted legal action against various IWA locals, and harassed IWA members. The American Northwest was almost in a state of civil war before intervention by the Governor of Oregon forced a truce upon both belligerents. By the middle of 1938, the violence had somewhat subsided and the organizational activities of both unions were intensified.

Besides this external menace, the IWA was being divided internally as well. Because of their leadership abilities, obvious organizational talents, and their contribution to the founding of the union, the Communists were elected to most of the decision-making positions in the union. But the rank and file was predominantly non-Communist, and for four years the struggle between the two groups seriously endangered the survival of the IWA. The consequent internal strife stunted organizational work and little headway was made in organizing the thousands of unorganized lumber workers on the west coast.

To investigate this unhealthy situation, in early 1940 John L. Lewis appointed the CIO director of organization, Michael Widman. Despite the violent opposition of Pritchett and his allies, the CIO forced the IWA to agree to undertake a broad organizational compaign under CIO leadership. On Widman's recommendation, the CIO also threw its full support behind the anti-Communist rank-and-file opposition. At the 1940 convention, which Pritchett was unable to attend because American immigration authorities refused to allow him across the border, an amendment to exclude Communists from membership was defeated by only ten votes – 134 to 124.[5]

Furious with the CIO, the IWA leadership, which was still controlled by the left, pushed through a resolution condemning the CIO. And immediately following the convention the IWA executive demanded the removal of Adolph Germer, the CIO director in charge of the IWA organizational campaign. In order to avoid an election at the convention, upon its conclusion, Pritchett, who still had one year more as president, resigned and turned the job over to his supporter, Orton. As an American, Orton would not have to worry about immigration officials.

In February 1941 the IWA leadership officially terminated its organizing agreement with the CIO. The anti-Communist opposition responded by setting up the CIO Woodworkers' Organizing Committee with funds and organizers from the CIO. In effect the IWA was now split into two almost autonomous factions – one under the control of the Communists, the other under the CIO. But as was happening in other unions, after the Nazi invasion of Russia, the party changed tactics and began to co-operate with the CIO. At the 1941 convention, taking advantage of the party decision to abdicate its control over the so-called "paper locals" – locals with no dues-paying membership but with a Communist executive – the right wing completely dominated the proceedings. They swept the executive positions and even adopted a resolution barring Communists from membership in the union.

This convention marked the end of Communist control over the IWA in the United States. But it made no impact on the Canadian IWA where Pritchett was strongly entrenched as president of the British Columbia district. Indeed, the results of the convention only served to weaken the international's control of its Canadian district and to strengthen the independent character of the British Columbia membership.

This self-sufficiency and pride was enhanced by the rapid growth of the union in British Columbia. In 1938 the IWA in that province had been almost demolished after an eleven-month strike at Blubber Bay. It took years for the union to recover from this setback. But in 1943, without any help from the international, the district won its first general contract covering the Pacific coast area. Between the Blubber Bay strike in 1938 and 1943, the union membership in British Columbia increased from little more than a hundred to well over 15,000. The district also loyally tacked about in line with the tortuous zig-zags of party policy. Before June 1941 Pritchett denounced the war as "imperialistic" and the district adopted a slogan of "raise the pay a dollar a day." Following the invasion of Russia the union changed its slogan to "production for victory" and it loyally adopted a no-strike pledge.[6]

Within the CCL, the IWA was in the forefront of the left-wing opposition. At the very first convention, the IWA's Nigel Morgan ran unsuccessfully as the left-wing nominee against Mosher. At a meeting of the executive committee in October 1941, the IWA was severely reprimanded for issuing "biased" reports of Congress minutes and threatened with suspension. In 1943 the district was in fact suspended because of the support it gave, against Congress orders, to the left-wing leaders in the Boilermakers' union. Soon afterwards it was reaffiliated and granted national union status by the Congress executive committee.

The Congress made several half-hearted efforts to control its Communist members in British Columbia, but after its fiasco with the Boilermakers (see chapter 5) it was overly cautious. Attempts to discuss the "problems" of the British Columbia district with the CIO and the international executive of the IWA came to nothing. Millard's efforts at the 1944 IWA convention to work out policies with the CIO and the IWA executive to undermine the British Columbia leadership were similarly fruitless. The Congress, in Conroy's opinion, could do nothing about the Communist domination in British Columbia unless it was prepared "to eject Communists of any and every description," and this, he suggested, could not yet be done. Instead Conroy adopted a policy of attempting to mediate between the left and right and of not interfering in the affairs of the IWA in British Columbia. This prompted Eileen Tallman, the Steel representative in Vancouver, to inquire angrily of Congress leaders when "the Conroy policy of appeasement to the LPP [was] going to stop."[7]

With the approval of the Congress, and at the instigation of the IWA, on 30 September 1944, the British Columbia Federation of Labour, consisting of most of the CCL unions in the province, came into being. From the beginning it was controlled by the left and its policies were usually in line with those of the Communist party. Its president was the Congress regional director in British Columbia, Danny O'Brien.[8]

Though he had warned Mosher in January 1945 of the dangers of the Communist domination of the Federation, O'Brien was shortly espousing the leftist position. And the provincial secretary of the CCF in British Columbia was soon complaining to David Lewis that O'Brien was "a tool of the LPP" and was acting as its "chore boy." He added, however, that since most of the Congress unions in the province were controlled by the Communists, it was "natural enough that the CCL office" should be controlled by them as well. "Only when the CCF influence within the CCL here outweighs the LPP influence," he added, would O'Brien 'succumb' to the former. Mosher's attitude, according to Lewis, was to "support Danny very strongly," and though he admitted that perhaps O'Brien was "too much under the influence of the LPP unionists" he still had "very great confidence in him." Ironically, if the Congress had confidence in O'Brien, the party had even more. For four consecutive years the Communists, who controlled the Federation, made sure that O'Brien retained his position as president.[9]

As the official voice of the Congress in British Columbia, the Federation proved an embarrassment to the CCL. Its pronouncements on many issues ran counter to what was being issued from Congress headquarters. Yet attempts to root out the Communists seemed futile. Party members had been active in the British Columbia labour movement long before the creation of the Congress. These men were largely responsible for the organization of the CIO unions in the province and were genuinely admired and respected by many rank-and-file union members. Any attempt to oust these men – Pritchett, Murphy, MacLeod, and others – would incense most local members.

Unlike the situation in eastern Canada, the CCF in British Columbia would be of little value in assisting the Congress to defeat the Communists. McAuslane complained to Conroy that in British Columbia the CCF was "just one unholy mess." He added that the party's actions have "alienated the sympathy of a great many workers who are far from being LPP, but have a sense of trade union principles." Eileen Tallman, a CCF organizer, complained that the CCF in British Columbia reminded her of the CCF in Ontario in the late 1930s – "they don't seem to have any conception of how to go about winning labour support." As Eamon Park of the Steelworkers, a staunch CCFer, sadly lamented, the British Columbia CCF "had its beginning in the old Socialist Party of Canada and it retains considerable of the doctrinaire intellectual approach which reveals itself in an almost naive approach to the labour movement." Similarly the Congress representatives in the province, Dan Radford, O'Brien, and McAuslane, seemed helpless. Eileen Tallman, who was leading the anti-Communist opposition within the CCL unions in the province, complained bitterly to Conroy that the Steelworkers and Packinghouse Workers were conducting the fight by themselves since there had not been "any evidence ... of any closer co-operation between the CCL officials and the anti-LPP bloc." In reply Conroy promised that the Congress was still considering methods to overcome the Communists, but until a "comprehensive approach" was adopted, little could be done.[10]

The first step in the "comprehensive approach" was to send a Congress representative to British Columbia to undertake the onerous task of ousting the Communists from Congress organizations. For two years, Eileen Tallman and Pen Baskin, the Steelworkers' representative in British Columbia, had bombarded Conroy and Millard with requests that such an appointment be made. In 1947 Eamon Park toured British Columbia on behalf of the Steelworkers and suggested to Millard that a Steel representative should be sent with the power to "clear out the Communists." At the 1947 Congress convention the British Columbia situation was discussed at length at a private meeting of Millard, McAuslane, Mosher, and Conroy. They decided that Bill Mahoney, Millard's protégé in the USW, would be sent to take charge of a two-year campaign to rid the Congress unions in the province of their Communists.[11]

Officially, Mahoney was named the Congress' western director of organization to "co-ordinate the organizational work in the western district from Manitoba to British Columbia." Unofficially, his sole responsibility was to "co-ordinate" all the activities of the anti-Communist forces in British Columbia. His task would be exceedingly difficult. Eamon Park warned him that he could expect little support because Congress officials and the CCF were "divided" amongst themselves. In the IWA, Park noted, Mahoney would "be compelled to start almost from scratch [because] the anti-commie leadership ... had been basically Trotskyite." He added that there was some anti-Communist feeling in Mine-Mill but that it was not well organized. Finally he stated that though Harvey Murphy of Mine-Mill was the "king pin" of the party leadership in the province, there was "some feeling" between him and Pritchett "as to who is going to play the leader."[12]

The Congress buttressed the Mahoney mission at the 1947 convention by passing resolutions condemning "Soviet imperialism" and "world communism." This prompted Pritchett to announce that his union, at least, would "spurn" this policy of opposing communism, and he urged others to do the same. On his return to Vancouver, the *B.C. Lumber Worker,* the district paper, published several articles attacking the "red baiting" of the Congress. It charged that the Congress executive had "wasted three and a half days at the convention in advancing a programme whose central theme was red baiting." This program, the paper went on, was planned by Mosher, Conroy, and McAuslane and had been discussed with Jay Lovestone, the AFL's Notorious "red-baiter," David Lewis, CCF leader M.J. Coldwell, and Walter Reuther.

The Congress swiftly replied to these charges. Mosher wrote to Pritchett terming the articles "a tissue of falsehood and misrepresentation from start to finish," and warning that unless the IWA quickly apologized for intentionally "injuring the Congress and besmirching its executive officers," the union would be suspended from the Congress. On 13 November, the day on which Mahoney's appointment was announced, Mosher laid charges against the district for publishing "false, misleading and mischievous statements." Four days later, the IWA issued a half-hearted apology, but refused to retract anything stated in the articles. Obviously, the Congress was not satisfied and at the December council meeting, it warned the IWA to publish a "satisfactory" retraction within thirty days, or the union would be suspended. Pritchett then agreed to sign the retraction drafted by Conroy.[13]

But at the same time, the IWA candidly stated that it would not stop its public attacks on the Congress. Addressing a Mine-Mill convention with Mahoney in attendance, Pritchett and Ernie Dalskog, a district board member, vowed to carry on their battle against Congress policies. Though the union had apologized for the articles attacking the Congress, they promised that the district would not "sacrifice the right of criticism." A bulletin from the district to its stewards accused the Congress of committing the labour movement "to partisan politics ... to red baiting and disunity instead of united action against boss attacks, and to a foreign policy of tying Canada to the tail of American big business."[14]

Meanwhile, Mahoney had spent his first few weeks in British Columbia attempting to "knit" together the several anti-Communist groups in the province and to warm the "definite coolness" between the Congress staff and the various international representatives. In this he was remarkably successful. Though he thought himself "overly optimistic," he maintained that "with the necessary leadership and co-ordination" he could "change the situation considerably in the proposed two-year attempt to set things in order."[15] In fact, it took him less than a year.

His first real task was to unseat the Communist executive on the Vancouver Labour Council. He ordered Dan Radford, a Congress representative, to make certain that every chartered local in the city sent delegates to the next Council meeting. A series of caucuses was held amongst the anti-Communist delegates and a slate of candidates for each of the twenty-one elected Council positions was drawn up. For the first time the non-Communists were doing what the Communists had been doing for years; and with the same results. At the Council elections on 27 January 1948, the entire Congress slate was elected; not one single leftist retained his seat on the Council. Delegates from all the Congress-chartered locals in the city, including some from locals that many Council members did not even know existed, attended and voted for the Congress slate. It was a considerable victory for the Congress. After many fruitless attempts, the right had captured from the left a major Congress organization in the province.[16]

The next job, a smug Radford told Conroy, would be to take on the British Columbia Federation of Labour. This, he added, could not be done unless the IWA, which controlled most of the Federation delegates, could be "broken down." And this, in turn, was not the impossible task that it at one time seemed to be. The IWA – as seemed its wont – was undergoing another of its periodic internal disruptions.

Since the ousting of the Communist leadership in 1941, relations between the British Columbia district and the international had been consistently cool and occasionally hostile. At one stage the connection was so strained that president Ballard of the IWA requested Millard to keep him informed of Congress policy and developments since he could not depend on his British Columbia section to give him "a true picture." Personal contact between the leaders of the international and the British Columbia district were kept at an absolute minimum, more especially since the Canadian leaders were unable, because of American immigration law, to attend international conventions. Most disturbing to the Canadian section was the international's power to appoint and dismiss organizers without consulting the district. In 1945 devoted party followers, Mike Freylinger and Hjalmar Bergren, were fired as Canadian organizers by the international and replaced by men loyal to the international.[17]

By 1948 relations were at a breaking point. At the district convention in January the delegates voted to remove the new international president, Jim Fadling, because he had suspended a Canadian trustee, Jack Greenall, for refusing to sign the non-Communist affidavit stipulated by the Taft-Hartley Act. When Fadling and other international executives spoke in praise of the Marshall plan, and condemned the leadership of the British Columbia district and the Communist party, they were jeered off the podium by the delegates. Speeches by Harvey Murphy, Pritchett, and Jack Greenall, attacking the Marshall plan, American foreign policy, and especially the international executive were greeted with jubilant cheers from the audience.[18]

It was a sadly disillusioning experience for the international officers. But it also drove them to consider drastic measures to remove the district leadership. Immediately, three organizers in the province who had supported the motion to remove Fadling were dismissed. Advertisements were placed in the Vancouver daily press by Fadling attacking the district's objectives and methods. To compete with the district's regular weekly radio broadcast, the international set up its own weekly program. In addition, Fadling promised to underwrite a Congress newspaper which would restrict itself solely to answering the charges made by the various publications used by the district and the Communist party "to get their line of thinking out to the members."[19]

Taking advantage of the IWA disunity, Mahoney began working with the anti-Communist forces within the district, particularly the strongly anti-Communist Local 217 in New Westminster led by Stewart Alsbury and George Mitchell. The Congress was naturally pleased with these developments. But Conroy felt that more action was necessary if Mahoney was to succeed in his task of "co-ordinating" the Congress unions in the province "to make a substantial dent in the Communist strength before the next convention." This, he said, could best be done only on a "step to step" basis. He agreed that it would be "impossible to clear out the Federation" without "doing something about the IWA," and urged that a list of "tactics" and "objectives" be decided upon quickly so that the entire British Columbia situation could be "cleaned up."[20]

First priority was given to reaffiliating the large number of Congress locals which had withdrawn, against Congress advice, from the British Columbia Federation of Labour in protest against its pro-Communist leanings. Radford had argued with them that it would be "far better if [they] stayed in and fought the issue," but so "tight" was the "party control" that most unions felt no useful purpose could be achieved by remaining. Acting on Conroy's request that Congress officials "do all they can to get these locals inside the Federation," Mahoney decided to reduce the Vancouver Labour Council's per capita tax from five cents to three cents so that affiliation to the Federation, whose dues were only two cents, would mean "no added cost [to Congress locals] above what was formerly being paid to the Labour Council." This, he said, would give the Congress "a great deal more to say about who is on the executive and what the Federation policy shall be."[21]

Other tactics were also adopted. Congress organizers were warned not to organize any new locals which might conceivably support the left-wing elements in the Federation. A massive public relations campaign was initiated. Mahoney even arranged for a weekly radio broadcast, which in his words, would publicize the "official views, policies and activities of the Congress" and its "dependable" affiliates. Superfluously, Mahoney added that no air time would be allowed to Mine-Mill, the IWA, "or other such unions". These tactics succeeded. Within a month the number of Congress locals affiliated to the BCFL had doubled.[22]

But the major objective was still to "break up" the IWA, which, according to Conroy, was the "backbone of the Federation." How difficult this would be was made clear by the IWA election in March. The anti-Communist or "white bloc" in the district which was supported by the Congress was completely smashed. It won a majority only in the New Westminster local, and not one member of its slate was elected. In most locals, the "white bloc" candidates were defeated by margins ranging from four to one to eighty to one. A disgusted Radford informed Conroy that there was absolutely no hope for the Congress "to make any headway in the IWA."[23]

It seemed that Mahoney's anti-Communist drive had lost its momentum. At a Vancouver Labour Council meeting in late March, the delegates, led by Pritchett and Harvey Murphy, pushed through a motion, over Mahoney's adamant opposition, asking the Congress executive to reconsider its decision barring from Canada American union officials with Communist connections. This issue provided the left with a substantial immediate victory. It would soon cause them a catastrophic defeat.

On 8 and 9 April the British Columbia Federation of Labour conducted a "Labour Lobby" in Victoria to protest against the provincial government's labour legislation. As part of the "Lobby" a banquet, presided over by Pritchett and attended by all the Federation representatives, was held on the evening of April 8. After a good deal of drinking and carousing, the speeches began. One of the speakers, Harvey Murphy, perhaps having drunk a bit too much, launched into a bitter and sometimes profane tirade against the Congress officers for their activities against Mine-Mill president, Reid Robinson (see chapter 6). Among the less lurid of his statements were that the Congress officials were "phonies" and "red-baiting floozies" attempting to break up the union movement. It was his highly distasteful remarks about the private lives of some labour leaders, however, which prompted Mahoney to take action.

At a meeting of the Federation on the following day, Mahoney read some of Murphy's statements to the assembled delegates and warned that unless Murphy and Pritchett apologized and issued an "unconditional retraction" he would withdraw from the meeting and "recommend that all loyal CCL members and affiliates do likewise." In reply, Murphy stated that he had spoken not as a vice-president of the Federation but as a member of Mine-Mill. He added that he had merely "made general references" and had "mentioned no names of people in the labour movement who are behind the deportation of Reid Robinson." He said he was "fully prepared to substantiate" his statements and face any charges laid against him. After a stormy session in which, supported by Pritchett and Danny O'Brien, Murphy refused to retract his statement, Mahoney and sixteen other "loyal" CCL members stalked out of the meeting leaving the remaining seventy-five delegates "to carry on as if nothing had happened."[24]

Ever the opportunist, Mahoney at once set the Congress machinery into motion. He phoned Mosher and told him of the incident and of his intention to lay charges. He sent a copy of Murphy's speech to Conroy and informed him that the delegates who had walked out of the meeting with him were prepared to sign affidavits that Murphy had indeed said what Mahoney claimed. Mahoney asked for Conroy's permission to lay charges against Murphy and against Pritchett as well, "for having acted as chairman of the public meeting and permitting such an attack to be made unchallenged." Significantly, he added that though Murphy was "undoubtedly drunk," this was "a perfect opportunity to nail him down and Pritchett along with him."[25]

Mahoney also encouraged Murray Cotterill "to figure out some angle of capitalizing to the greatest extent possible" on Murphy's blunder. He admitted that he hadn't "had so much fun in years" and that the only thing he "could appreciate more would be the opportunity of sitting in when the party boys rake Murphy over the coals for his drunken stupidity." In addition, he asked Cotterill to "line up" support in the executive council "to push these charges ... so that if Sol Spivak or anyone of his ilk tries to be a nice fellow and pussy-foot, it will be a hopeless proposition."He pointed out that the Communists, especially Murphy, had "stuck their necks out, and the [the Congress] would be more than stupid if [it] did not take full advantage of it." Finally, he reminded Conroy that the opportunity was now at hand to "eliminate" Murphy and Pritchett from the Federation. It would be "much easier," he added, "to handle anyone who substitutes for them."[26]

In reply, Conroy urged him to have the charges laid by the Vancouver Labour Council "as the representative agency of many [Congress] unions in the area" because this would "lend more weight" to the charges than if they came from "a lone individual." This suggestion angered Mahoney. He argued that it was best to use the Labour Council simply as "a sounding board" since the Congress majority was still quite slim. He stated that "the only method of approach to this problem [was] capitalizing on all opportunities" and there was "not the slightest possibility" that he would use the Labour Council "for dealing with matters" that were essentially between the Congress executive and himself. He also complained to Conroy over the lack of confidence that the Congress seemed to be showing in him, something he was not used to as a "trusted officer" of Steel. Tactfully Conroy assured him that he had the greatest confidence in him, and that recommendations from the Congress were not meant to indicate "lack of confidence" but merely to be used as suggestions which might "be of help in the given situation."[27]

Within a few days the Congress received from Mahoney an official copy of the complaint as well as twelve affidavits from union members substantiating Mahoney's charges. In his official complaint Mahoney demanded that Murphy be suspended for his "slanderous" attacks on Congress officials at a public meeting "with newspapermen, wives and friends of the delegates, and representatives of political parties present." Pritchett, he added, should also be punished for his failure to repudiate Murphy's statements, though privately he admitted that Murphy was much "more vicious" than Pritchett and that the Congress purposes would be served "if some way could be found of nailing Murphy and simply reprimanding Pritchett."[28]

Mahoney's charges were discussed at the Congress executive council and committee meetings in June and it was decided to set up a sub-committee to investigate the situation. This committee met with Pritchett, Murphy, and Mahoney immediately following the council meeting. Murphy admitted to the committee that he had indeed maligned the Congress leadership, but explained that "he had consumed some liquor before attending the banquet" and that he was "boiling over" at the Congress' treatment of Reid Robinson. Pritchett explained that he was merely acting as master of ceremonies at the banquet and that other Federation officers were present, none of whom "had seen fit to object" to Murphy's statements. Consequently he had "not considered it worthwhile to make a personal objection." Mahoney reminded the committee, however, that neither Murphy nor Pritchett had apologized or issued retractions. The Committee then adjourned to consider its report.[29]

Keeping relentless pressures on the Congress, Mahoney suggested to Conroy that "the thing to do is to rule Murphy ineligible for the next two years to hold any office in a unit chartered by the Congress and to give Pritchett a severe reprimand which will put him on the spot." With this suggestion in mind, the committee recommended that Murphy be barred from attending meetings of the Congress or of any of its chartered organizations for two years. It also suggested that Pritchett and all officers of the British Columbia Federation be reprimanded "for their laxity in not repudiating the slanderous attack by its First Vice-President Murphy upon the Congress and its officials." The report of the committee was discussed and adopted by the executive council on 24 August. Though the Federation vigorously protested, and Murphy termed the Congress action "outrageous," there was little either could do.[30] This was Mahoney's second great victory and would do much to prepare the way for his third and greatest triumph, the capture of the British Columbia Federation of Labour.

On 2 June 1948 Mahoney informed Conroy that he was now ready to launch a massive Congress campaign over the next few months to get every possible union affiliated with the Federation in order "to take it over if it is humanly possible." Whether possible or not, it soon became an absolute necessity. On 12 June, the Federation executive repudiated the Congress for its actions against Reid Robinson. In direct opposition to the Congress it passed a resolution supporting "the free movement of Labour representatives across the International Border for Union business." At once, Conroy ordered Mahoney to ask the Federation to "surrender" its charter before the Congress "lifted it." Mahoney excitedly replied that events in British Columbia were "moving so rapidly" that the Congress would soon "have a much better issue than the Reid Robinson case to rap the Federation on." In any case, he added that there was much sympathy even among the non-Communists for Robinson, and because "things are moving so well" for the Congress, it could "well afford to pick an issue that is particularly good for the real opening of hostilities against the Federation."[31]

To defeat the Communists, issues, as Mahoney realized, were helpful but not essential. What was essential was an organization that could outmanoeuvre that of the party. Creating this organization in time for the 1948 Federation convention would be Mahoney's next task.

He visited most of the Congress locals in the province to make sure that the delegates they elected to the convention would support the Congress slate. But there were many small locals outside Vancouver which could not afford to send delegates to the Federation convention. Shrewdly, Mahoney arranged to transfer their credentials to Congress officers in Vancouver who could then represent them at the convention. He even ordered the Congress officials to take out memberships in these locals. In an attempt to counter Mahoney's tactics, the Federation executive decided to bar from the convention the many locals which had affiliated in 1944 but which, because of the leftist orientation of the Federation leadership, had stopped paying their dues, but were now being urged by Mahoney to reaffiliate. Informed of this move by Mahoney, Mosher immediately ruled that the Federation had "no authority to exclude from representation any chartered union of the Congress ... or any locals ... in British Columbia." This ensured that Mahoney's efforts had not been in vain.[32]

Despite all the exertions of Mahoney and Congress representatives in British Columbia, the most significant step toward capturing the Federation was taken in Ottawa. On 24 August, at the same meeting that suspended Harvey Murphy, the Congress executive council also suspended the entire Mine-Mill union (see chapter 6). An ecstatic Mahoney wired Conroy pleading with him to make sure that the Mine-Mill suspension would not be lifted, at least not before the BCFL convention because the Congress now had "a fair chance" of capturing the Federation. The "absence" of the twenty-two Mine-Mill delegates, he added, would "undoubtedly improve that chance." He was immediately reassured by Mosher that the Congress had no intention of ever reinstating Mine-Mill.[33]

For weeks before the convention, Mahoney pleaded with Conroy and Mosher to send a major Congress personality to the convention. The issue was still in doubt, he said, and "a thing like the prestige and assistance of a top Congress elected official may be the deciding factor." But Mosher replied that he could not find "anyone suitable" to represent the Congress, and that, in any case, "without Mine-Mill delegates the situation was controllable." Bitterly,

Mahoney responded that the "whole proposition [was] touch and go." Since there was "always a certain group who can be swung either way at a Convention" he was "extremely anxious" that an influential Congress officer attend. Eventually his perseverence was rewarded. Just three days before the convention, the Congress informed him that Harry Chappell, a leader of the CBRE in western Canada, would attend.[34] As it turned out, every bit of help was needed.

The 1948 convention of the British Columbia Federation of Labour was, according to Mahoney, his "most nerve-racking experience." Undoubtedly, it was one of the most exciting and rancorous labour conventions in Canadian history. With the Mine-Mill delegation suspended, the left was frantically fighting for its life; the right, sensing victory, was relentless in its attack. So evenly matched were the two sides that one vote often spelled the difference between victory and defeat. Before the convention met, the Federation executive bitterly condemned the barring of Murphy and the suspension of Mine-Mill and perversely extended a "cordial invitation" to Mine-Mill representatives to be the Federation's "guests at the forthcoming convention."[35]

The convention opened on 4 September with a plea from President O'Brien to the delegates to "lift the deliberations" of the convention to a "high plane" and to "have orderly and dignified discussions on all questions." No sooner had he finished speaking than a disorderly and undignified fight broke out over the executive appointments to the convention committees, appointments which were usually automatically approved. This time the Congress forces disputed three of the appointments and were successful in having one of these changed. In turn, the left raised the question of the ten anti-Communist delegates from the IWA local in New Westminister who, it claimed, had been "irregularly" elected. O'Brien ruled that these delegates would not be seated until the convention had decided whether their election was legal. Over the stiff opposition of the Congress delegates, O'Brien's decision was upheld by a vote of 73 to 52. An overconfident Pritchett then moved that the convention vote to seat these ten delegates. This was his fatal mistake. Some of those who had voted to uphold O'Brien's decision were not, to Pritchett's surprise, supporters of the left wing, but merely delegates who felt that the convention had a right to decide on the legality of the election of delegates. These, along with the ten delegates from New Westminister, would provide the votes which would end the domination of the left over the Federation.

For two days, the convention was in turmoil. Though his union was suspended, John Clark, president of Mine-Mill, was allowed to address the delegates and denounce the Congress. Speaker after speaker from the left attacked the suspension of Mine-Mill and charged that it was "part of a carefully laid plot to disrupt organized labour in British Columbia and in Canada ... for the purpose of gaining control of the British Columbia Federation of Labour convention." They pointed out that the "loyal and devoted" members of Mine-Mill who had played a large role in creating and supporting the Federation were barred from the convention, while unions which had "always refused to be part of the Federation, to pay their per capita, and to take part in Federation activities have suddenly received credentials to sit and vote in the convention." Led by Pritchett and Jan Lakeman, a fiery Communist and a leader of the CCL forces in Alberta, the left denounced the Congress, the CCF, the Steelworkers, and the press. In turn, the right, under the direction of Mahoney and Chappell, criticized the Federation leadership, the Communist party, Mine-Mill, and the IWA.[36]

When the time finally arrived for the elections, the delegates were physically exhausted. Indeed five delegates to whom Mahoney had carefully catered, and whose votes were promised to the Congress slate, did not even bother attending the final session to vote. None the less, Congress officials were confident that they would sweep most of the leftists out of the executive. For weeks they had been busy lining up support, and during the convention they kept up their unceasing pressure on delegates. In addition, in conjunction with Fadling, Mahoney had hired a hotel suite "for entertaining some of the delegates" on whom "work" still had to be done.[37]

In the vote for president Mahoney was not too surprised when O'Brien defeated Radford by 68 to 64. He was shocked, however, when Bill Stewart of the left defeated Pen Baskin of Steel 66 to 65 for one of the vice-president positions. So carefully had Mahoney calculated how the delegates would vote and so closely were the Congress supporters watched that he knew at once that one of the latter was "double-crossing" him. Immediately he dispatched a Congress representative, George Home, to sit beside the suspected "rat," a delegate from the Retail-Wholesale Union and "the only Congress delegate not being properly watched ... to help him mark his ballot."[38] Sure enough, with Home's "help," on the next vote for the position of second vice-president the Congress candidate Alsbury defeated the leftist Alex McKenzie by the same 66 to 65. In the most important election, for secretary-treasurer, with the recalcitrant delegate from Retail-Wholesale being closely observed, this time by several nervous Congress officials, Home defeated Pritchett also by 66 votes to 65. John Cameron, Bill Symington, and Stewart Mackenzie, all Congress supporters, were elected to the Executive Council along with Pritchett and Malcolm MacLeod of the left. Of the nine executive seats, the Congress had thus captured five, the left three. The remaining member, Danny O'Brien, in

Mahoney's words, would "always gravitate toward power." The BCFL was now firmly in the hands of the CCL. The capture of the Federation was the greatest triumph for the Congress over the Communists since Millard "cleaned up" Steel; an even greater one was soon to follow.

How complete was this defeat was soon apparent. Immediately following the convention O'Brien called a meeting of the executive board. But Mahoney had no intention of allowing the Federation executive to meet until he had discussed strategy with Congress officials. In addition each of the four labour councils in the province was also entitled to elect a member to the Federation executive council. Mahoney was therefore anxious to put off an executive meeting until he could make sure that no leftist would be sent by any of these councils. The Federation constitution stipulated that three executive council members were necessary for a quorum. The two leftists on the Council, Pritchett and MacLeod, announced they would attend the meeting. The three Congress members, Symington, Cameron, and Mackenzie, were ordered by Mahoney not to attend because the Congress had found it "necessary" to get rid of some of the board members first.[39]

O'Brien complained bitterly that the business of the Federation was "being unduly held up and the Federation authority usurped by a minority of the executive board," but there was little he could do. The left charged that the Congress had used "machine tactics" and "paper locals" to gain their majority – the same charges that Congress supporters used to hurl at the left with the same nugatory results. The Federation was now firmly in the hands of the Congress.

As Conroy reminded Mahoney, however, "the solution of our problem in British Columbia ... lies in the solution within the International Woodworkers of America ... a maximum concentration of our energies ought to be made on this problem. Certainly until we solve this problem, we shall be on unsafe ground in British Columbia." With the Federation and the Vancouver Labour Council in "safe" hands, and with Mine-Mill suspended, the IWA remained as the last large bastion of opposition to the Congress in British Columbia. To the task of assaulting and seizing this bastion, Mahoney vowed to "devote all [his] energies."[40]

The task was less difficult than he had expected. The British Columbia district had come under simultaneous attack on three fronts – from within by its anti-Communist opposition, the "white bloc," from above by its international, and from without by the Congress. Understandably unnerved by this well co-ordinated onslaught, the harried British Columbia district leadership reacted rashly, and at times irrationally, providing its foes with the long sought for opportunity to pounce and capture the union.

The most significant step in this campaign was taken by the so-called "white bloc" within the union. At a quarterly district council meeting in April 1948, two members of the anti-Communist New Westminster local, repeating a claim they had earlier made on the international's radio broadcast, charged that approximately $9000 was unaccounted for in the district's yearly audit. Reacting sharply, the district officers ordered a complete audit of union books for 1946 and 1947 by a respected firm of chartered accountants, Riddell, Stead, Graham and Hutchison. The district also decided that if the books were found to be accurate the New Westminster local would be required to pay the entire cost of the audit. Little did the district officers realize that by approving the request for an audit, they were signing their own death warrants.

On 12 May, the audit was completed. A more damaging indictment of the district's financial practices would have been beyond the abilities of even the most talented and vigourous of its enemies. Indeed so explosive was the audit that the district council refused at first to show it to its membership, or even to admit that it had been completed. Somehow, however, Mahoney obtained a "pirated copy" and sent it "in the strictest confidence" to the Congress office in Ottawa for suggestions from the Congress research director, Eugene Forsey, and from Conroy "as to its usefulness in blowing up the people now in control."[41]

The auditors reported that a total $150,633.15 had been paid out by the district officers without "supporting vouchers," and that this was contrary to both the laws of the district and of the international. Though there was no evidence that these funds had been misused, there was also no evidence to the contrary. Certainly the district was guilty of what Pritchett now calls "terribly sloppy bookkeeping." Without these vouchers, the audit, of course, was almost totally worthless. The auditors themselves complained that nothing but can- celled cheques were available for their inspection and there was no way for them to substantiate expenditures. They also questioned some dubious loans made by the district, and stated that they did not have sufficient information to find out whether travelling expenses paid out to organizers and officers "were within the per diem limits as prescribed by the by-laws of the Council." They also noted that "bulk cheques" were made out to district executive officer Ernie Dalskog and to secretary-treasurer Melsness for which "no individual account was available."[42]

The audit, as Mahoney jubilantly told Millard, was "the break we have been waiting for for some time." Immediately upon receiving it, Mahoney attended an executive board meeting of IWA in Portland to "discuss strategy." At this meeting he was informed that the British Columbia district "was becoming very belligerent toward the International" and had publicly denounced it for its "partisan political expediency" and "arbitrary dismissals" of organizers in British Columbia. On Mahoney's advice the international issued a statement condemning the British Columbia district for "its continual harangue of half-truths, misstatements and deliberate falsehoods." In addition, the IWA executive decided to set up a committee of three members of its executive and one Congress official "to completely investigate the financial affairs of the District."[43]

On his return to Vancouver Mahoney wrote Conroy a full report of this meeting. He requested that the Congress appointment to the investigating committee be someone "who has not been too closely involved in the fight against the party," yet someone "shrewd," since the Congress had "never been in a better position to see the Party people in the IWA exposed, ... [but] a mistake in handling a judgment can very easily blow the whole thing up." "He also told Conroy that the international had no intention of openly "providing the necessary leadership" to the opposition forces in the district for fear "of leaving themselves open to a charge that the Americans are invading Canada." Consequently, as Congress representative, he would assist the "white bloc" by helping them "to prepare their case [on the audit], listening in on their presentation of it and consulting with them on ... strengthening of points they miss."[44]

Meanwhile the district leadership announced that the audit had given the district "a clean bill of health" and the "charges of shortages" had proven "groundless." For this reason the district bitterly denounced the international for setting up an investigating committee and particularly for appointing to it a Congress representative, on the grounds that "this was strictly an IWA matter." The district was warned by the international, however, that if it did not co-operate with the investigation "an injunction [would] be taken out ... and [its] funds tied up until such time as the investigation [was] completed."[45]

In addition, Ernie Dalskog, the district president, complained to Conroy that Mahoney had no business attending a meeting of the executive board of the IWA and interfering in "inner union affairs." When Mahoney replied that he had been invited by the international merely "to extend fraternal greetings" from the Congress, and that his refusal to accept "would have been interpreted as an affront to the International Woodworkers of America," Dalskog responded that the district was well aware that Mahoney had been "advising the dissident group inside the IWA and had gone to the executive for that purpose." This, said Dalskog, was an IWA affair "and no business of the Congress representative."[46]

On 12 July the investigating committee, with Harry Chappell as the Congress representative, met with district officials to discuss the auditors' reports. The brief of the "white bloc," drawn up by Mahoney, pointed out that the constitution and bylaws of both the district and the international required that "all moneys paid out must be covered by a properly drawn and signed voucher." And this, of course, had been ignored by the district. Though Mahoney felt that there was little "possibility of getting anything of a criminal nature on the people involved," the Congress, he told Conroy, could "certainly build up a record of lack of administrative ability, which will carry with it, by innuendo, the impression that something could have happened to their funds, and likely did, even though it cannot be proven in court."[47]

The district officers raised strenuous objections to the Congress being represented and refused to answer any of the questions directed at them by Chappell. They also refused to permit the committee to examine the district's books or to allow a representative of the auditing firm to testify. After one abortive session the committee warned the district to present a brief at the next meeting or it would write its report without "hearing their side of the story." At the next meeting, Dalskog admitted that the district staff "did not make any attempt to properly voucher their expenditures" and that other vouchers were "destroyed" when the district "housecleaned" its vaults just before the audit. With that, the committee adjourned to write its report.[48]

On 9 October 1948, fully three months after it finished its investigation, the committee finally released its report. It accused the district of "gross mishandling" of funds and "wholly inadequate bookkeeping," but it could find no proof of any "criminal activity." Mahoney called it a "pathetic piece of work coming out of the material they had to work with."[49] By the time of its release, however, the report was almost irrelevant; too much had happened in the intervening three months.

During this time, open warfare had broken out between the district and the international. For years the two sides had been sniping at each other, but had shied away from any extreme action. At the district's quarterly meeting in July, however, a resolution was passed warning that unless it was given complete autonomy and all the international representatives were withdrawn from the province, the district would take whatever steps were necessary "to save the union."[50] It was obvious to the international and Congress leaders that the district had finally decided to sever connections with both the IWA and the CCL.

Acting quickly, IWA President Fadling demanded Congress assistance in "undermining" the district leadership, and requested that his personal representative, Mike Sekora, "be allowed to work out of the Congress office." He also suggested to Conroy that it was "time for both the Congress and the International to openly accuse the Party of disruptive tactics ... and go to the membership with the full story." He bluntly ordered Conroy to use "the fullest facilities of the CCL office and staff" to help the international in its campaign.[51]

Though Conroy was not very impressed with the tone of Fadling's letter, and even less with the kind of leadership and ability manifested by the international, he told Mahoney that he would have to resign himself to "working with the material" that was available in the IWA. Mahoney agreed that the IWA officers "while having the best intentions in the world are not too competent," and that Fadling's "demanding tone ... was just an unfortunate choice of words." He added, however, that the large Port Alberni local of the IWA had already passed a resolution calling upon the district to hold a referendum on the question of seceding from the international. Such a resolution, Conroy told Mahoney, would be an "extremely fortunate development for the Congress," since it would save the CCL the trouble of expelling the district. He added that it should therefore be "encouraged" in a "subtle way."[52]

Encouragement, however, did not seem necessary. On 12 September, the IWA local at Mission, at a meeting attended by Pritchett, passed a motion to withhold the local's dues from the international. Three days later Dalskog condoned this act and by inference urged other IWA locals to follow the lead of the Mission local. Mahoney immediately told Fadling to inform him as soon as any IWA local had officially stopped paying its assessment, as such an action would automatically bar that local from attending a Congress or Federation convention.[53]

The impending secession did not seem to faze Fadling. He was more concerned that the district leadership and not the international be "clearly identified ... as taking the first step ... in cutting the people from British Columbia away from the International and the Congress." Though he had been informed that the district had already transferred its bank accounts "to the name of some individuals ... as a preparatory step for a switch in affiliation" he refused to act. He would "rather risk losing all the funds" he told Mahoney, if he could thus "retain the support of the membership through showing them who is responsible for the disruption."[54]

Meanwhile, the district president Ernie Dalskog had laid charges with the Congress against Mahoney for "participating in a factional meeting" of an IWA local that was called "without authority ... to foment disruption of the local and the district." Mahoney readily admitted that he had addressed a meeting of the anti-Communist "white bloc" in the New Westminster local and had urged them to align themselves with those "seeking to bring the IWA in British

Columbia in line with international and CCL policies." When Mosher rejected Dalskog's charge on the ground that it was more of a "complaint than a charge," Dalskog circularized all Congress unions in the province with copies of the correspondence to show how "unfairly" his union was being treated.[55]

In turn, Mahoney urged Mosher to accept the charges since the District position was "so ridiculous that it would give [the Congress] a perfect opportunity to really give them a lambasting and would deprive them of the angle to which they are now turning, – one of being deprived of the opportunity to air what they consider a grievance." At the same time, in order to make sure the district had no legal grounds of complaint, Fadling urged Mahoney "to accept credentials as an official International representative." He wanted Mahoney to take over "the responsibility of co-ordinating the activities" of the international supporters in the province on "an off-the-record unpublicized" arrangement. Mahoney could then "make on the spot decisions with regard to tactics, press releases and other pressing details" while staying in the "background" as much as possible.[56]

Though preferable, "remaining in the background" was no longer possible. On 20 September, after informing Conroy that secession of the British Columbia district was "imminent," Mahoney took over the weekly international radio broadcast and, for the full fifteen minutes, attacked the leadership of the district. He warned district members that they were allowing themselves to be isolated from fellow trade unionists in Canada and the United States and to be "dragged along" in pursuit of the "fantastic policy" of their leaders. At the same time, a new newspaper, *The Voice of the IWA,* which was published by the Congress but paid for by the international, was sent to each IWA member in the province. Its purpose, was "to reach the thousands of lumber workers in British Columbia who are at present cut off from their fellow workers by the disruptive activities of the British Columbia district officers." It charged that the paper of the district, the *B.C. Lumber Worker* had "kept up a regular barrage of abuse and accusations of lies and distortions" against the international and the Congress. It was therefore "necessary" to found a new paper to present the "real facts."[57]

At long last the district leadership made its decision. In the 29 September edition of the *B.C. Lumber Worker,* for the first time the district executive publicly urged all of its locals to reconsider paying their per capita tax to the international and to consider creating a "strictly Canadian" union of lumber workers. For well over a year there had been influential voices raised in the ruling circles of the district council urging that some action be taken to separate from the international and create a new Canadian union. When relations with the international worsened, these voices became more strident and more numerous. Pritchett resolutely withstood this advice. To the very end he believed that severing the connection with the international would be a tragic error.

But clearly by October 1948, Pritchett was no longer the master of the district's destiny. More radical and intransigent voices were being raised. They argued that because district leaders were barred from attending international conventions and executive meetings in the United States, on the grounds that they were "Communists," the Canadian section had absolutely no influence on the policy-making bodies of the union, but was none the less subject to all their decisions. They cited the large number of international organizers in the province, appointed over the opposition of the district, whose solitary objective seemed to be to "undermine the leadership of the district" and enhance the power of the opposition. They argued that the district's high per capita tax was being used to subsidize this work instead of being used to organize lumber workers in Quebec as the district had recommended. The left-wing elements in the district were appalled by the international's "embrace" of the Cold War – its support of the Marshall plan and American foreign policy, its acceptance of the Taft-Hartley Act, and its rabid opposition to Soviet policy. The activities of Mahoney and the Congress in support of the "white bloc" and the close co-operation between the international and the Congress in advancing the interests of this opposition group were further proof that the district was in great danger of being "seized" by these forces. Something drastic would obviously have to be done.[58]

By the middle of September 1948, after the Congress victory at the BCFL convention, the leaders of the district council, with the significant exception of Pritchett, decided to secede from the international. Pritchett argued forcefully against the move and finally suggested that a referendum be held on the issue. Other district leaders, however, were convinced that there was no time. The decision would have to be made at once and put into effect before the international could react. Fears were expressed that the international would make the first move, that by a court order it would freeze the funds of the district, appoint an administrator, and take over the operation of the district. Reluctantly, Pritchett agreed to go along with his more "hot-headed" colleagues.

Quietly and unobtrusively the district prepared for the disaffiliation. Funds were covertly removed from banks; some were transferred to secret accounts in other banks; others were handed to Harvey Murphy and Mine-Mill to be held until the situation resolved itself. On the day following the secession recommendation in the *B.C. Lumber Worker,* Pritchett made the same request on the district's radio program. On the next day leaflets appeared outside the various sawmills in the province advertising "important" local meetings to be held on the night of 3 October. On the same day, thirty-three district delegates on their way to the IWA convention were stopped at the United States border and refused admittance. On 2 October, "selected" shop stewards were told by the district leaders that a motion to disaffiliate would be passed at the district meeting on the following day, and that the local meetings called for the following night were to endorse this move.[59]

Meanwhile, posters, pennants, and buttons with the union's new name, Woodworkers Industrial Union of Canada (WIUC), were being printed – all in the strictest secrecy. On the night of 2 October, Pritchett recorded a statement officially announcing the disaffiliation of the district. At 2 pm the following afternoon the recording was broadcast. Three hours later the district council meeting voted to disaffiliate. At about the same time a flabbergasted Salsberg was informed by telephone by party leaders in the province of what the district had done. Frantically he asked them to reconsider. It was too late; the decision had already been made public.[60]

The quarterly meeting of the district council at which the secession motion was passed was by far the most tempestuous and chaotic in the union's history. For seven hours, from 10 AM to 5 PM, on that fateful first Sunday in October, delegates did little but exchange insults, and a full-scale brawl was barely averted. Though Pritchett's broadcast of the district's decision to disaffiliate was on the air at 2.00 that afternoon, it was not until 4.30 that a resolution calling for disaffiliation from the international was adopted. For those seven hours, time and time again Fadling requested permission to speak; each time he was refused. Delegate after delegate charged the international with "disruption," with "red baiting," with "betraying the labour movement" and with "going to bed with Taft-Hartley." In the end, by an overwelming vote the district seceded.

Immediately, Fadling and fourteen other delegates from the New Westminster and Kamloops locals stalked out of the meeting. With the opposition removed, the remaining delegates quickly voted to set up a new union under the same executive, authorized it to take over all the assets and contracts of the district, and to hold a constitutional convention on 11 October.[61]

That night at carefully arranged local meetings, resolutions supporting the district's action were adopted. At one of these, in New Westminster, in the home local of the "white bloc," a "rump" meeting of the strongly anti-Communist local 377 chaired by the BCFL president, Danny O'Brien, also adopted a motion supporting the secession. For the next few months the air would be full of claims and counterclaims as the IWA and WIUC competed for support amongst the thirteen locals and 25,000 workers of the district.

On the day following the secession, Fadling and Stewart Alsbury, president of the New Westminster local, received an injunction from the British Columbia Supreme Court ordering the district officers to turn over all the district's assets and books to the Court. They were too late. All night long and into the morning, furniture, files, and office equipment were being moved out of the district office to a "secret location." When the sheriff arrived to serve the writ on the secession leaders, he found them barred behind locked doors in their empty office. There they stayed for three more days before the sheriff was allowed to enter.

On 5 October the IWA claimed that it had received the support of four locals; on the same day, WIUC stated it also had won the backing of four locals – the same ones. And if this were not sufficiently confusing, on the following day, Dalskog claimed that "twenty thousand lumber workers had voted to follow the WIUC banner." On the same day, in the same paper, Fadling stated that the IWA had also won the support of twenty thousand union members. As there were only twenty-five thousand members when the district seceded three days before, either a great deal of organization had been done in those three days or both claims were somewhat exaggerated.[62]

The Congress immediately came to the support of the international despite Dalskog's assurance that WIUC had "every intention of maintaining its affiliation with the Congress." Unimpressed by the district's "loyalty" Mosher stated that no organization set up "for Communist political purposes" could hope to "achieve any status in the legitimate ranks of organized labour in Canada." And at the Congress convention in October 1948, by an overwhelming margin, the delegates denounced WIUC as a "pathetic imitation of a real trade union" and renewed their support of the "loyal" IWA members. At the same time, Stewart Alsbury, leader of the "white bloc" was chosen by the international as acting president of the district until a special district convention could be called to elect permanent officers.[63]

It soon became apparent that Pritchett had been right. Union members found it difficult to transfer their loyalty from their union to their leaders. The executive of the district had vastly overestimated their influence. For some few months after the secession this was not apparent. Some locals did indeed opt for WIUC. But under the relentless persuasion and pressure of the international and Congress organizers, these locals soon returned to the IWA fold. Neither management nor the provincial labour board would recognize WIUC as the legal successor to the IWA. Legally, therefore, the IWA was still the bargaining agent for the British Columbia lumber workers, and WIUC was consequently compelled to renegotiate the contracts of all the locals which voted to join it.

But for the few months that the battle lasted, it was intense. Families split, friendships were shattered, and in some areas open warfare broke out. Stewart Alsbury was badly beaten and taken to hospital after attempting to cross a WIUC picket line. Others – on both sides – were also bloodied and arrests were plentiful. But in the end, the superior resources of the Congress and the international triumphed.

Directed by Mahoney, organizers from both the CCL and the IWA travelled far and wide across the province lining up support for the international. When the IWA complained that it was short of funds and men, the Congress sent in extra organizers to help in the campaign. It also committed all its officials in British Columbia to the effort.[64]

But neither organization was satisfied with the effort of the other. Mahoney complained that the IWA had taken over the publicity campaign from the Congress and was attempting to "Americanize" the campaign by expounding the "glories of free enterprise." When the IWA balked at accepting the political action programme of the CCL, the Congress threatened to withdraw its organizational assistance. So disillusioned did the Congress become with the "immaturity" of the IWA, with Fadling's "lack of grasp" and with the union's internal squabbling that at one time, "through disgust with the whole confused situation," Mahoney considered keeping the Congress "pretty well clear of the IWA." The IWA, on the other hand, complained that, except for the Congress, "no other Canadian organization had contributed to the fight" and that "outsiders" such as Mahoney were exerting more influence over IWA members than were international officers. Despite these grievances enough harmony was maintained to ensure the successful conclusion of the campaign.[65]

One organization which did a great deal to support the secessionists was the British Columbia district of Mine-Mill. Long before most district members knew of the secession, Harvey Murphy had been told. He attended the district council meeting at which the resolution for disaffiliation was passed, and on the same night he addressed the membership of the New Westminster local urging them to join the WIUC. Funds were hastily transferred from district locals in Mine-Mill. For example, IWA Local 71, at a hurriedly called meeting on 1 October, voted to turn over $2500 to the union attorney, $5000 to the union printer, and $9000 to the Mine-Mill district strike fund. By 4 October approximately $29,000 in district funds had found their way into Mine-Mill hands.[66]

On 30 October, vice-president Hartung of the IWA requested that Murphy return these funds. Two days later Murphy replied that all the money that had been left with him had long since been returned "in strict accordance with instructions" given to him by the "owners." Again, on 5 November, Hartung specified the amount of money transferred from each local to Mine-Mill and directed Murphy to inform him to whom he had returned these funds. Murphy refused to elaborate. On Fadling's recommendation, Phillip Murray, president of the CIO, appointed a committee under CIO director Adolph Germer to make "a speedy investigation" into what had happened to the missing IWA funds.[67]

The committee held its hearings in Vancouver on 25 March 1949. Acting on the advice of his lawyer, Murphy refused to testify. On behalf of the IWA, Fadling presented evidence that the funds were still in Mine-Mill hands. With no other testimony offered, the meeting adjourned. Mahoney then wrote Germer that there was "not a shadow of doubt" that Mine-Mill was guilty and that it was absolutely necessary to "stamp our friend Murphy down" in order to defeat the party in British Columbia. He therefore urged that the committee ask the CIO executive board to order Mine-Mill to dismiss Murphy as a sign of "good faith."[68]

At the beginning of May, the committee reported to the CIO that Murphy "knowingly and willingly aided the movement to secede" by diverting funds, attacking the IWA and the CCL, and encouraging the secessionists in every way. His conduct, it reported, was "reckless and inexcusable."[69] Unhappily for the Congress, the CIO had no power to compel Mine-Mill to dismiss one of its organizers, so no action was taken against Murphy.

Though Mine-Mill and the Shipyard Federation supported the secessionists, their support was hardly sufficient for the WIUC to survive. Danny O'Brien also lent his support to WIUC. When the executive of the BCFL criticized him for supporting the secession, a disgusted O'Brien compared "the intolerance" of the Congress majority "to the tactics of Hilter" and resigned as president.[70] Malcolm McLeod, the last Communist on the Federation executive council, died several days later. With O'Brien's resignation and McLeod's death, the Congress was now in complete control of the Federation executive.

Most important, however, for the ultimate victory of the IWA was the attitude of the courts. After a long and complicated series of legal actions, the international finally recovered most of the assets of the district. On many occasions sheriffs were ordered to confiscate forcibly property with which WIUC refused to part. The "Loggers' Navy," the small cruiser owned by Local 71 and used by district organizers to visit the many logging camps on the coast and Vancouver Island, was discovered, after four months of concealment, in a remote bay on Vancouver Island and returned by the court to the international. In addition the *B.C. Lumber Worker* and the weekly radio broadcast were also judged to be the property of the international. In the end, most of the district's assets though few of its records were recovered. But as the IWA newspaper remarked, "our most precious asset, the loyalty of the membership, was intact."[71]

In the face of this concerted opposition – from government, from industry, from the courts, as well as from organized labour, – the WIUC, after some initial success, lingered precariously for several more years and finally disappeared – a demise lamented by very few. Its entire membership, except for a local in Cranbrook, returned to the IWA.

One can readily understand the frustration which precipitated the secession. Ideologically, the international and the district were at opposite poles. Organizationally they had antipathetic views. Financially, the British Columbia district felt deprived of the nearly $600,000 in dues it had sent to the international between 1943 and 1948 – only $235,000 of which, it claimed, was spent on union activity in the province.[72] These disagreements, along with such irritants as being barred by immigration authorities from attending international policy meetings and conventions and being subject to attacks from both the Congress and the international, combined to create in the minds of the district leaders an almost fanatic desire to be on their own. For once, party discipline collapsed. Though at the time, Tim Buck was calling for the Communists to work within the labour movement to strengthen the forces of unity,[73] the district went its own way.

Perhaps it had little alternative. Unlike the UE and Mine-Mill which were also at odds with the Congress, the district was, in addition, confronted with a hostile parent organization. Mine-Mill and UE could always count on the full support of their internationals in their disputes with the congress. The district had no one on whom to rely.

Tactically the former two unions were also much shrewder; they took no precipitate action but waited instead for the Congress to expel them. By seceding, the district became a "pariah" organization, supported by the Communists and some other leftists, but by no one else. At the time of its gravest crisis, the union's leadership failed it. Instead of bracing itself for a last-ditch effort to fight off the incursions of the international and the Congress and calling for a referendum among its membership to gain a mandate for whatever action it took, the district leadership reacted rashly and irresponsibly. It cost them dearly.

On 16 November 1949, Mahoney formally submitted his resignation as Congress representative in British Columbia and returned east, his job done.

8

The United Electrical Workers and the United Automobile Workers 1940-50

No union was more troublesome to the Congress leadership than the United Electrical Workers. No less than six times between 1943 and 1949 the UE was either suspended or threatened with suspension. But at no time was the primary cause of these suspensions – that the UE leadership was predominantly Communist – ever publicly enunciated by the Congress. Rather such secondary reasons as "non-payment of dues" and "libelling Congress officials" were usually found.

Of all the Congress unions, the UE was most continuously and accurately identified with the Communist party. Organizers dismissed from other unions for their Communist connections or sympathies – Harry Hunter, Jack Douglas, and Alex Welch amongst others – invariably found positions on the UE staff. To a large extent this redounded to the benefit of the UE. Most of these men were experienced and capable union organizers and, in a country short of these, UE was in a fortunate position. As well, because of its close links to the party, the union could rely – and often did – on the advice and assistance of such talented and knowledgeable party functionaries as J.B. Salsberg.[1] With such a reservoir of talent to call upon, UE was in a unique position amongst Congress affiliates. Other CIO unions – Mine-Mill, the IWA, the UAW – were to a large degree influenced by Communist policy. But only the United Electrical Workers was completely and consistently dominated by the party in both Canada and the United States.

The UE in Canada has been the creation and instrument of one man – C.S. Jackson. In early 1937, temporarily laid off from his job as an auditor for the Thor Washing Machine Company in Toronto, Jackson began visiting workers in plants around Toronto's west end, urging them to join the CIO. Shortly afterwards, Jackson quit his job and became an unpaid CIO organizer. With Dick Steele, he set up an office in a vacant store near the large General Electric plant in Toronto and began organizing workers from the various factories in the area. Immediately following the Oshawa strike, in Jackson's words, he and Steele "needed several pairs of hands, night after night, to meet the demand for membership in the newly born CIO unions of which Dick and I were the only organizers in Toronto."[2]

Meanwhile the United Electrical Workers, of America had held its founding convention in 1936 and, almost as an afterthought, had appointed its Buffalo vice-president to be responsible for Canadian organization. The first Canadian UE charter was issued in March 1937 to the Westinghouse local in Hamilton organized by Bert McClure. Charters soon followed to Thor and General Electric locals organized by Jackson, who by this time was travelling through southern Ontario and Quebec attempting to organize electrical plants.

He met with little success. Led by Westinghouse and General Electric, the electrical companies, with one significant exception, would not negotiate with the new union. The exception, the Phillips Electrical plant in Brockville, concluded the first agreement with a UE local in Canada in July 1937. Perhaps as a reward, but more likely because the UE had neither the time nor the inclination to organize in Canada, the second UE convention in Philadelphia set up a special autonomous district for Canada, with Jackson as its president. For the next three years, the Canadian district made no progress at all. Only with the onset of the war did the UE membership begin to expand, culminating in 1944 to a peak of some 30,000.

Though Jackson was one of the founders of the Congress, he was also its most vocal critic. An articulate experienced unionist he became the leader of the so-called "left" opposition, dominated by the UE, IWA, Mine-Mill, and Auto, which was usually at odds with the Congress leadership. As a focal point for the left, the UE bore the brunt of the counter-attacks from the right – from Steel, CBRE, and the Congress executive.

No other union in the Congress so closely, and at times stubbornly, adhered to the Communist "line." Jackson and Harris were in constant contact with party headquarters in Toronto and particularly with Salsberg who set down the party's union policies.[3] Before 22 June 1941, no union was more harshly critical of the war and more bitterly opposed to the Congress support of the war than the UE. Thereafter, no union was more patriotic and more passionate in its attacks on the Congress for its supposed lack of enthusiasm for the very same war.[4]

The UE was one of the few Canadian unions which adopted a no-strike policy after June 1941. "Class strife, strikes and lockouts ... are the weapons of the Fifth Column of Hitlerism," Jackson explained to his membership. The task of the UE was "to put aside everything that in any way interferes with the immediate opening and the full success of a second front in Europe."[5] Though the CIO had adopted a no-strike policy in the United States, the CCL refused to on the grounds that "Canadian unions did not have the same security guaranteed by law to American unions." This argument was in turn rejected by the UE.

In complete consonance with party policy, the UE also vigourously supported the re-election of the King government in 1945, though no union had been more vitriolic in its condemnation before then of that very same government. Indeed once the war was over, no union was more eager to strike, and none more savage in its denunciation of the King government, than the UE. It can be argued that the invasion of Russia did alter the nature of the war, and therefore attitudes and positions taken before the invasion were irrelevant in the new situation. But these changes in party policy came so suddenly and were so completely contrary to policies before the attack on Russia, that the UE, and other unions following the Communist lead, often looked foolish and inconsistent to admirers and critics alike.

At the very first Congress executive council meeting, Jackson established himself as the leader of the opposition. He criticized the Congress organization policy – or the lack of it – and the "dictatorial and unconstitutional" behaviour of the executive. Against Congress wishes he supported both the Stewards' Councils and the Ontario Executive of SWOC. Not surprisingly, when he requested help from the Congress for a strike the UE was conducting at the Electrolier plant in Montreal, the exececutive committee refused. Because of his suspension from the Congress in May of 1941 and his subsequent internment as a Communist at Petawawa from June until December of that year, it was not until the beginning of 1942 that Jackson again played an active role in Congress circles.

But before he was allowed to take his place on the council, Jackson was ordered to make an official apology to the Congress for his previous "misbehaviour." This he did in a series of three letters to the executive council. In these, Jackson stated that it was in the mutual interest of all Canadians "that nothing be allowed to stand in the way of our working together with the maximum unity." He promised that it was his "sincere desire to work in close harmony and cooperation with each and every individual and group which has as its basic aim the winning of this war ... and preservation of the democratic way of life," and warned that unless members of Congress were "able to submerge all of [their] past differences in the urgency of the present situation, it indeed bodes ill for the Canadian labour movement and for the Canadian people as a whole ... [because] there is much to be lost by the continuance of personal animosities within the ranks of labour."[6]

Despite these sentiments calling for greater unity and harmony within the CCL, Jackson continued to criticize the Congress for not making a greater effort in support of the war. He demanded that the Congress take up the cry for the opening of a second front, that it vigorously support a "yes" vote in the conscription plebiscite, that it favour conscription of all available manpower, that it call on workers to remain at their jobs on Labour Day, and finally, that the Congress adopt a no-strike policy for the duration of the war. He also bitterly rejected the decision of the Congress jurisdiction committee on the Anaconda Brass Company, and only the threat of another suspension forced him to reconsider (see chapter 9). Similarly, the same threat in December 1944 compelled Jackson to retract his criticism of PAC and Congress officials (see chapter 5). Thus by the end of the war, despite his appeals for unity and co-operation, Jackson had twice been threatened with suspension, and his opposition to Congress policy was no more restrained than it had been before his first suspension.

Whatever harmony had developed within the Congress during the war was irretrievably shattered only two weeks after Japan surrendered. On 12 September 1945, 10,000 workers at the Ford Motor plant in Windsor went out on strike. For the previous seventeen months, since April 1944, the UAW had been attempting to sign a contract with the Ford company. Some of the leaders of the UAW locals in Windsor, however, were either Communists or men who held their positions only with their support, and were therefore opposed to striking during the war. Despite this, a large number of impatient workers walked out in the early part of 1944 and closed the plant for several weeks. Deserted by their leaders, criticized by their national director, George Burt, and condemned by local Communists, who even paid for large newspaper advertisements calling for a return to work, the strikers reluctantly returned to their jobs with no gains.[7]

But with the end of the war, party policy suddenly reversed itself again, and strikes once more became an integral part of the Communist lexicon. Perturbed by the spectre of a resurgent Communist militancy, the executive council of the Congress offered to support the UAW's efforts in Windsor against the Ford company. It set up a subcommittee to consult with the UAW, but made clear that it was opposed to the calling of a strike. Equally concerned, the international executive board of the United Auto Workers rejected Burt's appeals for either a general work stoppage of all UAW plants in Windsor or a general strike of all workers in Windsor. The UAW board argued that both proposals were "bad strategy" and would alienate the public and the government. Instead, the board ordered Burt to call a strike at the Ford plant and explicitly ordered him to keep the other UAW locals in Windsor working. Speaking on behalf of the joint policy committee – a committee consisting of representatives from all the UAW plants in Windsor – Alex Parent, president of Local 195, protested the UAW directive and demanded in vain that the international call for a general strike.[8]

On 12 September the restive workers at Ford suddenly went out on strike and set up picket lines around the company's administrative offices and manufacturing facilities. The major issue of the strike was union security. Once again Burt and Parent argued with the international that the only way to force Ford to recognize the union and to intimidate the government to pass suitable labour legislation to protect the right of collective bargaining was to tie up the entire Windsor area. Again this proposal was rejected by the UAW executive board.

The reaction of the Congress to the strike was equally disappointing to the UAW. At a special executive council meeting called to discuss the strike, Burt received a hostile reception. Aside from Jackson who urged that the entire labour movement "take advantage" of the militant attitude of the workers during the reconversion period and "challenge" private enterprise, the other members of the council refused to endorse the strike. Angry that the Congress had not been consulted about the timing of the strike nor about the other issues involved, Mosher argued that the Congress should not make the strike a "national issue." He urged that the Congress should "endorse the demands of the Ford workers but should not endorse the strike itself." In the same vein, Millard thought the UAW had acted without "properly considering" the issues involved and warned that Communist "influences were already appearing." A motion to support the strike was withdrawn. Instead the council voted simply to endorse the demands of the Ford strikers, to urge all affiliated unions to give moral and financial support to the UAW, and to set up a National Ford Strike Committee of council members to aid in these efforts.[9]

The Congress was especially angered by the UAW's peremptory rejection of a government conciliation board's decision before either the Congress or its special subcommittee had read the decision.[10] There was no question that, under president Wallace Cambell, Ford was one of the most virulent anti-union companies in Canada and was determined to break the union. On the other hand, the Congress also felt that the UAW in Windsor was dominated by Communists. It was only with mixed feelings, therefore, that the Congress finally threw its full weight behind the strike.

On 15 October representatives of the union and the Ford company met with officials of the federal and provincial governments in Toronto. At this conference, Campbell told the federal labour minister, Humphrey Mitchell, that "if the government felt that the union shop and check-off was good for the people of Canada, then they should pass legislation, and if such legislation were passed, the company would go along with it." An embarrassed Mitchell in turn suggested a royal commission be set up to investigate "all the angles of the dispute." Burt demanded that the government establish a controller over the Ford plant as it had done during a Packinghouse strike earlier. He added that the union was only asking for the "same benefits ... as the same company has given the same Union in the United States," and he laughed off company claims that the Canadian Ford company was not controlled by the American Ford company. The conference broke up when Campbell announced that the company would not negotiate until the union lifted its picket line around the company's offices and power plant. And this, of course, the union would not do.[11]

On 1 November the Ontario government was informed by the Ford company and the Association of Insurance Underwriters of Ontario that, unless the strikers permitted maintenance men to enter the power-house, severe damage would result to the machinery and pipes of the plant. Immediately, and against the advice of Mayor Rheaume of Windsor, provincial police and RCMP officers were rushed in to reinforce the Windsor police should they decide to smash through the picket lines around the power house. On the following day in a well-planned strategic coup, union members and supporters drove into downtown Windsor, and over a stretch of twenty blocks around the Ford plant, parked their cars so that all the roads were completely blocked, turned off the ignition, locked their doors, and went home. The entire city was paralysed. Naturally the police were unable to reach the plant. This tactic shocked both the international and the Congress, but delighted UAW members in Windsor. The attempt to break in to the power-house had been foiled and was never made again.

To capitalize on this renewed sense of militance, against the wishes of both the international and the Congress, the joint policy committee sent off several hundred telegrams to various unions in the country calling for a nation-wide one-day general strike. This action was condemned by the Congress, and the request was ignored by almost all Congress locals. Similarly, against the explicit requests of both the international and the Congress, Chrysler Local 195 walked out in sympathy with the Ford workers, thus adding 8500 more men to the already over-taxed Congress and UAW strike relief lists.

It was apparent that Burt, the international, and the national Ford strike committee had lost control of the strike to the militants on the joint policy committee and in the locals. In a last desperate attempt to regain the initiative, the UAW secretary-treasurer, George Addes, met with Burt and Conroy. As a result of this meeting, the union offered to allow maintenance men into the power plant if the company would agree to start negotiations. Though the company refused, a settlement now seemed possible. At the UAW executive board meeting on 20 November, Burt urged the international to accept the recommendation of the federal government that a justice of the Supreme Court of Canada arbitrate the dispute. He added, resignedly, that he favoured arbitration but "the men on the line" did not.[12]

Burt's analysis was proven correct. On 29 November the workers rejected the union's advice to end the strike and to allow the issues to be put to arbitration. Two weeks later, however, after appeals from their own militant leaders, the men voted 72 per cent in favour of the government plan, and on 20 December Mitchell appointed Justice Ivan Rand of the Supreme Court of Canada as the arbitrator. On the same day the men went back to work.

In its significance the hundred-day Ford strike stands second to none in the post-war decade. The so-called "Rand" formula, which brought the conflict to an end, provided for a compulsory check-off of union dues, though union membership remained voluntary. It was to become the precedent for collective bargaining for the next generation. The strike put securely into the economic fabric of peacetime the gains and recognition that unions had achieved during the war. It was also an unhappy harbinger of the record number of strikes which were to take place following its successful conclusion, as union after union attempted to emulate the Ford workers and to gain victories which had been denied them by restrictive wartime legislation.

For the Congress, the Ford strike was equally significant. Aside from the impetus it gave to affiliates to follow the trail blazed by the Ford workers, it brought out into the open the fundamental conflict between the factions of the left and right which had been papered over during the war. From the beginning, Mosher, Conroy, Millard, and other leaders of the Congress had "questioned the wisdom" of striking Ford so soon after the war. They were opposed to the strike, and the tactics and speeches of the strike leaders alienated them even more.[13]

On the other hand, the left wing was openly critical of the Congress behaviour. On 9 November at a meeting of the Ford strike joint policy committee, Jackson charged that the Congress national Ford strike committee was "sabotaging the Ford strike." At a Labour Progressive party meeting a week later, George Harris, Jackson's second-in-command in the UE, condemned Millard and Conroy for "trying to sell the workers down the river in trying to get them to accept the company's terms." Communist hostility to Conroy and Millard was exacerbated by the Congress decision to oppose the call for a one-day sympathy strike, which the party believed "could conceivably have caused the police to be withdrawn and the government to step in and to take over the plants and commence negotiations." Explaining the Congress position Millard told Philip Murray that the Communists were "trying to use the strike to further their political ends" and that the strike call had to be rejected.[14]

Unquestionably, the Communists played an important role in the calling, conduct, and concluding of the strike. Salsberg, Harris, Jackson, Oscar Kogan, the LPP organizer in the Windsor area, and other prominent Communists were in constant communication with the joint policy committee and with strike leaders, Roy England and Alex Parent – neither of whom, however, were Communists. They gave advice, planned strategy, and organized support. Burt, nominally the strike leader, was often not privy to the decisions made by this group.

On the other hand it is quite inaccurate to argue, as does Gad Horowitz, that the strike was organized and directed by the Communist party for selfish political ends.[15] In fact, though the party was certainly influential, all the key decisions were made by the union itself. As Oscar Kogan and J.B. Salsberg remember it: "the party had nothing to do with the important tactical decisions that were made by the union during the strike. The massive picketing, the withdrawal of the power plant workers, the building of the auto barricade, the sending of the one day strike telegrams ... were all decisions made by the union itself with little Communist influence."[16]

The auto workers in Windsor after the war were impatient and militant. For nearly two years they had attempted to sign a contract with the Ford company. By September of 1945, frustrated and embittered, they could wait no longer. At the same time the Communist party which had counselled cooperation and passivity during the war had returned to its more accustomed role of encouraging defiance and activism. Since the Congress and the CCF were hesitant in supporting the strike, the UAW was receptive to the Communist offers of support. Because of the militance of the union and the constant presence in Windsor of leading Communists, the Congress naturally assumed that the party was playing a far more important role in the strike than it actually was.

In fact, as the strike progressed, with the support of the international the Congress national Ford strike committee began to take a more active part, and played a major role in bringing about a satisfactory conclusion to the strike. As well, under its auspices, more than $300,000 was raised to aid the strikers, though some funds from the CCF unions and clubs were held back in "fear that the money would find its way into the hands of the LPP."[17]

To counter what he felt was obvious Communist domination of the UAW in Windsor, Millard offered to help Burt in the "house-cleaning" necessary to replace the local leadership, but Burt politely, but firmly, declined the offer. Determined to undermine Communist influence in the Congress, Millard then laid formal charges against Jackson and Harris for their "treacherous, fraudulent and malicious" attacks against the Congress, Conroy, and himself, and urged that the executive council suspend the UE until its leaders promised to refrain from "such scurrilous attacks."[18]

These accusations were discussed at a stormy executive council meeting on 13 February 1946. Jackson and Harris did not deny the charges, though the latter argued that he had spoken as a member of the LPP and not as a member of the UE and that he thought every person "had the right to express opinions on public issues." Jackson claimed that he had made his statement at a private meeting and was not aware that a reporter had been present. Conroy, who was still attempting to act as a mediator between the two factions in the Congress, argued that he did not believe that "suspensions would serve any purpose." He urged instead that the UE "cut out this nonsense" and that a subcommittee be set up to examine the entire situation. Showing the strain, Conroy confessed that he was "fed up" with the "immaturity" of the Congress and that he longed to retire as secretary-treasurer before the job "killed him." Silby Barrett and J.E. McGuire demanded that the UE be expelled from the Congress because it was apparent that the Communists wished only to "tear down the good name of honest leaders in the labour movement." Barrett also threatened to pull the Mineworkers out of the Congress. By a vote of thirteen to eleven, a motion to suspend the UE was defeated, but the Council agreed to set up an investigation committee including Barrett and Burt to report back to the Congress on the situation.[19]

The decision not to suspend the UE was a victory for the left and an indirect slap at Millard who was the most forceful proponent of the suspension motion. Greatly perturbed, Millard suggested to Murray that, if suspension of the UE were not warranted, then at least Harris and Jackson should be suspended from all Congress positions and organizations to stop "them from using their position to attack the Congress and other CIO unions operating in Canada." In its report to the executive council, however, the investigating committee concluded that the statements of Jackson and Harris "constituted an offence" against the Congress and unless they apologized they should be suspended from the Congress. The two UE officers, hurriedly apologized and so the suspension was never put into effect. The incident, however, did serve to intensify the bitter acrimony between the two factions within the Congress.[20]

For the UE, the year 1946 was most rewarding. The large number of members lost when the war plants closed were regained in startling UE victories at the large Westinghouse and General Electric plants in Hamilton, Peterborough, and Toronto. These gains shifted the union's base from the machine shops which it had organized during the war to the electrical industry which, by the end of 1946, provided 75 per cent of its members. With a membership of 25,000, the Canadian section of UE became completely self-supporting for the first time.

Because of American immigration laws, the UE also became the most autonomous of the CIO unions in Canada. Since both the international and the Canadian leadership were suspected of being linked to the Communist party, Canadian members could not attend union conventions in the United States, nor could international representatives cross the border to meet their Canadian counterparts. From 1946 on, the UE in Canada had all the powers of a national union. It operated almost totally independently of its international headquarters in the United States.

Heartened by this new vitality, the UE increased the vigour of its attacks on the Congress. After the Ford strike, Jackson urged Mosher to call a special wage conference. The latter complained to Eugene Forsey, the Congress research director, that with the Ford strike over, Jackson was seeking another national issue to further the Communist policy of "continued disruption and agitation." In any case, Mosher felt the "timing of the agitation" for wage increases was "too soon" and that the amount suggested by the CIO below the border (30 per cent) was "too high." Forsey agreed. None the less, the Congress adopted a wage policy very much along the lines suggested by Jackson.[21]

In April 1946, Jackson issued a lengthy and detailed attack on the annual Congress memorandum to the government. It bitterly criticized it for not condemning the "vicious attack on the Soviet Union" by western governments and newspapers which were "obviously designed ... to provide a smokescreen on the domestic scene behind which to disrupt the labour movement." He further suggested that not "sufficient emphasis" had been given to attacking the "onslaught of big business on the living standards of the Canadian people." Some of these suggestions must have found their way into the memorandum since Jackson had been appointed to a committee to redraft certain sections. The militance of the memorandum unnerved the ordinarily placid Mackenzie King who, for one of the few times in his public career, lost his temper and delivered a severe tongue-lashing to the assembled Congress leaders for their candid criticisms of his policies.[22]

Jackson's attacks were not reserved solely for the government. During most of 1947 and 1948, Jackson kept up his sniping against Congress policies. In addition, the UE resolutely opposed Congress approval of the Marshall plan, and its delegates at the 1947 Congress convention spoke out forcefully against the resolutions condemning Soviet imperialism and Communism. In direct opposition to the Congress, the UE supported the jurisdictional claims of the Communist-led AFL Textile Workers in its continuous battle with the CIO Textile Workers Union. Only threats of suspension from Philip Murray and Conroy brought the UE back into line. In vain, the UE also led the fight in the Congress against the suspension of Mine-Mill and the British Columbia district council of the IWA. Closely adhering to party policy, the UE in 1948 also supported the CCF and provided assistance to CCF candidates in the Ontario election, support and assistance most CCF candidates did not want.[23]

At the 1948 Congress convention it was evident that the UE did not have much of a future in the Congress. The convention opened with a plea from Mosher to all unions to "free themselves from Communist leadership." Because the schools did "nothing to inculcate in the minds of their pupils the facts with respect to the Communist threat to the peace and well-being of this world," Mosher urged that the labour movement leave "nothing undone to awaken the people to the menace of Communism." Throughout the convention both Mosher and Conroy informed the delegates that they "were going to clean the Communists" out of the Congress and that they were "not going to permit ten or fifteen percent of the delegates" to disrupt Congress policy and "obstruct" the convention. Mosher specifically warned the UE that "unless you change your tactics and damned soon, whether you leave or not, you will be thrown out. Your tactics and your philosophy shame the convention." With the Berlin blockade and the coup d'état in Czechoslovakia, still freshly imprinted on their minds, the delegates were caught up in a frenzy of anti-communism, which culminated in Conroy's fervent entreaty that "every local union must clean the Communists out of the unions and out of the trade union movement if it wants to live, if it wants to grow and flourish, if it wants to preserve its right to think and plan and if it wants to get on with the job of bringing security and freedom for the great mass of the workers."

With both Mine-Mill and the British Columbia district of IWA suspended from the convention, the UE bore the full brunt of these attacks. Jackson bitterly informed his union that the Congress had singled out the UE as the "target for the day" and that the UE had been the victim of "name calling and slanderous lying attacks." Isolated but not cowed, the UE delegates stood their ground and opposed, in the face of heated threats, the resolutions which condemned Communism, Soviet foreign policy, and other programs and policies supported by the party. They were badly outnumbered. In the election for president, Jackson could only garner 154 votes against Mosher's 564. By the end of the convention, it was clear that the Congress had committed itself to ousting the UE, with only the timing and the method still in doubt.

Shortly after the convention a method seemed to present itself. The Congress had undertaken to organize the workers of the Sovereign Potteries plant in Hamilton who had decided to disaffiliate from the AFL Pottery Workers union. Just when arrangements were being completed for the union to become a Congress local, the UE announced that it intended to bring these workers into its union. Mosher immediately wired Jackson that the UE had no jurisdiction in the plant and unless it "withdrew immediately" the Congress would undertake disciplinary action. Ignoring the order, the UE continued its campaign and at a meeting on 25 November 1948 the workers rejected pleas from two Congress organizers and voted to join the UE. The unhappy Congress organizers reported to Mosher that the meeting was "packed" with UE members from other plants in the Hamilton area.[24]

Incensed, Mosher ordered the Congress organizers "to drive the UE out with everything at their disposal." Within days most large CCL affiliates in Hamilton – Steel, Textile, Rubber – circulated leaflets to the Pottery workers warning them of the UE's Communist connections and urging them to join the Congress. At the same time the Congress issued a charter to the union.[25]

At the executive meetings in December, the UE was ordered to give up its organization in the plant or face suspension. Jackson protested, quite correctly, that other unions had organized outside their jurisdictions, but only the UE had been threatened with sanctions. It was the feeling of the UE, he added, that all workers should have the right to join the union of their choice. Accurate as well was the UE charge that the Congress was not dealing with the Sovereign Potteries issue "on the basis of jurisdiction as such" but as an "attempt to victimize and weaken the UE." There was, therefore, little the UE could do to dissuade the Congress. Confronted by the relentless hostility of the council, Jackson stated that "rather than be suspended" his organization would give up Sovereign Potteries.[26]

Thwarted in this attempt to expel the UE, the Congress was soon presented with another. At its quarterly district council meeting in Welland on 30 January 1949, the UE strongly condemned the Congress for encouraging "wild and reckless" raids against Mine-Mill and itself. It criticized the Congress wages and contracts policy, called the North Atlantic alliance a "war pact," denounced the Marshall plan, and strongly objected to the Congress decision to withdraw from the World Federation of Trade Unions.[27]

Two weeks later, at a rowdy Ontario Federation of Labour meeting in Toronto, the UE valiantly attempted to pass resolutions condemning Canadian foreign policy, the Congress wage and political policies, and especially the "raids" conducted by Steel and the Congress. These resolutions were beaten back by a militant and vocal anti-Communist faction. Explaining the defeat to its membership, the UE leadership charged that a "closely controlled group of delegates led by Millard's Steelworkers held numerical strength sufficient to steamroller through decisions which were obviously pre-arranged ... and to stifle debate." To underscore its bitterness, the UE published an editorial in its paper condemning the OFL leadership for aligning itself "with every anti-union and union-busting individual and organization in Canada," for using "Hitler-like" tactics, for subjecting the UE delegates to "red baiting, hysteria and war-mongering," and for "attempting to disrupt, divide or capture the trade union movement for narrow partisan or personal aims."[28]

The OFL reacted promptly. It laid charges with the Congress against the UE for printing "vicious and slanderous" accusations. The OFL warned that if the UE's actions were ignored it would "spur other Communist organizations to the utmost to blackmail everyone in the Canadian Congress of Labour who disagrees with them." These charges were discussed by the executive council which decided that an investigation would be held. But until it was completed, no representative of the UE would be allowed to participate in any Congress meeting; Jackson was therefore forced to leave the meeting. There was some protest from council members that the UE had not been given advance notice in order to prepare a defence, and even louder cries were raised when Mosher announced the investigating committee would consist of J.E. McGuire of the CBRE, Millard, Baron of Textile, Dowling of the Packinghouse workers, and William England of Rubber, all of them militant anti-Communists and passionate foes of Jackson and the UE. With such a committee, the findings, as well as the unanimity, were assured beforehand. To make certain that no one misunderstood its intentions, on the day before the committee was first scheduled to meet, the Congress issued a press statement assuring the Canadian people that it would soon rid itself of its Communist-dominated unions.[30]

The investigating committee met on 14 April in Toronto at the Royal York Hotel. Jackson had requested all UE locals to send representatives to the opening session. When the meeting convened, it was found that the room in which it was to be held was too small. Fortunately, Jackson had taken the precaution of renting for the UE one of the large Royal York diningrooms, and the hearing took place there. Five officers of the OFL, including George Burt, presented the case for the Federation. They argued that there was no justification for the "slanderous and grossly misleading statements" in the UE editorial, and that these attacks "were made for the specific purposes of assassinating the character of honest trade unionists and to destroy the trade union movement itself." For the UE, Jackson presented a thirty-page brief tracing the history of his union, its contributions to the Congress and the labour movement, and accusing the Congress and the OFL of "disrupting" the labour movement.[31]

Though Jackson's presentation was certainly thorough, the committee found that "practically everything in it was irrelevant." The committee also felt that Jackson had used the hearing to "slander" other labour leaders and their organizations, "and to thoroughly discount and discredit the efforts of every other National and International Union affiliated with the Congress." The committee predictably concluded that the UE had "failed to substantiate any of the alleged slanderous statements" in the editorial, and that it was "guilty of willful and calculated slander against the officers of the Ontario Federation of Labour." But even before the committee had reached its verdict, at its quarterly meeting, the indomitable UE passed a resolution condemning "certain elements within the CCL [who] parrot the anti-union employers in their red-baiting hysteria ... and certain union leaders, notably those of the United Steel Workers of America [who] carry on open raiding against established unions within the Congress."[32]

The committee released its report on 5 July. Surprisingly, though it found the UE guilty, three of its members, Dowling, Millard, and England, did not feel that the entire union should be disciplined. Both Baron and McGuire had demanded that the union be expelled permanently, but with their reluctant acquiescence, the committee recommended that only the UE leaders – Jackson, Chambers, George Harris, Ross Russell, and Jack Douglas – be suspended from all Congress activities for five years.[33]

When the decision was made known to the executive committee, Mosher angrily demanded the UE be expelled "for good" from the Congress. He was supported by McGuire, Dowd, Baron, and Barrett. However, the strong opposition of Burt, who was supported by McAuslane, Millard, Conroy, and Spivak, defeated this motion. Instead, the executive committee decided to suspend the UE from representation on the executive council and to warn the union that any further incident would lead to its "total suspension" from the Congress. This decision was approved by the Council though four members, Burt, Roy England, Bob Haddow and Stewart, were opposed, while Dowling abstained because he thought the penalty too severe.[34]

The decision was not entirely unexpected by the UE. Even before the executive council decision was known, Jackson had sent a letter to all UE staff members suggesting how they react. He told them that as soon as the Congress decision was made public "it will be necessary that your locals immediately issue strong protests to the Congress against the interference in the internal affairs of the union and the abrogation of democratic rights, and of taxation without representation." They were also told to hold discussions with other unions in their area to gain their support, and were given a list of six subjects, including the suspension and the problems of unemployment and foreign policy, from which to present resolutions to the next Congress convention.[35]

Once the Congress decision was made public, the UE sent a searing telegram to Conroy protesting the "whole series of violations of fundamental principles and ethics which have characterized the whole period" during which allegations were made against the UE and the investigation carried on. In an equally bitter press release the UE called the Congress action "an alarming invasion of the democratic rights of the membership" of the UE. It accused the Congress of attempting to stifle "legitimate criticism" unconstitutionally by setting up a highly partisan investigating committee – "most of the members of which have been on public record as attacking the UE over a long period of time" – and of carrying on a vicious campaign against the union in the newspapers during the entire investigation period. Nevertheless, the UE emphasized its intention of remaining within the Congress in the hope that "rank and file ... when fully appraised of these developments ... will ... gladly support the position of militant and progressive struggle epitomized by the membership of the UE." Unmoved by the protests Conroy replied that "democratic rights are in no way invaded by the imposition of restrictions upon those who seek to vilify their associates on every conceivable occasion. Democratic rights cannot properly be used as a cloak to carry on a campaign of sabotage and character assassination."[36]

This was only the beginning. For the next few months, resolution upon resolution, charge and counter-charge, filled the pages of union papers. At its quarterly district meeting in July, the UE declared that "silencing opposition by suspension or threats leads only to destruction of democracy" and claimed that its officers were barred by Congress officers who wished "to rid themselves of the conscience of the working people when they cannot stand being faced with the hard facts of life which expose the errors of their policies." In a letter to all Congress affiliates urging them to support the UE, George Harris claimed that the reason for the suspension was the Congress' desire "to eliminate all forms of real opposition from the floor of the convention" and was therefore "in violation ... of all principles of trade union democracy." In turn, George Burt, who had voted against suspension, informed his UAW locals that he thought that the Harris letter and the other statements and press releases issued by the UE since the suspension ignored "the substance matter of the charges which were laid against the UE." He urged his UAW locals not to support the UE until it "began to clean its house" and desisted from "character assassination" and "slanderous statements."[37]

It seemed, the more numerous the attacks on the UE, the more unyielding became its resolve. At the UE annual convention in September, instead of behaving more "responsibly" and cautiously, the executive let loose a devastating tirade against Congress policy and officials. The UE officers devoted approximately half of their 65-page annual report to a stinging attack against the Congress, the Marshall plan, American foreign policy, the CCF, and especially against their own suspension. Addressing the convention, Jackson and Harris spent most of their speeches maligning the Congress leadership. They accused it of "carrying out the dictates of the employing class of this country, in creating division throughout the ranks of labour," and charged that "Mosher, Millard and Conroy are out to get this union because we opposed them on policy." Though they admitted that Mosher had threatened to "kick the UE out of the Congress," and that the Congress leadership obviously wished to manoeuvre the UE into leaving the Congress, Harris, and Jackson vowed to the UE delegates that the union had "no intention whatsoever of walking out of the CCL."[38]

But whatever their intention was, there was little the UE could do. At the 1949 Congress convention, Jackson and Harris pleaded with the delegates to overturn the executive's recommendation. It was useless; by an overwhelming margin the convention voted to uphold the suspension of the UE leadership. It was the last time Harris and Jackson ever addressed a Congress convention.

In November 1949, at its eleventh convention, the CIO at last made its move against its "Communist" unions. It barred Communists from its executive board, it authorized "trials" for nine board members and ten unions accused of "following the party line," and most significantly, it expelled the UE and chartered a new union, the International Union of Electrical, Radio and Machine Workers of America (IUE) to organize in UE's jurisdiction.[39] (The leaders of the new union were one-time UE president James Carey and the three men who had been defeated by the left-wing slate at the 1949 UE convention in Cleveland.)

Orders immediately went out from the CIO to the Congress to help bring "into the fold of the CIO all UE members." Conroy had already consulted the Congress lawyer, E.B. Jolliffe, to discuss the "legal status" of UE in the Congress, and had called a meeting of Millard, Cotterill, Henry Rhodes, and Jack Williams to "reassess the Congress position." The leaders of the right-wing opposition group within the UE were also active and on 12 November, John Morton, who had been appointed the IUE director in Canada, applied to the Congress for affiliation on behalf of UE locals 508 in Guelph, 524 in Peterborough, and 534 in Cobourg.[40]

As with Mine-Mill, the Congress was once again in a quandary. It could not affiliate the new IUE without expelling the UE, nor could it constitutionally expel the UE. Congress organizers in Peterborough and Toronto, who were already hard at work lining up support for the IUE in UE organized plants, found themselves in the untenable position of "raiding" a Congress affiliate on behalf of an unaffiliated union.

Countering their efforts, Jackson suspended Morton and his adherents from the UE. He also announced that he had received "votes of confidence" from most of the UE locals in Canada. At the same time he laid charges with the Congress against Congress organizers Fred Hanna and Henry Rhodes, David Archer of the OFL, and Mike Fenwick, Murray Cotterill, and Millard of Steel, for "raiding, disruption, division and the deliberate destruction of organized labour ... by openly encouraging and assisting secession" from the UE. In fact, however, all these men who were assisting the UE secessionists, were operating directly under Congress orders.[41]

Faced with the absurd situation of a Congress affiliate laying charges against Congress organizers for following Congress orders, Mosher agreed despite the protests of Millard, Barrett, and Rhodes, to bring Jackson's charges before the executive council. Because Jackson was suspended, they believed that the Congress could "not recognize any communications from a person who had no status in the Congress." But at the same time, Mosher sent letters to all members of the executive committee enclosing copies of the IUE application for affiliation, and requesting committee members to advise him if they approved the affiliation. He admitted, however, that if they approved affiliating the IUE, he was not sure what could be done about the UE.[42]

The response only added to the perplexed Mosher's confusion. Most of the committee, Joe Mackenzie, W. Robitaille, Donald MacDonald, Sam Baron, and J.E. McGuire, voted for the IUE's immediate affiliation. But other members were not so explicit. Harry Chappell thought it would be better to wait for the next meeting of the executive committee, though he enthusiastically approved the affiliation. Barrett stated that he would not vote for affiliation until the UE was expelled. This, he proposed, should be done at once. Millard argued that affiliation of the new union would "automatically cancel" the affiliation of UE and thus he was "delighted" to vote for the IUE.[43]

The most formidable opposition came from Alex McAuslane and George Burt. The former drew Mosher's attention to the fact that the CIO had first expelled the UE before chartering IUE and therefore had the "clean-cut position" which the Congress lacked. In addition, he warned that the UE seemed to be successfully withstanding the secession movement and he feared precipitate action by the Congress would put it in "an utterly ridiculous position." Aware that chartering the IUE would give the UE "a platform to fight from, inasmuch as they are being raided by another CCL union while they themselves are still maintaining affiliation," McAuslane refused to vote for the IUE affiliation. Burt's position was similar. He admitted that since the CIO had already "kicked" the UE out, the Congress would obviously follow suit, but he wished to do "these things in an orderly way because of the repercussions which may follow." He warned that by acting too rashly he would be "threatening" the unity of his own organization, and he saw no way of affiliating the new union until the Congress had found a way of expelling the UE.[44]

Because of this divergence in opinion, Mosher was unable to inform the IUE whether its application had been accepted or rejected. Instead he shelved the problem until the next executive committee meeting with the fervent hope that some way could soon be found to "get rid" of the UE.

There were many suggestions from Congress officials as to how this could be done. Rhodes even recommended that the UE be notified that it was suspended, and that it be left to the UE to "show cause why the suspension should not take place." This, he argued, though unconstitutional, would place "the onus on the UE to satisfy the executive council, [and] then you could throw the book at them." Mosher rejected this and other such proposals for fear that any blatantly unconstitutional action "would be repugnant to organized labour generally." Two things were certain, however: with the example of the IWA before it, the UE would not voluntarily withdraw from the Congress; and the Congress would therefore be forced to find a way to expel it. In response to a resolution passed by his largest local in Hamilton calling for the UE to leave the Congress, Jackson stated that the UE had "no intention or desire to pull out of the Congress."[45] Within two weeks, however, whatever the UE's intentions, the Congress at last found a way to oust its most troublesome affiliate.

Sometime in the middle of November 1949, Dowd informed Mosher that the UE had not paid its per capita tax for two months, probably because the international, which paid the tax to the Congress, had decided to withhold its dues from the CIO and had forgotten to send the Canadian share to the Congress. Fully aware that, according to the Congress constitution, "any union in arrears of per capita tax for a three-month period" was liable to suspension, Mosher asked Dowd "not to reveal the situation to anyone, including executive committee members, lest the word get out and the UE pay its overdue fees."[46]

For ten anxious days Mosher and Dowd awaited the morning mail, praying that it would not contain the overdue cheque. On 1 December the triumphant Mosher "grinning like a cheshire cat" informed members of the executive council of his coup. In telegrams to all the council members, Mosher told them of the UE's failure to pay its per capita for three months and reminded them of the suspension of the UE officers and of the desperate attempts of the newly chartered IUE to gain affiliation. He warned them of the danger to the future of the Congress if it did not take action at once. He then informed them that he had suspended the UE because of its "failure to pay its dues" and he asked each member for his approval of this action.[47]

Though the UE was not directly informed of Mosher's action, late that afternoon Jackson received the news from several executive council members. He immediately contacted the international office which informed him that "solely due to inadvertance" the per capita cheques had not been sent out. On the following morning, Jackson wired Mosher explaining why the dues had not been paid, and stated that the overdue tax was now in the mail, and that, in any case, the UE's per capita was paid on the 15th of every month and therefore the "three months of arrears does not elapse until December 15." At the same time Jackson sent copies of the telegram to all council members. But, as Jackson must have known, nothing he could do would alter the situation.[48]

Even before the council members had begun to reply to Mosher's telegram, the Congress president had contacted the IUE representatives and had promised them the Congress's "full cooperation and all necessary assistance." On 5 December, Mosher rejected Jackson's claim and informed him that the decision of the executive council to suspend the UE was final. However, some hours before he sent this letter, the overdue UE per capita tax arrived in the mail. Mosher immediately ordered Dowd to send the cheque for $1,297.68 back to the UE with the remark that the UE was already suspended.[49]

In fact, many of the Council members had not yet responded to Mosher's appeal for approval of his suspension of the UE. Indeed the last reply arrived in the Congress office on 10 December – fully five days after Mosher had informed the UE that its suspension was "final." Of the thirty-two council members, only fifteen had responded when Mosher issued his suspension order. Even more questionable was Mosher's decision to affiliate the IUE though the UE had merely been suspended and not expelled. He had taken this decision himself without consulting any council or committee members. Predictably, when the results were all in, the executive council members upheld Mosher's suspension of the UE though they had no opportunity, of course, to vote on the affiliation of the IUE. Twenty council members supported Mosher;

three – Roy England, Haddow, and Stewart – did not; and, surprisingly, nine – including Burt, Spivak, and McAuslane – abstained.[50]

Commenting on Mosher's hurried suspension, McAuslane complained that "frankly it leaves one in a hell of a positions when they are asked to vote on something that is already an accomplished fact." The most telling response, however, came from Burt. Charging that it was "not the practice in the labour movement" to suspend affiliates "who are in arrears of per capita tax," especially when it involved the suspension of 20,000 workers and when the overdue tax had already been paid, Burt reminded Mosher that the UE was not the first nor would it be the last affiliate to be behind in its dues. He admitted that it would be "almost impossible to keep [the UE] within the ranks of the Congress," because of the opposition of all the CIO unions, but he objected to the course of action the Congress had taken. Would the Congress, he asked, suspend for non-payment of dues a union like Steel or the UAW which "was in agreement with the policy of the Congress?" He further reprimanded Mosher for announcing the UE suspension before the council had finished voting and stated that there was no way of affiliating the IUE before the UE was expelled.[51]

Mosher's reply was short and, for once, to the point. "You know as well as I do," he told Burt, "that a large number of executive council members wanted to get rid of UE, at the very first opportunity, though there might be some hesitancy in again preferring charges against the organization and going through the procedure of a trial." He also admitted that, with regard to the affiliation of the IUE, he did not wish to wait until the next executive committee lest "those who had broken away from UE might have sought affiliation with some other central body." He therefore, had taken it upon himself, once the UE was suspended, to affiliate the new union.[52]

Constitutionally, the Congress position was dubious. As Jackson pointed out in a letter to council members, though the constitution provided the executive council with the authority to suspend any union three months in arrears of its per-capita tax, it also stipulated that the per capita tax had to be sent in "within fifteen days after the first day of the succeeding calendar month." This, Jackson maintained, allowed the UE until December 15 to pay its tax. Mosher naturally dismissed this argument out of hand.[53]

There was little Jackson could do to reverse the decision. His plea to present the UE case before the next meeting of the executive council was rejected by Mosher on the grounds that only the convention had the right to deal with appeals against council decisions. The UE nevertheless forwarded an appeal to the council charging that even if the suspension were constitutional, which it was not, the entire issue was "based upon a technicality." The UE also raised the matter of its charges against Congress representatives who were "promoting dissension and disruption and attempting to break up the membership" of the UE, charges which the Congress had ignored. The union pointed out that the Congress raids had failed, and that the UE membership had remained loyal and united, but that "divisions [were] being created in labour's ranks by those who raid or condone raiding."[54]

At the Congress executive council meeting in January, Burt raised the question of the UE suspension. He declared that he disagreed totally with the way the Congress had handled the situation, since other unions had been "in arrears for even longer periods than the UE." McAuslane felt that the Congress position would have been stronger if the UE had been suspended after the charges against it had been discussed. Articulating what everyone else was thinking, Dowling stated that the UE failure to pay its dues was merely an opportunity for the Congress to suspend it – something it wished to do long before, for other reasons. Conroy added that he could not understand why anyone should wish to defend an organization "which had done everything possible to destroy the CCL." Millard saw it as a "life and death struggle" against the UE and he argued that the Congress had a moral obligation to support the new electrical union. Because the suspension was not debatable, the committee merely confirmed Mosher's action in affiliating the IUE.[55]

Only one hope remained for the UE, an appeal to the convention. But this was really no hope at all. Indeed, by the middle of 1950 the Congress was well caught up in the frenzy of anti-communism which swept the continent in the wake of the onset of the Korean war and of the dramatic anti-Communist crusade of Senator McCarthy. At its July meeting the executive committee recommended that a constitutional amendment be adopted giving the council the power to expel any union "which was following the principles and policies of the Communist Party." And at a later meeting in September, the committee adopted Conroy's proposal to "draft a positive statement concerning the menace of Communism and the way in which it could be met." Within two days, with the help of Barrett and Chappell, Conroy had drafted a ten-page "Declaration of a Positive Economic Philosophy" which was discussed, amended, and printed so that it could be distributed to delegates attending the convention two days later.[56]

It was one of the most remarkable documents ever issued by the Congress, certainly its most savage piece of propaganda. It saw two great forces in the world – communism and democracy – engaged in a life-and-death struggle. Communism, it warned, was "the greatest tyranny the world [has] ever known" and was everywhere "on the march." It promised freedom, bread, and equality, and instead provided dictatorship, poverty, slave labour camps, and the "sound of firing squads." The document charged that communism had "replaced truth and morality by their opposites," had applied "a ruthlessness, the like of which has never yet been seen," and had used "every diabolical and devious method in pursuing its ultimate goal." Finally, the document concluded that communism "has set up a Fifth Column in every nation, consisting of devoted fanatics ... [which] has polluted every institution into which it has penetrated and has sought to dominate every organization it could reach [and] ... it has sabotaged and will continue to sabotage every nation where it has been established." With such a document in the hands of each delegate, the UE appeal was merely a waste of time.

Nevertheless, the UE persisted. When Mosher ruled that the appeal could not be presented by any of the five officers suspended in 1949, Jackson asked George Aldridge, president of UE Local 521, to read the 34-page appeal. It was a well-organized and well-written presentation of the UE's position on everything from finance minister Abbott's 'baby budget' to the causes of the Korean war. It attacked Mosher, Conroy, Millard, the CIO, the Marshall plan, and "big business," and stated, quite accurately, that the UE had not been suspended for its tardiness in paying its dues but because "on some fundamental policy questions ... the UE ... found itself in sharp disagreement with the Congress officers ... and carried forward a consistent fight within the Congress in support of [its] point of view." The appeal concluded with a ringing plea for the delegates to "stand and fight together," to vote for the "unity of the labour movement," and to defeat any attempt to expel the UE.[57]

In rebuttal, Conroy referred to the UE appeal as an "unctious, sniffling document," a "seventy-minute song and dance" full of "captious and piffling" excuses. Every UE leader and staff member, he claimed, was "a prisoner and political slave of the Communist party ... and a complete vassal of Uncle Joe Stalin ... crawling on their bellies to Uncle Joe Stalin to obtain leadership at the expense of the Canadian workers." Conroy begged the convention to support the action of the executive council "so that the leaders of the UE who have sold their souls to Uncle Joe Stalin will be told in unequivocal and unswerving language there is no room for you among free men in the trade union movement. Go your way. You are out and you are going to stay out." In overwhelming numbers, the delegates decided that there was indeed no room in their Congress for the UE.

To oust the UE proved to be relatively simple for the Congress. But to persuade UE members to join the new IUE proved infinitely more difficult. The UE held its own against the combined forces of the CIO and the CCL, the press, and some portions of the clergy. The bishop of Peterborough, for example, in an extraordinary Christmas midnight mass sermon, warned Catholic workers to join the IUE.[58] Members of the UE, like members of Mine-Mill, proved more loyal to their union than the Congress had anticipated, and organizers for the IUE proved more inept than the Congress had expected. Year after year, the IUE attempted to break the UE by gaining the bargaining rights for the thousands of electrical workers in the huge General Electric plants in Peterborough and Toronto, and year after year they were beaten back.

Explaining away the IUE's abysmal failure to make any progress in Ontario in the first eight months after its formation, David Lewis and E. B. Jolliffe, the union's lawyers, blamed the lack of experienced personnel, the "weak opposition" inside the UE to its leadership, and the fact that the Ontario Labour Relations Board – in order to preserve its "strict impartiality" – often leaned over "backwards to be fair to the UE." They also claimed that in Canada unlike in the United States the opposition to communism was "a calmer more tolerant kind." Because the anti-Communist issue was not succeeding, they urged the Congress to adopt a "positive programme of union benefits which the IUE can present" to the workers.[59]

For the next decade the IUE made little headway against the UE. So hopeless was the IUE position, that several times Millard suggested that Steel be allowed to organize the electrical industry; he once even suggested that his "trouble-shooter" Bill Mahoney be put in charge of the IUE organizing campaign. In addition, friction developed between the IUE and the Congress concerning the organizational procedure to be used. The IUE accused the Congress of promoting an anti-international union attitude, and the Congress charged that the IUE organizational policies were "bankrupt." Only in the province of Quebec where the Labour Relations Board decertified every UE local on the grounds that it was a Communist organization did the IUE manage to score some victories. In fact, despite the efforts of the labour movement, the church, government, and, in some cases, industry, the UE actually has increased its membership in the years after its expulsion. At the present time it has a much larger membership in Canada than the IUE.[60]

With the UE out, there remained in the Congress only one fairly large international union with close Communist ties – the International Leather and Fur Workers Union. It would not remain much longer. With the adoption of the constitutional amendment at the 1950 convention permitting the council to expel unions "following the principles and policies of the Communist Party," it was only a matter of time before the Congress moved against the Fur Workers' union.

In March 1951 the Congress acted. At a meeting of ILFWU locals in Winnipeg attended by Canadian district president, Bob Haddow, a resolution was passed charging the leaders of both the CCL and the TLC with "a rank and cynical betrayal of the working class" by committing the Canadian labour movement to a wage stabilization policy. When informed of this statement by the Congress representative in Winnipeg, Mosher indicated to Conroy that the statement was "not good enough to use ... as a basis for suspending the Fur and Leather Workers." In turn, Conroy argued that since the union was going to be suspended as soon as a "reasonable cause" was found, it would serve no purpose to delay. When he indicated that there would be no problem in rounding up the votes to expel the union, Mosher was won over.[61]

On 9 April, charges were brought against the Fur Workers at the executive committee meeting. The committee decided that if Haddow admitted that the statement was correct, his union would be expelled on grounds "that it was following Communist principles and policy." On the following day at the council meeting, Haddow presented a long statement defending his union's right of criticism but admitted that the statement was substantially correct. On this basis, the council voted to expel the ILFWU and to oust Haddow from the council, though Haddow protested that the resolution adopted by a handful of fur workers in Winnipeg did not necessarily represent the official position of the union.[62]

Following the usual procedure, the Fur Workers appealed the expulsion to the convention. The union claimed that it was being expelled merely for criticizing the Congress and its policies.[63] In his usual role, Conroy rebutted the union's arguments and demanded its expulsion because it was a Communist organization "following the Party line down to the crossing of the last "t" and the dotting of the last "i" ... " As had become its wont, the convention voted by an overpowering margin to expel the IFLWU.

Thus, by 1951, there was left in the Congress no large Communist-influenced union, though there were still the relatively small Longshoremen's Union, and some tiny national unions and locals with a leftist leadership. For the last five years of its existence the Congress would be free of the issue which dominated its first ten.

Both the Congress and its left-wing affiliates were victims of the Cold War; the latter because they were purged for undertaking the same activities that had gone relatively unpunished for the previous decade; the former for being stampeded into using the methods of those they opposed to rid themselves of this opposition. The fact that Communists were never very concerned with civil liberties in their own unions or even elsewhere does not excuse the same lack of concern by men who were championing "democracy" against "totalitarianism." What the opposition groups in the UE and Mine-Mill failed to achieve by the ballot the Congress tried to achieve for them by the purge.

Unquestionably, very few members of the expelled unions were Communists. Their sole crime was simply their insistence on electing leaders to whom the Congress objected. Men such as Jackson, Harris, Murphy, and Pritchett were men whose contribution to the industrial labour movement in Canada cannot be denied or easily matched. That their membership was devoted to them despite their political ideas seems to indicate that the rank and file were satisfied with their leadership. If the opposition to these men in their own unions could not defeat them democratically, then that was hardly sufficient reason for the Congress to help them with undemocratic procedures. In the process, not only were substantive guarantees and procedural safeguards undermined by the Congress, but the CCL found itself with some strange and unseemly allies. The only provincial government openly to support the Congress action by decertifying all "Communist-led" unions was that of the reactionary and corrupt Maurice Duplessis. And the Congress, wasting no time in protesting this obvious anti-democratic procedure, shamelessly moved in to organize some of the decertified workers into its own unions. In addition, the Congress often found itself on the side of labour-hating industrialists in jurisdictional battles and legal actions against Communist-led unions. In truth, however, they also found themselves aligned against these same industrialists and the Communist unions in other jurisdictional disputes.

The reasons given for the expulsion of the left-wing unions were spurious and almost fatuous. At any other period and against any other unions they would have been dismissed out of hand. The entire Communist purge was not one of the Congress's finer achievements.[64]

This is especially true in comparison with the manner in which the Congress dealt with the United Auto Workers. Because of the major role played by Communists in organizing the UAW in Canada, for years the union was closely attuned to party policy. For most of this period the three largest UAW locals, 200 and 195 in Windsor and 222 in Oshawa, were strongly influenced by the left. No less than the UE, Mine-Mill, or the Fur Workers, the UAW was often in opposition to Congress policy. And like the other three unions, many of the UAW's organizers were party members or supporters.

In a union which was almost evenly divided between party supporters and opponents, George Burt, the union's Canadian director, was forced to straddle.

His major priority and overriding objective was to ensure the unity of his union by not alienating either faction.[65] At times he lined up with the Congress and fought the party. At other times he lined up with the party and fought the Congress. But, as the Communist element in the union began to recede, Burt became less tolerant of it. Finally, when he felt it safe, and with the union firmly in his control, he broke all ties with the party and dismissed from his staff most of those who were closely connected with it.

Yet during the entire decade in which the UAW joined with the left in combatting Congress policy, not once – unlike the other left-wing unions – was it suspended or threatened with suspension. Though in convention after convention the majority of Auto delegates – like the majority of delegates in the UE, Mine-Mill, IWA, and Fur Workers – voted for the left-wing policies and slate, rarely did Congress officials publicly denounce the union. Condemnations of Congress policy were no less common or critical in UAW papers than in those of the other left-wing unions, but the union was rarely even reprimanded. Congress leaders were determined to avoid a showdown with the UAW. Its "crimes" were no less serious and its attitude no less hostile, but the UAW was left to solve its own internal dissensions without overt Congress interference. That is not to say, however, that the Congress was not determined to change either the UAW's policy or its leadership. Quite the contrary. Mosher, Millard, and Conroy and even David Lewis kept up unceasing covert pressure on Burt, Addes, Thomas, and, finally, on Walter Reuther to force a "volte-face" in the UAW's attitude. In the end they succeeded, but only because the party had lost much of its influence in the union.

Only by catering to the left wing was Burt able to maintain his position as director of the union in Canada. He defeated Millard in 1939 with the help of the party and was therefore in no position to support Congress policies which were opposed by the left-wing sympathizers in his union. In votes at conventions, and at meetings of the executive committee or council, Burt's would usually go to the left wing. For this he was roundly condemned from the beginning by Congress leaders. In January 1942, Mosher wrote to UAW president Thomas complaining bitterly that the Canadian section of his union was "allying itself with Communist party policies" and was voting "the wrong way" at Congress conventions. For the next seven years similar letters from either Conroy or Millard reached the UAW headquarters in Detroit with little result.[66]

When criticism from the Congress or from the right wing in his union became too fierce, Burt simply did an about-turn and for a time supported their policies. In this manoeuvering, Burt was a master. His "political nose," as David Lewis derisively called it, was of necessity almost infallible. He knew precisely when and how far to support each faction before pulling back. In no other way could Burt have been so successful in uniting his union and entrenching his position as Canadian director. In March 1944, for example, according to Lewis, Burt had made "a clear and unequivocal statement that the trade union movement must support the CCF" and had "signed an application to become a member of the CCF." At the same time, however, Lewis was informed by Walter Reuther that not only did Burt "always vote with the Communist gang on the [UAW] international board," but he had made "an antagonistic speech about the CCF at a board meeting," and had opposed the international board's decision to allow UAW locals to affiliate with the CCF.[67] And in April 1945, along with Harris, Pritchett, and Gary Culhane – all closely identified with the Communists – Burt resigned from PAC because of its decision to support the CCF. Shortly thereafter, with the support of the Communists, Burt ran for Parliament as a Liberal – and lost.

During the Ford strike, he shifted from a position of total support for the left-wing militants at the beginning of the strike to resolute opposition at the end. Encouraged by this change of attitude, an optimistic Millard wrote Burt offering whatever assistance he needed to overcome the Communists in his union.[68] The offer was ignored. Burt was convinced that he could handle the left wing in his union without any help. The Congress was not. By 1947, it appeared that the CCL was right and Burt wrong.

At the 1947 Congress convention, 50 of the 75 UAW delegates voted for the left-wing slate and for most of the left-wing policies. To combat the Communists in the UAW, an anti-Communist association was set up to oppose the left-wing administrations of locals 200 and 195 in Windsor. The association was vigourously denounced by Burt. Appalled at, but not surprised by Burt's attitude, the Congress leadership decided some sort of chastening would be in order. For three consecutive years Burt had been a member of the executive committee. At the 1947 convention, following Burt's decision to oppose the Congress's anti-Communist policies, Mosher, Conroy, and Millard met secretly and decided to nominate Tom Brannagan, a leader of the Local 200 anti-Communist association for Burt's position on the executive committee.[69]

Though Burt was defeated by a vote of 496 to 294, he received the overwhelming support of his own UAW members. The executive's purpose in replacing Burt was twofold. First, because Burt was critical of many of the committee's decisions, the Congress leaders preferred to have someone less fractious in his place; second, the executive wanted to humiliate Burt and weaken his position within his own union so that he would either be removed from office or would, at the very least, become more amenable to recommendations from his union's anti-Communist element.

What the executive achieved, however, was to outrage Burt. He publicly denounced the "slimy, mean, dirty, rotten, underhanded campaign to destroy the union" led by the "supporters of Reuther, Conroy and Millard." But the Congress' action also had its desired effect. At the UAW international convention Burt retained his position by only eight votes. His small margin of victory was probably the result of his opposition to Walter Reuther whose slate swept almost all the executive positions. Most of the Canadian delegates deserted Burt and voted for Reuther despite Burt's vigorous campaign in support of R.J. Thomas. Politically, it was now necessary for Burt to make peace with Congress; strategically it was essential that he come to terms with the right wing in his union.

He accomplished both. By releasing two of the union's left-wing organizers and by announcing his intention of "going down the line" with the Congress policy of supporting the CCF, he pleased both groups. At the same time, however, he kept on staff several party members, temporarily placating the left. Not fully assured, Conroy and Millard wrote a series of letters to Reuther urging him to "put the spurs" to Burt to get the UAW in Canada "into a healthy trade union condition." Reuther confidently reassured them that Burt had pledged himself to rid the union of its Communists.[70]

As Reuther became more solidly entrenched as international president, Burt became more responsive to the Congress and to the right wing in his own union. As part of a "bargain" reached between the Congress and the UAW in 1948, the CCL executive agreed to put Burt back on the Congress slate for election to the executive committee, if he would "clean up" his union.[71] But at the same time, Burt was also on the left-wing slate. Not surprisingly, at the 1948 convention, he received the highest vote ever polled at a Congress election to that time. Conroy felt that the Communists had included Burt on their slate merely "to maintain a strained relationship between Burt and the Congress" because Congress officials would doubt his "true status." He was shaken, however, when the large UAW local in Windsor, Local 200, bitterly attacked the Congress leaders, accusing them of "ruthlessly distorting" resolutions, "torpedoing labour issues," and of "subverting every issue with a Communist bogey." Conroy felt that it was now obvious that Burt could not control his own union and the Congress would have to take more direct action. Millard, however, urged that Burt be allowed "to handle this thing in his own way."[72] In the end this was the position the Congress adopted.

With occasional prods from Reuther, Burt drifted further and further away from his erstwhile allies on the left. Some were removed from union positions; others left of their own accord. None the less, Burt could still be counted on to oppose some major Congress policies. Though he was critical of the tactics and policies of the UE and Mine-Mill, he bitterly opposed the Congress action in expelling them. In 1950 he was severely reprimanded by Conroy for signing a "ban the bomb" petition sponsored by the Canadian Peace Congress. But by 1951, Burt was in the forefront of the PAC campaign to elect the CCF and though there were still several left-wing sympathizers on his staff, there was little doubt that he had them under control.[73]

With the diminution of the Communist influence in Auto and with the expulsion of the three major left-wing unions, there was, for the last five years of the Congress' existence, little opposition to the political and economic policies of the Congress leadership. This proved to be disastrous to the Congress. With no common enemy, the fragile ties between the national and international unions were soon sundered. Whereas in the past they could always unite to beat back the left, there was no longer that binding factor. The simmering conflict between the national and international unions could no longer be suppressed. Always overshadowed before by the struggle to exorcise the Communists, the strife between national and international unions would dominate the Congress's centre stage for its last few years. It was a battle which more nearly wrecked the Congress than the war with the left. The latter could be won; the former could not.

9
The CIO versus the CCL 1940-50

For the Congress, the Communist problem was at once more serious and at the same time more soluble than the international union problem. With the merger of the ACCL and the CIO, strongly nationalist unions found themselves in the same fold as unions controlled from the United States. Both were intensely committed to their respective philosophies. The former wished to build a powerful, strictly Canadian labour movement, controlled by its Canadian membership. The latter also wished to build a strong labour movement, but were less concerned with where the control lay. The former were concerned solely with Canadian labour problems; the latter with continental problems. The former wished to sever all ties with the CIO; the latter wished to strengthen them. This alliance of antipathetic philosophies bedevilled the Congress for years, and indeed would never be resolved. Thus the Congress proved to be less of a fusion than a coalition in which each faction attempted to maintain its individual identity.

Part of the problem lay in the inability or the unwillingness of the international unions to meet their financial commitments to the Congress. Meetings between Mosher and Conroy and international union presidents resulted in many promises, but little else. Even some of the international representatives in Canada complained to their parent organizations that the CIO unions were not doing their share for the Congress. As a result of this financial squeeze, the Congress continued to rely on its own chartered unions for the bulk of its revenue. The natural corollary of this was that the Congress fought all attempts of the international unions to take over the chartered locals within their jurisdiction. This only exacerbated the strained relationship between Congress offices in Ottawa and CIO headquarters in Washington.

From the outset it was apparent that the merger was something less than perfect. For the first few months after the founding convention, the *Canadian Unionist,* the official journal of the Congress edited by Norman Dowd and dominated by the CBRE, published a series of editorials emphasizing that in Canada, the CIO "no longer exists," that it had "withdrawn fully and absolutely from Canada" and that its policies "do not affect or influence in the slightest degree the policies of the Canadian Congress of Labour." This so outraged CIO affiliates that the SWOC policy conference in April 1941, reprimanded Mosher and Dowd for their anti-CIO editorial policy. Perversely, the SWOC delegates then unanimously passed resolution re-affirming their allegiance to the CIO and denouncing any attempt "to abolish the CIO in Canada."[1]

The difficulties with the left could be dealt with – either subtly or crudely – with little fear of repercussion. The difficulties with the international unions could not be handled quite so easily. A prime grievance for the sensitive leaders of the ACCL wing of the new Congress was that the CIO unions in Canada still paid dues to their international office. In the merger agreement these unions had agreed to continue sending the monthly per capita tax of five cents per member to the CIO in Washington. The Washington office would then send two cents of this to the Congress office in Ottawa. Congress officials, particularly Mosher, complained that it would "be far better to have the Canadian membership pay the per capita tax directly than to have it come to us from headquarters in the United States." Mosher warned Conroy that some "narrow-minded" people might think "that so long as the Congress receives a cheque for the per capita tax from ... the United States, it is taking instructions as well from the source of its revenue, and that does not help us in putting it across that the Canadian Congress is an independent Canadian labour body." He further lamented that he could not understand "why the Canadian membership of international unions should pay any per capita tax to the CIO if the CIO is extinct so far as Canada is concerned, and it is going to be a difficult task for us to show that the Canadian membership of these international unions is wholly autonomous if they continue to pay per capita tax to the CIO and send delegates to CIO conventions."[2]

So annoyed was Mosher that he travelled to Washington in January 1941 to meet the CIO leaders and discuss his grievances. He met with Philip Murray and Allan Haywood and bluntly warned them that unless the CIO unions in Canada began paying their dues directly the CCL he would resign as president and take his ACCL unions out of the Congress. Taken aback by Mosher's threat, a flustered Murray promised that henceforth the CIO affiliates in Canada would pay the two cents per month directly to the Congress while continuing to send the remaining three cents to CIO offices in Washington.[3]

Mosher's other proposals to limit CIO influence in Canada met with less success. To the executive board of the CIO, Mosher outlined a program which, he thought, would "be in the best interests" of both the CIO and the Congress. The CIO executive, however, felt differently. Mosher recommended that all international unions in Canada "undertake an intensive organizing campaign," but those unions which could not afford to do so should temporarily "place their Canadian membership under the direct control" of the Congress. These unions would pay all their dues directly to the Congress, and in return, the Congress would undertake the necessary organizing activities. He also suggested that CIO unions with Canadian memberships of under one thousand should be turned over to the Congress. Finally, he demanded that all publications, pamphlets and other advertising matter used in Canada should be "of Canadian origin," and that the international unions should "emphasize the CCL affiliation and not that of the CIO since so much prejudice had been created against the CIO ... the problem of organizing the unorganized is far more difficult and costly under the CIO banner than under that of the Canadian Congress of Labour."[4]

These proposals were discussed at length at a meeting of the six CIO vice-presidents in February and were rejected. They agreed that a major organizing effort should be made in Canada, but these men, who were themselves presidents of large international unions, refused to set a precedent by allowing any CIO affiliate to give up its jurisdiction in Canada. They further argued that publications and pamphlets from the United States did not "in any way jeopardize" the Canadian workers, nor were they "injurious to the interests of the Dominion itself and its citizens." On the contrary, they insisted that the affiliation with the CIO be stressed and "kept out in front." "There is no reason why people in Canada should not know what our movement stands for," they said; "It has nothing to apologize for." In an obvious rebuff to Mosher, they added: "We shall expect that the name CIO will not be held in the background but will be there for everyone to see as the institution which stands for our democratic way of life."[5]

This decision enraged Mosher. He angrily accused the CIO of ignoring the interests of Canadian workers and of "returning to the AFL psychology" in its treatment of the Canadian situation. He pointed out that the national unions had not "raised any objection" when the Algoma Steel Workers' union was transferred to SWOC. He therefore could not understand why "the international unions and the CIO fail to apply this principle in the same broad-minded way in a reverse situation." The CIO unions, he argued, were "in honour bound either to conform to the true spirit of the [merger] ... or withdraw their affiliation." The Congress, he claimed, was not meant to be "a recruiting agency for the international unions" nor should international unions be "treated any more favourably than national unions." The Congress could not achieve its organizing goals, he argued, if some international unions refused both to mount organizing campaigns and to give up their jurisdictions. He reiterated once more that the emphasis on the CIO connection was detrimental to Congress organizational activities. Finally, he accused the CIO of refusing to respect Canadian sovereignty and of not permitting its Canadian affiliates "to determine their own policy and administer their own internal affairs."[6]

Mosher's protests made no impact on the impervious CIO leadership. Nationalism, especially Canadian, in the trade union movement was something they neither accepted nor understood. They bluntly told Mosher that the CIO would do all in its power to maintain its identity in Canada though it had no intention of "injuring the standing or prestige" of the Canadian Congress of Labour.[7] The matter was therefore left in abeyance to be settled at a later date. Predictably, it never was.

The autonomy issue was raised once again at the 1941 CCL convention. In his presidential address, Mosher had made clear that the Congress was completely "autonomous and independent." To make certain that this was understood and against the advice of the convention resolutions committee, Mosher introduced a motion demanding that all international unions with a Canadian membership of less than five hundred leave the CIO and become chartered locals of the Congress. Needless to say, the resolution was opposed by the CIO unions and was decisively defeated.[8]

Of much greater significance, however, was the election by the delegates at this convention of Pat Conroy as secretary-treasurer, and chief executive officer of the Congress. It had taken a great deal of persuasion on the part of Millard and David Lewis, as well as the promise that he would be made director of organization, before Conroy had agreed to accept the position. Previously, Millard had complained about the "timidity" of the ACCL leaders in refusing to adopt an "aggressive organization policy" for the new Congress. With Conroy in the key position of secretary-treasurer, Millard was certain the attitude of the Congress leadership would be more favourable for the CIO unions. As he smugly told Philip Murray: "As director of organization, Conroy will be in a position to better serve *our* organizational needs." In addition, the Communists had been assured by "Big John" Stokaluk, their leader in the Alberta coal fields, that Conroy was a "reliable man."[9] The election of Conroy – a CIO partisan – to the most influential position in the Congress, seemed to have resolved the conflict between the national and international unions in favour of the latter. The CIO leadership, the Communists, and the international unions were all to be rudely surprised.

Friction between national and international factions was not only the result of disagreements over policy but also of the great incompatibility in temperament between the essentially conservative ACCL and the more radically oriented CIO. To Millard, the outlook of the ACCL officers was "timid"; while to Mosher, Millard and his CIO allies were "naive and adventurous." Just two months after the founding convention Norman Dowd had urged the Congress executive to condemn Millard for his criticism of Hepburn and the labour policy of the Ontario government, since this had made "things more difficult" for the Congress. He complained that Millard's "notoriety" gave the Congress a "black eye" and a great deal of publicity, "none of it favourable." Surprisingly, Conroy agreed that Millard had shown a lack of "finesse" by alienating a government whose co-operation the Congress greatly desired.[10]

Some months later, an unchastened Millard issued a statement bitterly criticizing the federal government's labour policy. He was immediately reprimanded by Mosher for not first consulting the Congress executive. Mosher warned him to withhold his critical comments because "we have to live and work under the present government whether we like it or not." And to compound Millard's unhappiness Mosher refused to pay for a study of the textile industry he had already commissioned. The angry Steelworker leader complained of the "damned poor cooperation" the CIO had been receiving from the Congress executive and warned Mosher to "smarten up."[11]

Within a few months, (in May 1941) Millard resigned as Congress regional director in Ontario because of his opposition to Congress organizational policies, and he harshly condemned the appointment of Elroy Robson of the CBRE as his replacement. The appointment by Mosher of H.B. Histon also of the CBRE to a government board further enraged Millard. He complained that there was "a question of balance within the Congress" and he thought it "unwise to give the impression that only the CBRE is to be called upon to provide personnel." In turn, Dowd charged that Millard was acting independently of the Congress and not following Congress policy.[12]

The Congress, less than a year old, was coming apart at the seams. The hostility between the CIO and the ACCL, rather than lessening, seemed to be growing. Millard and Mosher, the leaders of the two groups, were scarcely on speaking terms. The national unions and the CIO unions were apparently working at cross-purposes. Organization was at a standstill. Acrimony rather than fraternity seemed to be the hallmark of the new Congress. It was into this deteriorating situation that a reluctant Conroy was thrust. Only he had the confidence of both sides. It would be strictly up to him whether the merger would succeed or fail. The future of the Canadian Congress of Labour was in his hands.

Conroy was admirably suited to mediate between the warring factions in the Congress. A devout Catholic of Irish parentage and a strict though tolerant teetotaller, the Scottish-born Conroy had had a thorough training in trade unionism. At thirteen, he went into the mines. At twenty he was badly beaten by company "goons" in the infamous town of Ludlow, Colorado, and several weeks later he was jailed in Los Angeles for attending a meeting addressed by Upton Sinclair. From 1922 Conroy was a leader of the mine workers of Western Canada and it was in this capacity that he helped found the Congress. He was witty, eloquent, belligerent, and very, very obstinate. Most important, he was trusted by both the CIO and ACCL forces.

His first few months in office were spent attempting to heal the ever-widening breach between the national and international unions. The Congress, as he so correctly saw, was "splintered into fragments." Somehow he would have to glue the fragments together. He started by telling Mosher that henceforth all nominations to government boards would be equally divided between the two elements in the Congress; Mosher reluctantly agreed. He then wrote Haywood urgently requesting the CIO to pay the entire five cents per capita collected from its Canadian affiliates directly to the Congress. After several meetings with Murray and other CIO leaders, Conroy finally convinced them to send the five cents to the Congress instead of the two cents per capita they had been sending. But the obstinate Haywood doggedly insisted that the extra three cents be given to Millard and that it not be used for the "general purposes" of the Congress; rather, he stipulated "that it be deposited in a separate CIO Organizing Fund ... to be used specifically for CIO purposes."[13]

This demand both angered and humiliated Conroy. He complained to Haywood that he saw no need for Millard to act as an intermediary or "pay-off man in the background" who could "superimpose himself" on the office of secretary-treasurer. As a "respected officer" of the UMW, he could not understand why he needed "supervision" from Millard. More significantly, he rejected the proposition that the money be set aside in a separate CIO organizing fund. This, he said, would "contradict and belie the entire function" of the Congress and would undermine its "autonomous" nature and make it the "infant equivalent of the CIO" in Canada. He warned that Haywood's recommendation was "impracticable and incongruous" and would "undoubtedly lead to the breaking up of the Congress." He chided Haywood for "setting up a Congress within a Congress" and for not understanding the Canadian situation. The bulk of the Congress activities, he added, were "being directed towards the interests of the growing international unions, though seventy-one

percent of the Congress revenue came from national and chartered locals."
Finally, he emphasized that he had taken office much against his better judgment and at the insistence of "most of the Congress unions," and unless he
received the co-operation promised by the CIO he would immediately resign.
He also personally berated Millard for setting himself up as an intermediary
between the CIO and the Congress and charged that this was "a complete
breach of the basis of understanding that brought the Congress into
being."[14]

Taken aback by Conroy's tirade, Millard met with Conroy in early January
1942 and agreed to ask the CIO to forward all funds directly to the Congress
to be used "as the Congress saw fit." But for the next few weeks, the CIO office
in Washington stubbornly insisted that all funds must be used strictly for CIO
organizational purposes in Canada. Only after Conroy threatened to alert
Canadian customs officials that some CIO affiliates were ignoring wartime
customs regulations and "exporting" money to the United States did the CIO
finally accept the Congress position.[15] First blood in this never-ending battle
had been drawn by Conroy.

More victories were soon to follow. Over the opposition of the American
Newspaper Guild, the Congress chartered a newspaper local in Vancouver.
Conroy explained to Haywood that in its four years in Canada the Guild had
a total membership of only forty-six, largely because its leadership thought
"they were establishing an industrial branch of the Communist Party." He
added that if the Guild was "prepared to rout out its Canadian leadership"
and begin a concentrated organizing effort, the Congress would then turn over
to it the Vancouver local. He also suggested to Haywood that the Guild (which
by April of 1942 had lost thirty of its forty-six Canadian members) withdraw
from Canada and turn over its jurisdiction to the Congress. Though the Guild
decided not to relinquish its jurisdiction, Conroy insisted that the CCL would
continue organizing in that area.[16] In this way, he was able to assert the para-
mountcy of the Congress over the smaller CIO affiliates in Canada.

More important triumphs were yet to come. Despite the endless protesta-
tions of Dowd, Mosher, and now Conroy, that both the Congress and its
affiliates were completely autonomous, it nevertheless remained true that jurisdictional conflicts among international unions were invariably resolved in the
United States. How autonomous and independent could the Congress be if it
could not settle disputes among its own affiliates? This would be the litmus test
of the Congress' autonomy in Canada. If it could somehow persuade CIO
affiliates to have their quarrels settled directly by the Congress without referral
to the CIO, then the "autonomy" question would be resolved. The issue came
to a head in 1942. Jurisdictional as well as personality conflicts among the

Auto, Steel, and Electrical unions threatened to tear the Congress apart. Largely because of the tact, resolve, and ability of Conroy, the Congress was saved.

The dispute first broke out in June 1942 when Steel accused the UAW of organizing a plant in Hamilton which was within Steel's jurisdiction. Burt angrily denied the charge but charged that Steel had organized the Massey-Harris plant in Toronto which, he claimed, was within the jurisdiction of the UAW. Conroy's suggestion that the two unions meet with him to discuss the matter was rejected by Burt. The UAW leader also complained that, although the Congress had turned over to Steel the large Algoma steel union, it had refused to hand over to Auto the equally large Fleet Aircraft Workers' Association which was within the jurisdiction of the UAW. Conroy replied that the Congress was not prepared to force the Fleet Aircraft Workers into the UAW, but if they voted to affiliate with Auto, the Congress would have no objection. But above all, Conroy pleaded with the CIO unions to stop "scalping" each other and settle their disputes before the AFL unions "cash in" on these conflicts.[17]

Following the 1942 Congress convention at which the entire tangled question of jurisdiction was referred to the executive council, Mosher complained to Murray about the "tangles of the UAW, UE, and USW in Canada" and urged that the international presidents of these three unions meet with Conroy at the forthcoming CIO convention in Boston in November.[18] The meeting never took place. Conroy spent a full week at the convention for the sole purpose of meeting these three leaders. But they were too busy to see the Congress secretary-treasurer.

On his return to Ottawa, Conroy wrote C.S. Jackson that he was "fed up" and "damn disgusted" with the CIO. He had made several "fruitless trips" to the United States to discuss Canadian problems, he said, but found instead that "no one on the CIO has, apparently, any time to discuss anything with anybody." So Conroy decided to settle the jurisdictional disputes himself. He ordered Steel to hand over its organization in the Massey-Harris plant to the UAW and the UAW to compensate Steel for its organizing expenses. The UAW was further ordered to eschew any organizing attempts in the Acme Screw and Gear plant in Toronto. Conroy had also insisted that both unions should launch a joint organizing campaign in the Massey-Harris and John Inglis plants, with the former to go to Auto and the latter to Steel.[19]

Millard at once agreed. Burt, however, did not; he thought it unfair that the UAW should have to reimburse Steel for organizing a plant "where they have no business to be." Above all, he did not wish to launch a campaign in the Inglis plant because this would bring him into conflict with the International Association of Machinists, who, in retaliation, might raid other UAW-organized plants. Conroy berated him for "making a laughing stock" of the Congress and of "bending backward to co-operate" with the IAM, an AFL union, while refusing to co-operate with fellow Congress organizations. And to irritate Conroy further, the UE and the USW had also become involved in a vicious conflict over jurisdiction in the Anaconda Brass plant in New Toronto. By now thoroughly annoyed, Conroy urged the three unions to "come to their senses" as they had become "a source of jocular observations by those on the outside," and their "fratricidal warfare" was threatening the existence of the Congress.[20]

The intolerable situation was discussed at the Congress executive meetings in November 1942, and Conroy, Mosher, and Spivak were appointed to deal with the problem. The executive also decided that any further jurisdictional disputes would be referred to an arbitration committee of three officers of the Congress appointed by the executive committee. Its decision would be final and binding. Any union which ignored the committee's decision would automatically be suspended from the Congress.

A few days later, the executive board of the CIO decided that the presidents of the UE, USW, and UAW, would meet with Congress representatives in Ottawa to discuss the jurisdictional problems. On 18 December, R.J. Thomas of the UAW, David McDonald of Steel, and Jackson, substituting for Albert Fitzgerald, president of the UE, met with Conroy and Mosher. They agreed that henceforth their unions would consider the decision of the Congress jurisdictional committee "final and binding in any disputes which may arise in Canada" involving their unions.[21]

Agreement on paper was not necessarily agreement in fact. The dispute between the UAW and the USW was settled on the basis of Conroy's decision. This time Thomas ordered Burt to accept Conroy's recommendations. But the decision of the Congress jurisdictional committee – Conroy, Mosher, and Spivak – on the Anaconda problem met with a vastly different reception.

The committee decided to ignore both the claims of the UE and the USW and to turn the plant over to Mine-Mill. But because Mine-Mill was in no position "to undertake the organization and servicing of the workers involved," the committee ruled that the Congress would establish a temporary chartered local. The USW and the UE were requested to turn over all their members in the plant to the new local. Both Millard and Jackson were peeved. Though Philip Murray had warned Millard against organizing Anaconda, the latter had proceeded with the campaign because he felt that neither the UE nor Mine-Mill were capable of organizing the plant. More importantly, Millard warned Murray that the Canadian leadership of the UE, the UAW, Mine-Mill, and the IAM were "part of a political alliance" bent on undermining the position of both Steel and the Congress. It was therefore better for all concerned he argued, for the USW to organize Anaconda. Nevertheless, albeit reluctantly, Millard accepted the Committee's decision.[22]

On the other hand, Jackson was not so easily dissuaded. In a letter to Nigel Morgan he stated that the real purpose behind Mosher's request for full jurisdictional rights in Canada was "to give him the ... balance of power and position against the increasing strength of the international unions in Canada ... in other words, that Mosher would use these powers in order to build up national unions at the expense of the international unions." The Anaconda decision, he added, was "the first shot of the gun in this drive." Jackson thought that the UE would be "the main target of the attack" and he therefore urged that all international presidents "protest against such high-handed decisions which show a tendency to defeat the organizational efforts of the international unions."[23]

His advice was accepted by at least one international president – his own. On 6 January 1943, Fitzgerald repudiated the jurisdiction agreement and informed Conroy that he did not accept the committee's decision on Anaconda. He added that any future jurisdictional disputes must be settled by the international unions involved and not by the Congress. One week later, Jackson informed Conroy that the UE intended to appeal the Anaconda decision at the next Congress convention.

Because the Congress had taken the position that decisions of the jurisdiction committee were final and binding on all parties, the UE was suspended at the executive council meeting of 7 March 1943. But immediately following the meeting, Jackson pleaded with the council members to reconsider and promised that the UE would accept the jurisdictional decision. On the strength of this promise, at its meeting on the following day, the council voted to reconsider the suspension and to allow the UE fifteen days to accept the jurisdictional decision. Two weeks later the chastened UE agreed to abide by the decision of the jurisdictional committee.[24]

Thus by March 1943, just a little more than one year after Conroy became secretary-treasurer, the Congress could boast that it was fully autonomous. Not only did it receive the entire five cents per capita per month ordinarily paid by international unions to the CIO, but it had also acquired the power to settle all jurisdictional disputes involving its affiliates, and to create, if it wished, chartered locals within the jurisdiction of a CIO union. Yet for the next few years, the Congress would often be forced into battle to assert its newly-won independence.

This struggle took many forms, some serious, some less so. Among the latter for example, in July 1943 Conroy suggested to Haywood that he stop using the term "our Congress membership" in his letters to the CCL and substitute "your Congress membership" because the former expression fanned "the prejudices of some executive members" who thought it "undermined the autonomy of the Congress." More seriously, Haywood complained that the Congress had 203 chartered locals with a membership of over 50,000. These unions, Haywood argued, "should have been turned over long ago" to the appropriate CIO union. He ordered Conroy to begin the transfer at once. Conroy refused. He explained that because of the "unique Canadian situation with its regional and racial differences," many local unions would leave the Congress rather than join an international union. This explanation made no impact on the wrong-headed Haywood. The Canadian situation, as he saw it, differed little from that in the United States. He therefore persisted in his demands that all the Congress' chartered unions be immediately transferred to the appropriate international.[25]

He naturally received support from the CIO unions in Canada who were greedily eyeing the chartered locals. Because the bulk of the Congress revenues came from these locals, Mosher denounced the CIO unions for preparing 'to sell out Canadian unions.' The CIO unions, he complained, were not ready to accept Congress policy. They were "destroying confidence" in the Congress, he claimed, and were acting irresponsibly and indiscreetly. Unless they could be brought quickly into line, Mosher threatened to resign as president and to withdraw the CBRE from the Congress.[26]

An equally critical issue for the Congress leadership was whether the CCL would be compelled to accept as affiliates all CIO unions operating in Canada. It had been decided at the first executive meetings of the Congress that the CIO could not charter any locals in Canada without first consulting the Congress. Not until 1943 did the CIO contest this decision. In December of that year, the National Association of Technical Employees in Canada (NATE) affiliated with a CIO organization, the International Federation of Architects, Engineers, Chemists and Technicians (FAECT), and on the basis of this affiliation, applied for membership in the Congress. The opposition of the Congress was instantaneous. Conroy claimed that NATE had "a questionable status" because its executive was largely Communist. Millard added that the union was not a "bona fide labour" organization but rather an "unclean" and parasite union and that it was "completely controlled by Party people." He also claimed that, its organizational director had been interned at the beginning of the war as a saboteur and a Communist, and that he had been discharged by the CBC for stealing parts to build a mobile short-wave sending station. The new union he charged, was "dual" and "disruptive" to the USW. For these reasons, the Congress executive rejected the union's application to affiliate.[27]

NATE's complaint to its international office was forwarded to Haywood who informed Conroy that since FAECT was a CIO affiliate "there should be no question in accepting them into affiliation with your Congress." In reply, Conroy stated that in Canada at least, the union was "dual" and under Communist control and would therefore not be a "welcome addition" to the Congress. Haywood, however, continued to insist that, as a CIO union, FAECT must be allowed to affiliate with the Congress, while Conroy, persisted in his position that the Congress must decide for itself which unions to affiliate. Haywood eventually backed down. NATE would remain outside the Congress.[28]

At the same time another serious conflict had arisen between the Congress and the CIO. With the decision in 1942 of the United Mine Workers to leave the CIO, a new chemical union, the Gas, Coke, and Chemical Workers Organizing Committee, was created by the CIO to organize in the same jurisdiction as District 50 of the UMW. But because of the efforts of Barrett, Livett, and Conroy, John L. Lewis allowed the UMW to retain its affiliation with the Congress.[29] The Congress was at once assured the continued allegiance of its largest and richest union; but at the same time, because of the jurisdictional disputes between District 50 and the new CIO chemical union, it was soon faced with an increasingly embittered CIO leadership.

To alleviate this problem, Conroy and Millard suggested that the Congress create a chartered union in the chemical field "to do the job" of both District 50 and the new CIO union. Moreover, the large Congress local of seven hundred gas workers in Toronto which had decided to affiliate with the new CIO union was, in Conroy's words, "dominated, body and soul, by the Communist Party." He feared that if the CIO chemical union was allowed to organize in Canada it would mean that the Communists would gain control over another Congress affiliate. But because of the forceful opposition of both the CIO and the UMW, the Congress suggestion was not immediately implemented.[30]

In August 1943, an executive of the new CIO chemical union, Walter Harris, met with Millard and agreed to his proposal that the CIO and the Congress join forces in an organizing committee for the chemical field. In return, though he did not have the authority, Millard promised that all chemical locals in the Congress would eventually be turned over to the international union. Mosher, however, rejected this plan. An organizing committee, he maintained, could only be created by the Congress, and the Congress alone would decide whether to retain the chemical locals or turn them over to the international. He predicted that the UMW would vigourously oppose this proposal, and warned that the Communists, who had done most of the organizing in the chemical field in Canada, would likely control the new union in Canada. But Conroy agreed with Millard and at a special Congress executive committee meeting in September the affiliation of the CIO chemical workers' committee was approved.[31]

After discussions with Harris and Haywood, the Congress appointed Conroy as the director of the union in Canada and, as his assistant, Alex McAuslane. The Congress also retained for itself the right to hire and dismiss the union's organizers in Canada, and "to do whatever [it] saw fit to build a strong union." But this arrangement was rejected by Martin Wagner, the international president of the CIO chemical union. In addition, Silby Barrett threatened to withdraw the UMW from the Congress, unless the agreement was immediately terminated.[32]

The Congress now had no alternative but to abrogate the agreement. In its stead, the Congress demanded that the CIO chemical union "forfeit all claims to jursidiction in Canada and leave the organization exclusively under the Canadian Congress of Labour." The unyielding Haywood replied that the position of the CIO was clear and he would give "any support necessary" to Wagner and his union in organizing chemical workers in Canada.[33]

For the next six months the CIO vainly undertook to have the Congress change its policy. In a final desperate move, Wagner came to Ottawa to discuss the matter with Conroy. He was informed that because of the two-fold danger of the UMW disaffiliating and the Chemical workers in Canada becoming another Communist-dominated union, the only possible solution was for the Canadian district of his union to disassociate from the International and become attached "to the Congress as a national union." Wagner declined the invitation. At the same time, despite CIO demands, the Congress refused to affiliate Harry Bridges' party-dominated International Longshoremen's and Warehousemen's Union.[34]

Thus by 1944 the tension between the Congress and the CIO had reached a new peak. After discussing the situation with Murray, Haywood informed Conroy that the CIO was "disturbed" with the behaviour of the Congress. It was the CIO's position, he stated, "that all internationals who had local unions in Canada would be entitled to affiliate with the CCL." He added that when any international had "equity or locals in Canada ... that should be sufficient to entitle such locals to affiliate with the Canadian Congress of Labour." And since the Mine Workers were no longer members of the CIO, they "should not be a bar to membership of our unions in the CCL." Finally he reiterated that "the one and only condition for acceptance by the Congress" should be that the union involved was affiliated to the CIO. This was a position from which the CIO would not budge.[35] Similarly the Congress refused to be dissuaded from its position of refusing to affiliate Communist-controlled unions, and in Canada at least, all these prospective suitors were dominated by the party.

Whatever prestige had accrued to the Congress in its successful battle to ward off CIO pretensions was dealt a grievous blow at the World Labour Conference in London in February 1945. That organization, with the acquiescence of CIO representatives, refused to give Canada a seat on its executive body on the grounds that both the CCL and the TLC consisted of locals of the United States unions. What most rankled with Canadian labour leaders was that representation was given to smaller powers in Latin America and Europe even though Canada had a much larger labour movement and had done much more to help win the war. This "humiliation" further strengthened the determination of the Congress to assert its independence from American domination.[36]

In a letter to Haywood, Conroy complained that the CIO unions in the Congress were becoming "rag-bags," disregarding jurisdictions, and throwing overboard all the principles of trade unionism. "Ninety percent of Congress trouble," he added, was caused by international unions "who cannot agree among themselves on any basic issue." Finally he told Haywood that he was "becoming pretty tired of being a buffer in between a number of irresponsible union groups" and was giving "serious thought" to resigning his position "and letting the two groups of CIO unions meet head on and permit the two of them to pick up the pieces."[37]

To remedy this situation all Haywood could think of was for the presidents of the CIO unions involved to meet to discuss the problem. But Conroy believed that this was "merely postponing the issue." Rather he suggested a "top-level" conference between Murray and Haywood representing the CIO, and Mosher and himself representing the Congress. This meeting, he felt, would resolve the relationship which was now "definitely unsatisfactory." The Congress, Conroy stated, would insist on three things: the power to determine its own foreign and domestic policy, the right to determine on its own what organizations it should affiliate, and finally, the power to compel international unions to follow the policy set down by Congress conventions. And to underscore the Congress dissatisfaction, Conroy charged that the CIO had never explicitly endorsed the right of the Congress to decide its own policy on foreign affairs and that on many occasions international unions had refused to follow Congress policies when they were at variance with those of the CIO. Above all, he added that the Congress was "completely disgusted" with the lack of support the CIO had given it at the World Labour Conference.[38]

Haywood's reaction was predictable. So impervious was he to the sensibilities of the Congress that he argued that because the Congress was composed of locals of CIO unions it was very clear why Canada had not been given an executive seat on the World Federation of Trade Unions. And as far as accepting affiliates was concerned, in his opinion the Congress was no different than any CIO state council. "Every local of a CIO union must affiliate" with the CCL in Canada, he said, just as every CIO union must affiliate with a state council. Though Conroy's suggestion of a summit meeting did not appeal to him, he reluctantly agreed that there obviously were differences to be resolved. He suggested, therefore, that he meet with Canadian CIO representatives in Niagara Falls some time within the next month to "become more acquainted with the problems in Canada."[39]

Now, even some of the CIO allies in Canada were perturbed. In particular, Haywood's obstinacy and myopia had finally riled Millard. In a personal letter to Conroy he offered "whatever support was necessary" to ensure that the Congress "be recognized by the CIO, by the International movement, and by the World Trade Union Congress as an entity worthy of recognition and cooperation." He urged that the Congress refuse to affiliate with the new World Congress until Canada was given a position on the executive. Further, he enthusiastically seconded Conroy's three proposals and urged him to demand from Murray that all CIO unions be compelled to follow the lead of Steel and grant their Canadian affiliates autonomy in the field of wages, legislation, and political action. "Otherwise," he claimed, "they will be of no use to the labour movement in this country and no credit to the parent organization to which they belong."[40]

The Niagara Falls meeting was a fiasco. Haywood complained vociferously about the encroachments of District 50 on the jurisdiction of various CIO unions and charged that the Congress had requested all CIO unions in Canada to turn over their Chemical locals to District 50. This was heatedly denied by both Conroy and Millard, though Conroy did admit, however, that District 50 was causing the Congress a great deal of aggravation. But he charged that this was largely the result of the CIO's failure to come to terms with the Congress in creating a Chemical Workers Organizing Committee. When this effort had failed, Conroy explained, the UMW, which had agreed not to organize in the chemical field in Canada if the Congress could come to terms with the CIO, decided to establish a District 50 regional office in Canada. The UMW was now threatening to pull its 26,000 members out of the Congress, unless all Congress affiliates turned over their chemical locals to District 50. Now, Conroy complained, because of CIO stupidity, the Congress was faced with opposition on two fronts – from the CIO for allowing District 50 to affiliate, and from District 50 for not allowing it to take over Congress chemical unions.[41]

These complaints and arguments made no impact on Haywood. He thought of the Congress as simply a district council of the CIO and therefore subservient to it in every way. Millard "was burned up" with the attitude of Haywood, but hoped that at the very least he would carry back to CIO councils in Washington the impression that the Congress was not a "step child" or a "poor country cousin of the CIO." But dubious that Haywood would in fact deliver this message, Millard himself went to Washington to discuss Congress problems with Murray. He was joined by Conroy and after a lengthy discussion Murray promised to support the Congress request for a position on the ruling body of the WFTU. With this promise, the executive committee of the Congress overcame its reluctance and agreed to send Conroy to the WFTU conference in Paris in September 1945 provided that the CCL was given official recognition as an "autonomous representative of the Canadian labour movement."[42] Thus, by the end of the war, the Congress seemed to have achieved in the eyes of the world labour movement recognition as an independent organization, recognition that was still denied it by its CIO "guardian."

Yet at the WFTU meeting in Paris, the CIO reneged on its commitment to the Congress and refused to allow Canada a seat on the executive board. The CIO delegate, Sydney Hillman, who was chairman of the WFTU constitutional committee, brought in a constitution which provided that the CIO alone would represent North America on the executive board. He was immediately reprimanded by Conroy who told him that 'no one is going to represent Canada but Canada' and unless the constitution were changed, Canada would walk out of the meeting and leave the WFTU. Privately Hillman pleaded with Conroy to change his mind. He told the beleaguered Canadian that he had come to Paris "expecting trouble with the Russians" but that he had found instead that he was having "more trouble with Canada, one of the CIO family than with anyone else at the meeting." But Conroy would not be dissuaded. Finally the shaken Hillman agreed to redraft the constitution and Canada was given a seat on the WFTU executive board. But the CIO's "double-cross" was something Conroy did not easily forget.[43]

For the next few years the efforts of Haywood to 'show the flag' in Canada, and of Conroy to repel any such attempt often took on humorous tones. Haywood's insistance on treating Canada no differently from any American state and Conroy's persistence in reminding him of the difference led to some ludicrous statements. In 1944, for example, replying to Haywood's telegram soliciting a "solid labor vote for Roosevelt" as president, Conroy replied that Canadians were quite satisfied with their system of government, but if the

Americans really wanted to trade President Roosevelt for Prime Minister King, then a deal could conceivably be worked out. In the next year when Haywood urged Congress unions in Canada to "communicate to their senators their support of Henry Wallace as secretary of commerce," Conroy pointedly responded that Canadians had no desire to interfere in American affairs "though the contrary could not be said for some Americans." After Truman's surprise victory in 1948, Haywood congratulated the Congress for having "performed a magnificent job." In 1949, when Haywood urgently wired Conroy that "vigorous action from your state supporting President Truman's fight to win Senate confirmation of Leland Olds to Federal Power Commission" was needed at once, Conroy good-humouredly replied that since Canada had not yet been admitted to the American union, "it ... should meanwhile accept and recognize the sovereign status of United States and refrain from promoting Canadian imperialist tendencies in the internal affairs of the American people." Finally, in 1950, after Haywood had sent a barrage of wires urging the workers in Conroy's "state" to send telegrams and letters to their senators voicing their strong opposition to the policies of the American Congress, Conroy's patience ran out. He wrote to Haywood and Murray and informed them that the Canadian Congress of Labour was not a "state federation and could not be treated like one," that the 49th parallel was not simply a state line but an international border, and that after ten years it was "about time" that the CIO realized that Canada could not be treated like an American state. This was something the CIO was extremely slow to accept.[44]

Every CIO state federation was obliged to take into its fold all unions affiliated with the CIO. Because Haywood stubbornly refused to see the Congress as anything other than a very large state federation or to accept the international reality of the CCL, he continued to insist that the Congress must accept all CIO affiliates in Canada as members. Because the Congress had long before decided that it alone had the right to decide on which unions to affiliate, and because the Congress leadership refused to accept CIO unions with Communist ties, most of Haywood's demands went unheeded. In late 1945, Haywood asked Conroy to affiliate the United Papermakers of America. Because "members of the Communist party" had already been to see Conroy about "securing appointments from the CIO" to organize for the Papermakers, Conroy refused to consider the affiliation until he was assured that "the people who are appointed are legitimate trade unionists." Similarly, in the summer of 1945, when Haywood asked Conroy to affiliate the United Office and Professional Workers to the Congress, Conroy agreed that if the union could satisfy the Congress that it had rid itself of its "Communist elements," then affiliation would be granted. Three months later Conroy informed Haywood that the

Congress would not affiliate the union because it had done nothing to "cleanse its leadership." Instead, the Congress announced its intention of setting up its own Office and Professional Workers' Organizing Committee.[45]

Still undeterred, time and again Haywood adamantly enjoined the Congress to affiliate the CIO Chemical workers. And by 1947, the pressure from Haywood and the CIO had weakened Millard's resistance. Consequently he urged Conroy to affiliate the union since the Canadian section of about one thousand members was now "quite clean." Immediately, an indignant Conroy informed Mosher that he did not like the idea of Millard nor anyone else "making private dickers with the Chemical workers, or any other organization" since this was his "personal perogative." Affiliation of the Chemical workers, he wrote Millard, "would be extremely foolish" since this would "be going out looking for trouble of the first magnitude with the United Mine Workers [who] ... are not greatly concerned about being affiliated to a central labour body." "To court the loss of twenty thousand mine workers in Canada," he added, "in order to gain one thousand chemical workers would ... be an extremely one-sided bargain." And despite the periodic fulminations by Haywood, Conroy refused to capitulate. In the end the CIO finally gave in and accepted the Congress position that it alone would decide which unions to affiliate.

There were other critical problems which heightened tension between the two organizations in the late 1940s. For example, despite the lead given it by the CCL, and despite Conroy's complaints to Murray, the CIO was much more hesitant about expelling its left-wing unions.[47] But the Congress's most pressing and permanent problem was that of finances. For years the CIO paid to the Congress the monthly per capita tax of five cents per member, three cents from each union and two cents directly from the CIO office. At its 1948 convention in Portland the CIO raised its per capita tax to eight cents. Soon after the convention, Philip Murray promised Congress officials that the CIO would pay the extra three cents per member to the Congress. But when Conroy retured to Washington several months later, he was informed by the CIO secretary-treasurer, James Carey, that the three cents increase was earmarked for an organizing drive in the southern states and the Congress was not entitled to any increase.[48]

The incensed Conroy immediately relayed this news to the congress executive which demanded that the CIO refund the extra three cents to the Congress. In a letter to Carey signed by all the CIO directors in Canada, the Congress begged him to reconsider his decision. They warned that because of the suspension of Mine-Mill and of the problems with the IWA, the Congress was almost bankrupt and could not meet its expenditures. Pointedly, Conroy added that the "abnormal expenditures ... have been wholly due to the maintenance of international unions in Canada."[49]

Personal letters also were sent from the individual CIO directors to their international presidents. Millard wired McDonald that the financial position of the Congress was "grim." Burt told Reuther that without the extra three cents, the Congress would be unable to carry out any organizing activity. There was no response. Trying a different approach, Millard pointed out to McDonald that the major source of Congress income was derived from the dues of the chartered locals. This, he declared, tended "to enhance the development of more and more chartered unions." "Because the CIO unions were not paying their fair share," he pointed out that there was " a disposition on the part of some people in the Canadian Congress to push for organization on a national or industrial charter basis." This approach, Millard warned, could only be overcome if the internationals made larger financial contributions to the Congress so that their "influence in the shaping of policies of real benefit" for themselves and other CIO interests would be strengthened.[50]

Where Conroy's pleas had failed, Millard's threat succeeded. The international unions agreed to increase their per capita to the Congress to seven cents per month – two cents from the CIO, five cents from the internationals. To formalize this arrangement the executive council of the Congress voted to increase the per capita of all affiliated unions from three to five cents. Unfortunately, Carey informed all the CIO unions that any increase in their per capita to the Congress would have to be approved by the CIO itself. After discussing Carey's ruling with the Congress executive, Conroy coldly informed him that because of the "automony of Congress in Canada" it was "not necessary to secure the authority of the Congress of Industrial Organizations on this or other questions." He warned Carey that because the attitude of the AFL towards the TLC had "reduced the latter organization to a satellite group it was even more essential that the CIO recognize the autonomy of the Congress." And to avoid any further misunderstanding he asked Carey to advise all the CIO unions to pay their per capita directly to the Congress rather than through the CIO office.[51]

Instead of complying with Conroy's requests, Carey announced that the CIO would no longer continue to pay the Congress the usual two cents per capita because this amount was included in the increased per capita paid by the international unions. Conroy protested vehemently to Carey that the decision was unfair. Murray, he claimed, had promised that the CIO would continue its remittance of the two cents, and he had, therefore, made financial commitments for the Congress for the coming year on the basis of Murray's reassurance. Millard also sent a strongly worded letter to Murray demanding an explanation for the sudden changes in CIO policy.[52]

After a great deal of bickering between the Congress and the CIO, the latter eventually agreed in 1951 to send an annual grant of $50,000 to the Congress to be used only for purposes of political action, education and public relations, as Millard had recommended, but pointedly, not for organization, as Conroy had demanded. This latter restriction greatly annoyed Conroy. Naturally, he felt that it was an "intrusion on the autonomy" of the Congress and an "indirect slap" at the organizational policies of the Congress.[53]

The episode left the susceptible Conroy deeply disillusioned and humiliated. His suggestions and entreaties to the CIO had been rejected. Those of Millard, on the other hand, were quickly accepted. He felt that his position as secretary-treasurer had been badly undermined, and he was rudely apprised of how impotent he was to change CIO policy. For the proud and sensitive Conroy it was a searing experience. Undoubtedly, it would play a large part in the momentous decision he was to make several months later.

10

National versus International Unionism 1946-52

In the labour hierarchy, relations between Washington and Ottawa were cool; between Ottawa and Toronto, they were absolutely frigid. The chill between CIO headquarters in Washington and the Congress head office in Ottawa was understandable and probably unavoidable but not too dangerous for the Congress. The frostiness between the Congress office in Ottawa, however, and the Steelworkers' headquarters in Toronto was equally comprehensible but infinitely more hazardous. Millard's position was rather ambivalent. At times he joined with Conroy to beat off the incursions of the CIO; more often, he joined with Murray and Haywood to deflate the pretensions of the Congress. External pressure from the CIO was an annoyance which Conroy could withstand. The internal pressures from the international unions led by Steel were something else again. Probably the most talented and able man in the Congress, Conroy was also its most moral and intractable; compromise and fallibility were not part of his vocabulary. And in all these characteristics, Millard was not far behind. Because of these similar traits and their antipathetic viewpoints, the two frequently clashed – and when they did, the fragile structure of the Congress often reverberated unsteadily. Their last conflict proved to be disastrous for the Congress.

Conroy was brought into the Congress in the key position of secretary-treasurer because the international unions felt that the triumvirate of Mosher, Maclean and Dowd, all of the CBRE, did not represent the attitude and aspirations of the new unionism. In Conroy they thought they had found the "perfect man" to represent their point of view.

They were sorely disappointed. As the representative of the United Mine Workers, Conroy came from a union which "had more or less arrived." He had little in common with the leaders of the young and struggling mass-production industrial unions. More significantly, as secretary-treasurer, Conroy expected to be able to control the Congress – to delineate its economic and social programs, to decide on its organizational and political policies, and to make its staff appointments. But in all these powers Conroy found himself pitted against the spokesman for the new unions – Charlie Millard. In any show-down between the two, Millard usually had the votes. Often the matters in dispute between the two were minor and insignificant, but every defeat, every snub, no matter how inconsequential, added to Conroy's sense of help-lessness and frustration.

To help counter the strength of the international unions, Conroy became the champion of those arguing for more and stronger national unions. With the help of the CBRE he strove to root out the CIO infrastructure in the Congress. He asked unions to remove the "CIO" from their letterheads and to avoid mentioning the CIO connection.[1] He appointed as organizers men who were strongly committed to the idea of national unions. Some of these appointments were men ill-suited for organizing activity, but devotedly loyal to Conroy. Over the objections of many union leaders, Conroy reciprocated this loyalty, long after the usefulness of some of these men had dissipated. The most blatant example of this was his tolerance of Alex McAuslane, a man anathema to most of the international union representatives and to many other union officials with whom he came in contact.[2]

Unhappily for Conroy, his attempts to reduce the power of the CIO unions in the Congress failed. He had come to the Congress expecting to rule but found that he was powerless to do so. His fundamental objective was to arrogate to the Congress the power to control its affiliates; instead, he found to his dismay that the affiliates controlled the Congress. His efforts to get for the Congress the authority over its affiliates he thought so necessary were doomed. After ten fruitless years of effort, Conroy sadly lamented that in relation to its large international unions the Congress was "left without any authority ... thereby reducing it to the status of a satellite organization at the mercy of its affiliated unions."[3] His defeat was a victory for the forces of de-centralization – of Toronto over Ottawa.

That the United Steel Workers was the dominant union in the Congress is beyond doubt. Because of the broad outlook of Millard and the comparatively huge treasury at his disposal, Steel became the banker of the Congress. It underwrote Congress political and educational campaigns, paid for and provided the personnel to direct these campaigns, and could always be counted on to contribute more than any other union to the various strike and organizational funds in the Congress. In fact Millard complained to Conroy that Congress affiliates "were getting the tendency of letting Steel carry the financial burden for the entire Congress" and that the Steelworkers were beginning to complain about "the extra activities and expenses undertaken by their union." Without Steel's generosity, Mine-Mill would have succumbed during the Kirkland Lake strike, and Auto would have been hard pressed to hold out during the Ford strike.[4] Steel also provided the manpower and funds to organize the new unions – Packinghouse, Textile, Office and Professional Workers, and Retail-Wholesale. Indeed, during the first six years of the Congress, aside from being national director of Steel, Millard was at one time also national director of the Packinghouse, the Textile, and the Office and Professional workers. Just as south of the border the United Mine Workers provided the personnel for the leadership of the new industrial unions, so in Canada it was Steel. Fred Dowling, Eileen Tallman, Margaret Sedgewick, Bill Sefton, Arthur Williams, Murray Cotterill, and Eamon Park, all of whom played a major role in organizing the new unions, came from Steel.

Equally significant was the way in which Steel dominated Congress conventions. The Congress constitution provided that each local of every affiliate was entitled to send delegates to Congress conventions. Because Steel had many more locals than other unions it was able to send more delegates than unions such as Auto which had more members but fewer locals. At the 1947 convention, for example, Steel sent 138 delegates to represent approximately 25,000 members while Auto sent only 72 to represent about 27,000. More dramatically, Mine-Mill with a membership of about 17,000, but with huge locals in Sudbury and Trail, was represented by only 20 delegates. Naturally, Steel had more money to subsidize delegates, but there was little doubt that the Congress constitution worked in Steel's favour. Any attempt – and there were many – on the part of Auto, UE, or the other under-represented unions to change the constitution was beaten back by Steel, and by CBRE which was also vastly over-represented. In addition, Steel representatives attended conventions as delegates from other organizations. Again, in 1947 there were at least ten Steel members representing the various provincial federations and labour councils in the county as well as unions such as Retail-Wholesale, and Office and Professional Workers. Indeed, not until 1952 after the "Communist" unions had been expelled, was the constitution changed to allow for a more balanced representation. In any case, with its huge delegation, and with the support of such staunch and unswerving allies as Retail-Wholesale, Packinghouse, Rubber, and the Amalgamated Clothing Workers, Steel could ordinarily count on enough votes to push through whatever policies it wished.

Between the Congress and Steel there were two major areas of dispute: the Congress organization policies and its appointments, the latter, naturally, the corollary of the former. In order to build up the strength of Congress numerically, and especially financially, Conroy and Mosher were dedicated to a policy of organizing as many directly chartered locals as possible. To carry out this policy it was essential to hire men who agreed with it – men who supported national over international unionism. This brought a series of complaints from Millard that no "CIO men" were being given Congress appointments.[5]

Though Millard's complaint was exaggerated, it was undoubtedly true that while "CIO partisans" were in charge of the Congress' political and educational campaigns, few were given organizational responsibilities. Conroy favoured turning over to Congress affiliates chartered unions within their jurisdictions, but only if the latter agreed to such a transfer. But this conflicted with Millard's opinion that the Congress had no business whatever organizing locals within an affiliate's jurisdiction. He believed that "the function of the Congress organizers should be to assist and be of general help to affiliated unions in the Congress, but that they should not organize chartered locals." Millard's position was that "if the Congress charters these groups and then the affiliated union comes along later, [the Congress is] in the position of spending time and money in "organizing the organized" rather than the "unorganized." None the less, because of the desperate need of the Congress for the revenue derived from chartered locals, Millard reluctantly acquiesced in Conroy's policy of organizing locals which were "not clearly within the jurisdiction of an affiliated union." But he warned that he would "fight" unless these locals were turned over as soon as practicable to the appropriate affiliate which "claims the group."[6]

Relations between Steel and the Congress were further strained by the innumerable jurisdictional disputes involving Steel. In his crusade to oust the left-wing unions, Millard organized raids on Mine-Mill and UE locals, often without the sanction of the Congress. In explaining his policy to Philip Murray in June 1948, Millard said that he had "given up the hope ... that the rank and file would clean up the UE from the bottom" and therefore had decided to "offer the members" of this union the services of Steel. Within months Steel had moved into a UE plant in St. Catharines and had begun serious campaigns within plants and mines organized by Mine-Mill. When Jackson protested to the Congress against these Steel "raids," Conroy replied that since some Congress affiliates, namely Steel, UE, Mine-Mill, and District 50, had refused to abide by the decisions of the Congress jurisdictional committee, Congress officers felt that no purpose could be served by listening to "requests or complaints of unions on the question of raiding." He deplored the policy of one union raiding the jurisdiction of another, but stated that because some international unions refused to obey Congress decisions the Congress was helpless to assist the UE. Steel's determination to affiliate the Mine-Mill local in Port Colborne against the wishes of the Congress, further exacerbated tensions between the two, especially when Millard exerted extreme pressure on all Congress affiliates to support Steel's claim for the vacated Mine-Mill jurisdiction.[7]

One of the Mine-Mill locals sought by Steel was in the Anaconda Copper plant in New Toronto, the same local which, in 1943, the Congress jurisdictional committee had given to Mine-Mill over the heated protests of both Steel and UE (see chapter 9). In 1950, however, the Steel claim was contested by the UAW, even though Conroy had informed the Anaconda union that the Congress had designated Steel to take over all Mine-Mill locals and that therefore the UAW claim was invalid. At the same time Walter Reuther informed Conroy that Steel and Auto had made "arrangements" concerning the allocation of Mine-Mill locals in the United States. He asked that these same arrangements "naturally" be extended into Canada. Aware of Conroy's sensitivity, Millard immediately urged his international executive to deny any such arrangement "to dispel any impression given CCL people that there will be interference from our internationals with decisions made in Canadian problems." This Steel did at once. Relaying his union's decision to Conroy, Millard stated that the "principle at stake ... [was] whether our international union will stand behind the authority given the Congress to determine jurisdiction in Canada." He vowed that Steel would do so.[8]

Despite the efforts of Steel and the Congress, by a vote of 293 to 188, the Anaconda local voted to affiliate with Auto rather than Steel. Once again the Congress issued the local an ultimatum: either affiliate with Steel or become a chartered local of the Congress. But under no condition would the Congress allow it to affiliate with the UAW. Attempting a new ploy, Millard pleaded with David McDonald to ask Reuther to "pull the UAW out of the plant" since the Communists would "hail as a victory any success the UAW might have at Anaconda in hindering the implementing of the CCL decision and the Steelworkers' programme."[9]

Meanwhile, Burt announced that the UAW would issue a charter for the new local. Deeply perturbed, Millard wrote a personal letter to Reuther outlining his union's huge costs in attempting to take over Mine-Mill locals and thus helping to destroy communism in the Canadian labour movement. He complained that Burt's insistence on affiliating the Anaconda local was "provocative and irresponsible to a degree bordering on treachery." He also warned that, by ignoring Conroy's orders and challenging the authority of the Congress, the UAW would certainly be subject to "some disciplinary action ... [since] no Congress worthy of the name can abdicate in favour of one of its affiliates." Millard also complained to Conroy that Burt was undermining Steel's struggle "to build a strong clean labour movement in Canada." Finally he told McDonald that Burt was being "pretty much of a skunk" by helping the Communists and Mine-Mill do "a stab-in-the-back job" on Steel and thus "adversely" affecting not only Steel's campaigns, but in addition, those of the Congress. [10]

The struggle between Burt and Millard, and the former's refusal to accept Congress authority, deeply disturbed Conroy. In a long letter to Millard he revealed the extent of his disillusionment. The UAW, he said, likely felt that it was doing nothing that Steel had not done before in such plants as International Harvester, which were in the jurisdiction of the UAW but which had been organized by Steel. Since the Congress was obviously helpless to do anything concrete, Conroy bitterly declared: "My personal opinion is that I should resign from office, and let the Congress of Industrial Organization and its International Unions take over the Congress. I am quite sincere in this, as I have been mulling the thought over for some time. The Congress is supposed to be an autonomous body ... but ... in matters of jurisdiction ... the Congress is left without any authority, thereby reducing it to the status of a satellite organization at the mercy of its affiliated unions. These organizations choose to do whatever they want regardless of Congress desires, and in accordance with what their individual benefit may dictate they should do ... My own reaction is that I am completely fed up with this situation and within a few weeks it may be that I shall submit my resignation to President Mosher ... In short, the Congress is either going to be the authority in its field, or it is not. If it is not to exercise authority, then the more quickly the Executive Council appoints someone to hold a satellite position, the sooner the Congress will know that it is a purely subject instrument, with no authority and a servant of the headquarters of International Unions in the United States ... This thought has been running through my mind for the last three or four years, and I have not arrived at it overnight. It is just that as the chief executive officer of the Congress, I am in an untenable position, and I am not going to work in that capacity." [11]

If Conroy hoped that such a letter would change the attitude of the CIO unions, he was to be disappointed. Acting on the orders of the UAW executive board, Burt refused to give up the Anaconda local. Instead he charged that Steel had "no more respect for our jurisdiction apparently than we have for theirs." In support of Burt, the UAW international executive board unanimously voted to grant the Anaconda local a new charter. Burt was then warned by Conroy that the UAW was in danger of suspension if it continued to ignore the Congress jurisdictional decisions. The UAW leader replied that he was acting "under express instructions of President Reuther who was fully informed of all consequences." He added that Steel had not abided by Congress decisions in respect to the agricultural implement industry, and the Congress could not "make fish of one and flesh of another if they expect the affiliates to co-operate with jurisdictional decisions." If the Congress were going to "enforce its decisions" against his union, he demanded that it must also enforce them against Steel which, in the past, had refused to turn over to the UAW locals in the agricultural implement industry. At the same time, Silby Barrett announced that his union would also not abide by the Congress decision on the Mine-Mill jurisdiction. District 50, he stated, intended to take over all the chemical plants in the Mine-Mill jurisdiction. He warned that he would not "divide the jurisdiction of District 50 with the Steel Workers or any other organization affiliated with the Canadian Congress of Labour." "It belongs to us," he declared, "and we intend to maintain it."[12]

At this time the Congress was also at odds with the USW over another issue. Ignoring Conroy's protests, the national policy committee of Steel decided to organize workers in Ontario shipyards who were members of Congress chartered locals. Even before this decision, against Congress orders, Steel organizers had been busy lining up support in the Collingwood and Midland shipyards. A bitter Mosher charged that no union, not even Steel, "had the right to transgress the jurisdictional lines of the Congress." Meeting privately with Conroy, Millard urged the Congress to change its organizing policy and to transfer its chartered unions to its affiliates as soon as possible since the former were now directly competing with the latter. It was Millard's opinion that "in the organizational field Congress activities should supplement those of affiliates" not "compete with them." He demanded the dissolution of the chartered locals and told Conroy that Steel organizers were now busily at work achieving this.

On the other hand, Conroy argued that since "the upkeep and maintenance of the regional offices and staff throughout the country depend upon the revenue from the chartered locals," no wholesale transfer of these locals to affiliates would be advisable. He would, he told Millard, oppose with all the power available to him, the attempts of Steel, Auto, and other unions to take over the chartered locals.[13]

Whatever their differences in outlook and philosophy, however, both Conroy and Millard strove to avoid a public confrontation which both knew would irreparably damage the Congress. Unfortunately their differences were too deep, their temperaments too volatile, their attitudes too polarized, and their aims too conflicting for a peaceful and satisfactory resolution of their disagreements. In the end, they broke over a seemingly insignificant internal quarrel amongst executive members of one of the Congress affiliates, the Textile Workers of America. His authority challenged once too often, after years of frustration, Conroy finally went his own way.

Symbolically, it was only fitting that the Textile Workers should cause the final disruption. For years, no union outside of those dominated by the left-wing had given the Congress more headaches. At the very first Congress executive meeting, Millard submitted a study he had commissioned of the textile industry in Canada. This showed that textile workers were among the most "exploited" in the nation and therefore most needy of organization. Despite this, the Congress refused to act. It rejected Millard's plan for an organizing campaign on the grounds that such a campaign would be too expensive.[14]

Six months later, bowing to relentless pressure from Millard and his CIO allies, the Congress leadership underwent a change of heart and appointed the author of the report, Arthur Williams, as director of the Textile Workers' Organizing Committee. Both Millard and Williams felt that TWOC should simply be a 'holding company' until the CIO textile union headed by Emil Rieve was ready to move into Canada. But Conroy believed that the Congress could organize textile workers without the aid of the CIO. To him, TWOC was the first step in the formation of a Congress union of textile workers, and not merely an agent for a CIO union.[15]

In October 1943 Conroy appointed Jack Robinson, a Congress organizer, as co-director to work with Williams. Robinson, Conroy knew, supported national unions; Williams, he felt, did not. The former could be trusted; the latter, a protégé of Millard's, could not. Naturally Millard and Williams were outraged by the appointment and both soon left the organization – Millard resigned and Williams was fired. Unhappy over the change in leadership and, implicitly, in policy, some members of TWOC decided to leave the union and create their own organization without Congress assistance. With Millard as chairman they set up the National Union of Textile Workers. Despite Millard's efforts, the Congress turned down the affiliation of the new union and ordered it to reaffiliate with TWOC. It refused. Finally, after a year full of bitter recriminations, in 1945, on the invitation of the Congress, Rieve's Textile Workers Union of America sent in Sam Baron a notorious anti-Communist, to consolidate the fifteen locals in the two textile unions into TWUA.[16]

If Congress officials expected that this would bring a happy ending to the problems caused them by the textile workers, they were in for a rude awakening. Within a year, the Congress found itself at odds with some of its left-wing affiliates who disapproved of Textile's attempt to "raid" locals of the Communist-dominated AFL textile union. For the next few years the two textile unions carried on in an unseemly fashion. Kent Rowley of the AFL textile union labelled Baron a "red baiter," "the bosses' hatchet man," a "stool pigeon," and other more earthy epithets. In turn, Baron called the AFL textile leaders a "bunch of Communist slobs and traitors," and matched in earthiness the expletives used by his opponents. He also launched a successful libel suit against the leaders of the AFL union.[17]

By 1950, however, the abrasive Baron had turned his caustic tongue on members of his own union. At the 1950 international convention of TWUA in Boston, when Emil Rieve attempted to depose vice-president George Baldanzi from the executive, Baron denounced the union president and supported Baldanzi. With the support of Baron and the seventy Canadian textile delegates, Baldanzi successfully repulsed Rieve's attempt. This victory set into motion a chain of events which not only ripped apart the TWUA, but very nearly destroyed the Congress.

Because Baron was Baldanzi's most important supporter, the feud between the international president and Baldanzi rapidly spilled over into Canada where Rieve did everything within his power to undermine the position of Baron as Canadian director. He supported the pretensions of Baron's assistant, Edward Cluney, who began stirring up opposition to Baron amongst the Canadian locals immediately after the Boston convention. When Baron was appointed by the Congress to attend a regional conference of the ICFTU in Mexico, Rieve refused to allow him to go and advised Conroy that he would name the Textile delegate. Conroy replied that the Congress made its own appointments and had chosen Baron not because he was a member of Textile but "on account of his outstanding ability and general knowledge of the international situation."[18]

On 27 September 1950, stepping up his campaign, Rieve sent Baron four different registered letters. The first ordered him to fire three people on his staff. The second stipulated that he discharge a man who for four years had done part-time publicity work for the union. The third prevented Baron from appointing, as was customary, the Canadian delegate to the annual textile conference of the International Labour Organization. The fourth, ordered Baron to move the Canadian office from Montreal to Toronto.[19]

Baron vehemently protested all four directives, but particularly the last one, which he described as "the most blatant example of political persecution gone sadistic." He argued that such a move was "both administratively and organizationally unsound," that Montreal was "geographically in the center" of the textile industry in Canada, and that Quebec was the most important potential area for textile organization in the country. Despite the protests of the majority of textile joint boards in Canada, Rieve adamantly refused to reconsider and ordered the move to be completed by the first of February. At a staff conference in Montreal in January, Rieve declared that he could fire "anyone in the room," and that some "great changes" were soon to take place in the Canadian section of the union.[20]

For the next month Rieve sent out a series of directives to all Canadian textile workers attacking Baron and announcing a new organizational set-up. In turn, following each of these directives, Baron sent out one of his own, defending his position and calling for "greater autonomy" for the Canadian section of the union. Finally, on 6 March, Rieve fired Baron for "defying administration policy." Not to be outdone, Baron termed Rieve's letter firing him, "the most galling document ever concocted by one of the many poison pen artists whom the President has at his beck and call." He claimed that it was "simply a piece of fiction," and charged that Rieve was "guilty of the most ruthless campaign of political persecution" and that union members would "not for long tolerate the disruptive and dictatorial action which the President had taken in his mad lust for total power." Baron vowed that he would not give up the fight to prevent the union "from becoming a monolithic totalitarism, fear-ridden organization." He urged his fellow members to "stand shoulder to shoulder" with him "in the coming struggle to force [the] organization from the iron grip of selfish men who are interested in power for power's sake."[21]

In this battle, Baron had the support of most of the Canadian members. On 9 March the advisory council of the union in Canada voted to call a Canadian convention to discuss the dismissal of Baron and the relationship of the Canadian section to the international. Those voting in favour of this motion represented 85 per cent of the union membership in Canada, though Cluney called this advisory session a "rump-meeting" with no constitutional authority.[22]

The convention was held in Toronto on 31 March and was attended by delegates from the huge Cornwall and Hamilton locals as well as from locals in London, Toronto, and the Maritimes. These represented almost 90 per cent of the union's membership in Canada. By an almost unanimous vote, Baron was re-elected Canadian director. Though Rieve and his new Canadian director, Harold Daoust, called the meeting an "illegal conference" and warned Mosher not to send a Congress representative, Mosher replied that since "the majority of the Canadian membership of the union would be represented" he saw no reason why he should not send a representative. This was a highly unusual step for the Congress to take, for it meant publicly supporting one faction in an intra-union struggle. Never before, except when the issue at stake was Communism, had the Congress taken such a step.[23]

Delivering Mosher's message to the convention, Dowd stated that it was "a matter of deep concern ... that an officer ... of an affiliated union in whom we place a great deal of confidence is removed from office ... particularly ... when that officer is a valued member of the Executive Committee of the Congress and one whom his fellow ... members admire for his ability and integrity ... It seems quite evident that there is a strong feeling amongst the membership of the TWUA in Canada that there has been a miscarriage of justice, and that the Canadian membership has not received the consideration due them in the determination of policy and administration of the union in Canada." Dowd affirmed the right of Canadian workers to "a large share of national autonomy and self-determination," promised the textile workers the support of the Congress in their struggle to achieve their "legitimate demands," warned them that "the Canadian membership of the TWUA has rights and privileges with regard to administration of their union's affairs in Canada which should not be ignored by the international officers of that union," and deplored "any action that would deprive [the Congress] of [Baron's] counsel and cooperation."[24]

Astounded and enraged at the behaviour of the Congress, Rieve sent off a stinging letter to Mosher, accusing him of ignoring his request not to send a Congress representative to the "rump conference." He charged that this action had "encouraged those present in their defiant and unlawful conduct ... to ... deride" his administration, and had "aided and abetted anarchy and secession within the ranks" of his union. He also accused the Congress of "highly improper interference with the affairs of an affiliated international union" and of playing "a most ignoble role" in the entire affair.[25]

Both Conroy and Mosher were deeply unnerved by the entire affair. They liked and admired Baron. In Conroy's opinion he was a brilliant negotiator, a "crack" organizer, and an extremely intelligent and well-read man. He had done a good job for the textile workers in Canada and the Congress valued him as one of its most capable leaders. Significantly, Baron often supported Mosher and Conroy in their battles with Millard. Though he was the leader of a CIO union, he was no friend of Millard's. In fact, Conroy relied upon him as one of his most trustworthy allies. In the numerous confrontations between the two camps, Baron often sided with the Congress leadership against the CIO. Thus the Congress would react forcefully if Baron's position were threatened.

Furthermore Conroy and Mosher were outraged by Rieve's clumsy attempts to interfere in the affairs of the Congress. They saw this as simply another demonstration that the CIO regarded the Congress as its satellite, subject to all its wishes. Baron was a duly elected official of the Congress and no amount of bluster from south of the border could change that fact. They would support Baron with all their resources and would withstand any attempt by Rieve, or any other CIO leader, to remove him either as Textile leader in Canada or as a member of the CCL executive.[26]

Replying to Rieve, Conroy severely rebuked him for sending a copy of his complaint to the CIO. The Congress, he told him, was an autonomous body and, in this matter, the CIO was "irrelevant." He added that the official position of the Congress was one of "complete and unreserved neutrality" in the dispute. Because of the danger of the Communist-dominated AFL Textile Workers taking over some of the workers however, the Congress merely wished "to allay any fear on the part of the workers that while they were at odds with the International Union ... they were not going to be left to the mercy of raiding AFL Textile Workers." Conroy also urged Rieve to follow the practice of other CIO unions and give his Canadian workers some degree of autonomy. Canada, he told him, was a sovereign state, and "has problems that cannot be solved on the basis of its just being another state of the United States."[27]

Mosher's reply to Rieve was less restrained. Rieve's letter, he told the Textile president, was "one of the most abusive which I have ever received from an officer of a national or international union, and it is particularly ill-mannered and unwarranted, as coming from the president of an international union to the president of an autonomous labour organization in Canada." When invited to a meeting, he said, he did not "have to ask the permission of any international president, nor of the CIO." The cause of the Textile problem, he claimed, was Rieve's "evident determination to abuse and irritate and push around a group of Canadian workers, comprising more than eighty-five percent of the Canadian membership of the union." He could not understand why Rieve had "the impression that he could treat Canadian workers in such an arrogant high-handed fashion," nor was he surprised that "they have been greatly disturbed by your action in stirring up disunity among their ranks." He charged that Rieve did not "know or understand the Canadian situation" and should therefore stop his "persecution" and "leave the determination of policy in Canada to the democratic decisions of the workers immediately concerned." As president of the Congress he defended his right to address any group of workers affiliated to it and added that he had an obligation to speak to workers who were being "deprived" of certain rights by their own union. Finally, he charged that Rieve's "efforts to override the wishes of [the] Canadian membership, and stir up disunity in their ranks, have done more to hurt international trade unionism on this continent than anything else that has happened in the ten years since [the Congress was formed] ... The dispute that has arisen in your union should never have been allowed to come into Canada ... there is no reason why the Canadian membership should be disrupted and abused because of any differences of opinion between yourself and some of your Executive."[28]

Not surprisingly, both Baldanzi and Baron quickly come to Mosher's defence and criticized as "intemperate, insulting and arrogant" the behaviour of Rieve. The Canadian Textile Union Joint Boards also wired Mosher their support, as did George Burt who relayed to Mosher information he had received from Reuther that CIO officers had attempted "to heal this breach" but had failed because of the "stubbornness and bull-headedness of President Rieve."[29] Rieve, however, was shocked by Mosher's response. He called the Congress president "naive and immature" and sent Mosher a strongly-worded telegram reproaching him for levelling "the wildest unsupported charges," for engaging "in name-calling," and for "assuming an authority" which was not his. To Conroy he sent a longer, more thoughtful reply expressing his concern over Mosher's "highly abusive and irresponsible" behaviour and the partisan approach of the Congress to the dispute in his union. He had already dismissed the idea of giving his Canadian workers some autonomy, he told Conroy, since this would alienate members in the United States who would not "enjoy these rights and privileges." "Autonomy for our Canadian local unions," he said, "smacks of special privilege and independent unionism to me." He termed the Congress demands for these changes as "reprehensible trade unionism" and warned Congress officials not to interfere in the internal affairs of his union.[30]

The Congress was faced with a perplexing dilemma. Textile now had two Canadian directors – Harold Daoust supported by the international executive and a few Canadian members, and Sam Baron supported by Baldanzi and most of the Canadian members. Which one the Congress would recognize would have to be decided before the CCL convention opened in Vancouver in September 1951. Baron had previously been promised official Congress support for re-election to the executive committee. With his position as Canadian Textile director now in doubt, some members of the Congress executive urged that he be removed from the Congress slate so that the Congress could show its neutrality. At a meeting with Conroy in Toronto in August, Millard and Dowling took the position that the Congress must be strictly neutral in the dispute, and that neither Baron nor Daoust should run for the Congress executive until the internal dispute was resolved. Previously both Baron and Daoust had visited Conroy in Ottawa to press for support for their candidacies. Conroy informed them that he and the Congress would remain strictly neutral.

Both Dowling and Millard believed that Conroy would therefore not support either Daoust or Baron for the Congress executive.[31] But what Conroy meant by neutrality was not precisely what Millard and Dowling thought he meant.

To Conroy, neutrality meant simply not committing the Congress to any action against Baron until after he had been dealt with by the Textile convention. Until Baron appealed his dismissal before his union's convention, he was still a member in good standing of the Congress. He had been elected to the CCL executive, according to Conroy, because of his performance in Canada. And on the Congress executive he should stay until he was expelled from his union. The CIO unions led by Millard disliked and distrusted Baron. They were as anxious to keep him off the Congress executive as Conroy and the national unions were to keep him on.

Conroy was not keen on publicly announcing his position on Baron until the convention. However, succumbing to the relentless pressure from Mosher, Dowd, and McGuire who argued that the Congress ought to support openly and loudly its Canadian membership in their struggle for some degree of autonomy from their international – an argument which was particularly appealing to Conroy – and from Baron who argued that his loyalty to the Congress ought to be reciprocated at the time of his greatest need, Conroy decided, just before the Convention, publicly to endorse Baron for a position on the Congress executive.[32]

Unaware of Conroy's change of heart, Millard travelled leisurely to Vancouver arriving only one day before the convention. At the usual executive meeting to decide on the Congress slate, Conroy dropped his bombshell and Millard exploded. He accused Conroy of reneging on his promise and demanded that the Congress take a neutral position. Most of the executive, but particularly Mosher, Dowd, and Burt, supported Conroy. Realizing this, Millard resigned from the executive, announced his intention not to seek re-election "on the same ticket as Baron," and declared that he would run a Steelworker candidate, Bill Mahoney, against Baron in order to give Steel delegates "an alternative" and thus allow them to maintain their "position of neutrality."[33]

To offset Millard's strategy, Conroy devised a counter-stroke of his own. Just before the election, he "moved Silby Barrett up to run for the vice-presidency" vacated by Millard, and "put Mahoney in Barrett's place for election to the executive." The purpose of this move, as Millard ruefully explained to Philip Murray, was simple: "since CCL delegates must vote for a full slate of candidates this would have meant they had no alternative to voting for Baron or Daoust." The next move was Millard's. After an emergency caucus with some of his supporters, he put forward the name of a Steel official,

Pen Baskin, to oppose both Daoust and Baron. In this way, the CIO forces could remain "neutral" by voting for Baskin.[34] The stage was now set for the most dramatic election in the history of the Congress.

The first few days of the convention were uneventful. With the last of the large left-wing unions, the Fur Workers, expelled on the first day of the convention, there was little dissension or even rhetoric from the floor. Policies recommended by the executive were tediously debated and automatically approved. The genuine excitement which had prevailed almost daily while the left-wing unions were in the Congress came on the final day with the elections. As usual, Mosher was re-elected without much opposition and Conroy received his largest majority ever. With Millard's withdrawal, the four Congress nominees for vice-presidents – Barrett, Burt, McAuslane, and Spivak – were all handily elected.

Just as the tension was reaching its peak, a Miss Rhona Kickley, general secretary of the Council for the Guidance of the Handicapped of Civilian Rehabilitation was given the floor to speak on the problems of the handicapped. Then, at last, the election of the eight members of the executive committee was held. The first seven members – Alsbury, Dowling, Chappell, Leclerc, Jenkins, Mahoney, and McGuire – were easily elected. For the final position Baskin polled 287, Baron 248, and Daoust 103. Because a majority vote was necessary, a run-off election between Baskin and Baron was held for the final position. By this time many of the delegates, including most of the Autoworkers who supported Baron, had left the hall, not realizing that another election was necessary. With the solid support of Steel, Packinghouse, and the IWA, Baskin won the election 200 to 156.[35]

As soon as the result was announced a shaken and angry Conroy rushed to the podium. For several minutes he was unable to gain the floor while the victorious Steelworkers cheered their victory and tossed armfuls of paper into the air. At last, despite shouts that he was "out of order," Conroy got the floor and told the stunned delegates that since he was the "man around whom Baron's support revolved," Baron's defeat was a sign that the delegates no longer had confidence in his judgment. Then came his startling announcement that he had no alternative but to resign. While the delegates sat dumbfounded, poised, his head bowed, Conroy quietly turned and strode resolutely from the hall. Within moments pandemonium broke loose as confused and shocked Congress officials deliberated on what action to take. At last, they decided to set up a committee to beg Conroy to withdraw his resignation. With that, the convention was adjourned.

Despite the attempts of Mosher, Millard, Chappell, and many others, and despite the hundreds of letters begging him to come back, Conroy refused to reconsider. Philip Murray invited him to attend the CIO convention where he was royally entertained by Murray, Haywood, Reuther, and McDonald. But Conroy would not be swayed. Indeed, not until the council meeting of 12 November 1951 and after many vain attempts by a host of Congress officials and members, did the council reluctantly accept the resignation.[36]

Why Conroy had resigned puzzled everyone concerned. Mosher was "disturbed as well as mystified"; Millard was merely "mystified." But everyone had his own theory. To Millard it was simply a plain case of "misguided authoritarianism." It was impossible to justify the resignation, he told Murray, unless "you accept the principle that the executive have the right to dictate the election of officers." Sam Baron thought that Conroy was forced to resign because Millard and Steel wanted "to take over the Congress." This was also the opinion of Alex McAuslane who, in sympathy with Conroy, resigned his position as vice-president. The Congress regional director for Alberta, T.A. McCloy, sent out a circular to all locals in the province stating that Conroy had resigned "not on the basis of an election result, but strictly on the position of opposing the "octopus control" of a large union, and, of course, natural resentment at being 'double-crossed' on administration policy." He charged that Steel would not be satisfied with anything "short of a complete upset of the administration" and had committed itself to "no other programme than bringing about dissension" within the Congress.[37]

Outside the labour movement, opinions were also varied. The *Globe and Mail* saw it as a division between those officials like Conroy who were primarily interested in trade unionism, and those like Millard who were primarily interested in politics. According to the *Financial Times* what was at stake was "whether organized labour in Canada is to stand on its own feet, or whether it is to be directed and dominated by trade union bosses in the United States."[38]

In truth, the issue was probably much simpler than most people imagined. From his very first day as secretary-treasurer, Conroy had been threatening to resign unless he were given more scope in formulating Congress policy. In this he was confronted with the opposition of Millard and other international union leaders. Finally, frustrated beyond endurance, in one last, grand, defiant gesture, the proud and unyielding Conroy walked out of the organization of which he had been the chief architect. David Lewis, in rejecting a proposal that Conroy be offered the position of national secretary of the CCF, likely came closer than anyone else in analysing Conroy's problem. "His difficulty in the Congress," he wrote, "arose particularly from the fact that he does not consider it possible to run an organization when there are differences at the top, and that he does not consider it tolerable for an organization to refuse to follow leadership at any time."[39] Characteristically, certain that he had made the right and indeed the only possible decision, Conroy refused to reconsider his resignation. Partly, as Lewis surmised, this was based "on his determination not to have to work with Charlie [Millard]"; largely, it was because once he had convinced himself that his decision was right, the uncompromising Conroy was by nature incapable of reversing his stance. Because of this strength, or weakness, in character, the Congress lost its most valuable and most gifted member.

It was unfortunate, however, that of all the possible and valid reasons for his resignation, Conroy chose probably the least commendable, the defeat of Sam Baron. As Millard astutely pointed out to Murray, "by taking the position that unless the convention accepted his dictates in the matter of electing officers he would not hold office ... Conroy did himself almost irreparable harm ... It was the same sort of mistake as John L. Lewis made some years ago."[40] In an ostensibly democratic organization, for an executive officer to resign because the members of that organization refused to vote as he asked them to vote was inexcusable. Though by nature domineering and intransigent, Conroy was also born and bred in a strong democratic tradition – a tradition he attempted to impose on the Congress. By resigning because he failed in his attempt to persuade the convention to accept his candidate, Conroy made himself appear no less dictatorial than Millard was accused of being.

Even more destructive to Conroy's cause was the upshot of the entire Textile imbroglio. As soon as Baron was defeated at the Textile convention in Cleveland in 1952, he bolted the Congress and the CIO and became Canadian director for his erstwhile enemies – the AFL Textile Workers. At once he discharged its entire staff, and started "raiding" his quondam friends in the CIO. How much more embarrassing it would have been for the Congress if Baron had still been on its executive. Not without cause did the spokesmen for Steel and Packinghouse crow that despite the "terrible attacks" to which they had been subjected, there was no longer any doubt whose position at Vancouver had been vindicated. And, indeed, there was not.[41]

One of the more unpredictable results of Conroy's resignation was that it brought to a head a fierce internal struggle in the CBRE. In commenting on Conroy's resignation, the union's secretary-treasurer, and editor of its paper, J.E. McGuire, editorialized: "Big-hearted and high-principled, he quit because an unashamed drive for power, conceived in cunning and carried forward with craft, was aimed at changing the Congress from a vehicle for the many to a juggernaut for one. Conroy hoped his action would rouse the membership to the danger they faced, to the danger the Congress faced." Immediately, the nation's press picked up the editorial, concluded that it was 'aimed at Millard and at Steel," and that it marked a final break between Millard and Mosher. Millard himself reported that the editorial "came as a shock" and wired Mosher for an explanation.[42]

The CBRE president reacted immediately. He fired McGuire and wired back to Millard that the editorial, of which he had no previous knowledge, "was not aimed at the United Steel Workers of America" nor at Millard "but was another step in a long series of events confined to internal matters of the Brotherhood." In a following letter Mosher stated that the editorial in no way represented his opinion and that it was simply "the product of a sick mind." The next issue of the union paper – with a new editor – "wholly repudiated" the attack and apologized in a fulsome manner to the Steelworkers.[43]

That McGuire and Mosher had been at odds for years was common knowledge within the labour movement. What was not so well known was how deep and how acrid was this emnity. An independent, strong-willed person, McGuire was increasingly embittered by what he considered Mosher's autocratic behaviour in the union. Unquestionably, Mosher treated the CBRE as his own personal fiefdom. Surrounded by a coterie of devoted followers, he was able to override all of McGuire's protests and to carry out whatever policies and programs he favoured. At times he made some egregious errors. For example, in 1951, without consulting his executive, he personally affiliated the National Seamen's Association, a dubious company union led by the notorious Captain McMaster. Within two weeks, faced with the combined opposition of his own executive and of the Congress, Mosher was forced to back down and repudiate the agreement.[44]

Mosher could usually count on the support of his executive – with the significant exception of the union's number two man, McGuire. Aside from personality clashes, the major confrontation between the two men arose over the question of Mosher's retirement. At its 1939 convention, the CBRE had made it compulsory for all union members to retire at sixty-five. In 1942, when a union organizer, Joe Wall, reached the retirement age but refused to leave, the union's executive, led by Mosher, ruled that no exception could be made and that he must retire. In 1946, when Mosher turned sixty-five, McGuire insisted that according to the union's constitution Mosher must also retire. Supported by his cronies on the executive, Mosher refused.[45]

In 1950, the dispute flared anew. McGuire charged that not only was Mosher receiving his full salary from the Brotherhood and the Congress, but that he was also receiving full pensions from the union and the CNR. To overcome McGuire's opposition, Mosher demanded – and was given – the power by the CBRE executive to suspend any of its members at his own discretion. Mosher argued that as national president, "no officer had the right to boss [him] around." Undeterred, at the next executive meeting, McGuire again loudly demanded that Mosher be forced to retire. Again McGuire's motion was defeated. By 1951, after so many vain efforts, McGuire had become convinced that Mosher and the executive members of the union were "involved in a conspiracy" to remove him from the executive. His editorial on Conroy's resignation was the first step in his counter-attack. It was, as Mosher correctly stated, aimed not at Millard, but at Mosher himself, who McGuire felt had allied himself with the "alien" forces who were bent on "taking over the Congress."[46]

As soon as the editorial appeared, Mosher laid charges with the union's executive against McGuire, who, he claimed, was guilty of a series of offences including "vilification of a fellow officer and member, namely, the National President ... disregarding constitutional authority without proper approval ... and general disregard for supervisory authority." At the time, McGuire was under doctor's care for a heart condition and asked that his trial, scheduled for 18 March, be postponed until he was well enough to attend. The CBRE executive stated that since McGuire was healthy enough to "carry on extensive activities from his home," he was healthy enough to attend the meeting.[47]

Even though McGuire was not there to defend himself, the trial took place. At its conclusion the CBRE executive reported that it had "come to the irresistible conclusion that the charges have proven to be true" and that McGuire would henceforth be removed from office and expelled from the union. At once, the CCL executive council voted to remove McGuire from the Congress executive.[48]

Terming both acts "dictatorial," McGuire sought to defend himself by accusing Mosher of "lazy and ineffective administration ... wasteful and unwarranted use of funds," and "singular lack of any form of constructive leadership." He stated that he would present a list of sixteen charges against Mosher before the union's membership. These included accusations that Mosher attempted to "sell the workers down the river" during strikes, that he used his position to attempt to "secure a Senate appointment for himself," that he "liquidated eight other union leaders who refused to be dominated," that he used "spies and informers" and that he misused union funds. McGuire said that he had been "tolerating this mischievous and meddlesome individual" until the next convention when the union members "would take the matter in hand and require him to retire." The charges laid by Mosher against him, McGuire said, were "based on falsehoods, misrepresentations, common gossip ... and childish concoctions of his own to give his plan of liquidation a semblance of credulity." Mosher naturally denied all these charges but in order to ensure that McGuire made no more, he secured a court injunction restraining McGuire from "printing, distributing, publishing or repeating" any charges against him.[49]

These charges and counter-charges were heatedly debated in one of the wildest and most tumultous labour meetings in Canadian history – the CBRE convention in Niagara Falls in May 1952. For three desperate days McGuire presented his case against Mosher. He read from a lengthy memorandum, he lobbied with delegates and he pleaded emotionally "for justice." In the end in an embarrassingly close vote, Mosher was upheld by a count of 190 to 162. Immediately, Mosher announced that he would not run for re-election; his place was taken by Harry Chappell. Thus, in defeat, McGuire achieved one of his objectives – the removal of Mosher from the CBRE presidency.[50]

Undoubtedly there was a good deal of validity in McGuire's charges. Mosher had indeed been "dictatorial" and conceivably may have been guilty of some of McGuire's other accusations. But so obsessed with the justice of his cause had McGuire become, and so convinced was he that he was the victim of a "frightful conspiracy," that his behaviour became erratic and whatever chance he may have had of convincing a majority of the members of the righteousness of his cause was lost.

Meanwhile, the Congress reacted in its own way to Conroy's resignation. With Conroy gone, the international unions resolved to weaken the office of secretary-treasurer, so that Conroy's successor would be less bumptious and more easily controlled. They therefore did not oppose the executive's candidate for the job, Donald MacDonald. As a member of the United Mine Workers he was acceptable to the international unions; as a faithful Congress organizer for more than a decade, he was a favourite of the national unions; and as a one-time CCF leader in the Nova Scotia legislature, his political outlook was perfect. Nevertheless, MacDonald's honeymoon in office would be short.

It soon became obvious that his sympathies, like Conroy's, did not coincide with those of the CIO union leaders. Conroy's policy of drawing Congress staff from national unions and ordering them to organize and service these same national groups was continued. Similarly, MacDonald was as reluctant as Conroy to transfer chartered locals to the appropriate CIO affiliates. The international unions were still as insistent as ever that they be given a voice in making Congress appointments and that chartered locals be turned over to them as quickly as possible. MacDonald was equally adamant that he would not surrender these prerogatives. When Tom McCloy, the Congress regional director for Alberta, resigned, the CIO members of the executive demanded that they be given some voice in choosing his successor. As unyielding as Conroy, MacDonald refused. Dowling's resolution that such appointments be ratified by the executive council was defeated when MacDonald threatened to follow Conroy out of the Congress if it were passed.[51]

More serious, however, were the international incursions against Congress locals. Because of the low dues structures of the chartered locals and the open opposition of Congress organizers, few of these groups were handed over to the international affiliates claiming jurisdiction. Though the Congress jurisdiction committee ordered that the Congress natural gas locals in Ontario be handed over to the Oil Workers' international union, the opposition and hostility of the Congress regional director and of Congress organizers thwarted this move. A similar attempt by the Oil Workers to take over seven electrical utility locals in Saskatchewan was also rebuffed by Congress organizers. Efforts of Steel and Auto to take over a Congress needleworkers' local in Quebec failed when the Congress decided that since there were two claims for the local it was better that it remain in the hands of the Congress. Demands by Burt and Millard that their unions be allowed to take over Congress locals in Orillia were rejected by Congress officials on the grounds that in that area "psychological factors were against organization by international unions." Steel was even forced to hand back to the Congress a shipyard local in Pictou, Nova Scotia, which it had organized, but not before the union was upbraided by Mosher who termed the Steel action in organizing the yard "an unprovoked act of hostility wholly at variance with the basic understanding upon which the Congress was established, and must unless corrected without delay, lead to the dismemberment of the Congress." Mosher further warned that "if the Canadian membership of international unions want a Congress where neither agreement, assurance, nor understanding shall have any effect, I presume that is what they will have, but I am quite sure that they will be left alone to enjoy or suffer the consequences." "It is not," he added, "my intention to be a party to making a farce out of Congress regulations, nor will I remain inactive while the foundation upon which the Congress was built is under attack.[52]

Oblivious, Millard requested that the Congress turn over all its shipyard locals to Steel, the "one union which is capable of organizing and properly servicing them." He also warned Mosher that MacDonald's policy of "dividing them up into individual chartered unions" was doomed to failure. Irritably, Mosher urged the Steelworkers to "at least exercise a bit of patience" and to stop "trying to force their way into [the shipyards] in spite of the opposition of the local membership involved and of the Congress."[53]

Dismayed by the attitude of the Congress leaders and convinced that the only way to alter Congress policy was to change its leadership, Millard resolved to unseat either Mosher or MacDonald – preferably both – at the next Congress election. He first wrote Mosher to find out whether the elderly president was considering running again. He informed him that "many sound unionists are asking what is going to happen at the next Congress convention regarding leadership," and added that before he decided whether to stand for the presidency he wished to ascertain Mosher's intentions. It was his own personal opinion, he informed the Congress president, that he should have resigned when he reached his sixty-fifth birthday several years before. To Millard's query, Mosher replied that "in view of the developments which took place at the last convention" it was not his intention to decline nomination for another term in office.[54]

Instead of risking defeat by challenging Mosher, Millard decided that it was safer and probably more important to unseat MacDonald. In this he was supported by all the CIO leaders, particularly Burt, Dowling, and Spivak. Explaining to MacDonald why he felt it necessary to unseat him, Millard stated that at an earlier meeting "the head of one of the unions that helped form the Congress expressed considerable concern about the Congress and said that, in his opinion, the prestige of the Congress had slipped badly in the past year or two ... [and] something would need to be done and done without delay to correct the situation."[55] After that, Millard added, "it was only a matter of days until several other union heads expressed almost identical ideas." He sadly informed MacDonald that "it seemed to be the consensus of opinion that if the Congress was to perform its function in Canada, and in view of its present status, it would take someone who was stronger than you are in some respects." Millard added that these union heads had asked Steel to choose one of its men for the job, but he denied that it was "another of Charlie's plots." He warned MacDonald: "If you refuse to accept the judgment of the people I have referred to in this letter, I am certain you will do yourself a very great deal of injury, in their sight. On the other hand, if you abide by the action which has been taken, and thereby demonstrate that you put the welfare and progress of the Congress before any personal considerations, I am equally sure you will find friends where you may not have expected to find them."

For a time it seemed as if Millard would be unable to find a suitable candidate to challenge MacDonald. The only two possible contenders, Larry Sefton and Bill Mahoney, were busily engaged in their own personal dispute. The history of the Steelworkers in Canada has been the history as well of the bitter rivalry betweenHamilton and Sault Ste Marie – between the workers at Stelco and Algoma, and between the ambitious leaders of the two areas, Larry

Sefton from Hamilton and Bill Mahoney from the Sault. Involved in their own contest to succeed Millard as Canadian director of the union, neither wished to accept the invitation to stand for MacDonald's position on the Congress executive. Both desired to remain in Steel to be in a better position to succeed Millard when he retired. Finally, at a meeting of Steel area supervisors and national staff it was decided that Sefton would succeed the retiring director of Steel's District 6 – John Mitchell – and that Mahoney would run against MacDonald.[56]

When informed by Dowling of the campaign against him, MacDonald "blew his top," charged that it was a "stab in the back ... a double cross and an insult to the miners" and vowed that he would fight "to his last drop of blood" to retain his job.[57]

At first his task seemed hopeless. Of the 934 delegates at the 1952 Congress convention, more than 600 were from international unions – 234 of these from Steel alone. Every single leader of every single CIO union in the country with the solitary and insignificant exception of McLaughlin of the tiny Retail-Wholesale union promised to swing his union's support behind Mahoney. There was no doubt in anyone's mind – but MacDonald's – that he would be defeated. The astute Wilfrid List writing in the *Globe and Mail* stated unequivocally just before the contest, "the key policy post of secretary-treasurer will fall to a young but able man, William Mahoney." Even more emphatic was the labour writer for the *Financial Post,* Trevor Lloyd. On the second day of the convention he began his story with this comment: "This week it was definite. The international unions had won control of the Canadian Congress of Labour." Sheepishly, in the issue following the convention, he began his story in an entirely different manner: "The Steel spearhead for US–Canadian international unionism got a set-back last week." Somehow against all odds, in what List called "the greatest election upset in the history of the Canadian Congress of Labour," MacDonald managed to win.[58]

Throughout the convention his strategy was magnificent. He started off with a certain 200 to 250 votes from chartered and national unions, Mahoney with a probable 550 to 600 from the CIO unions. MacDonald consequently concentrated his effort on the latter. The fifty or so Communists and left-wing delegates soon promised MacDonald their support, as did the seventy-five delegates of the United Mine Workers. But it was even more essential that MacDonald win over to his side approximately 100 to 150 delegates from the other internationals. And in this he was surprisingly successful.

He was assured of at least a handful of votes from Steel itself – from delegates from his home base in the Maritimes and from traditional Mahoney enemies in the Hamilton area. Several other CIO delegates, upset by the "power play" engineered by Steel and by other Steel activities during the past years, promised MacDonald their support. But most important, despite his indefatigable efforts, Burt, as usual, was unable to deliver the Auto vote.

Nowhere was there more antipathy towards Steel than in the Autoworkers and in no other CIO union did Mahoney fare so badly. As Malcolm Smith, the president of Local 222 of the UAW sadly informed his members after the convention, "We believe that the UAW delegation was responsible [for Mahoney's defeat], as almost all of them supported MacDonald, when they were expected before the convention started, to support Mahoney."[59] With the key support of Auto, MacDonald out-polled Mahoney by 455 to 410. It was the most humiliating setback ever suffered by the international unions in the Congress.

But even in defeat the CIO unions triumphed. In the elections, aside from Mosher, only one other representative of a national union was elected to the fourteen-seat executive. Even the representative of the CBRE, Elroy Robson, was handily defeated in his attempt to retain the seat held for so long by McGuire. The CIO unions also took special delight in beating back an attempt by McAuslane to regain the position he had resigned out of sympathy and support for Conroy. But far more meaningfully, the CIO unions, over the heated and at times vituperative opposition of Mosher and MacDonald, managed to pass two constitutional amendments which further enhanced their control over Congress affairs. The first took the power of appointment out of the hands of the secretary-treasurer and gave it to the executive council; it also gave the latter body the power to set up a department of organization and to administer it. The second raised the dues structure of the chartered locals to the level of the affiliated and international unions, so that there would be less reasons for the former not to join with the latter. With these two amendments the CIO unions achieved the full control over Congress affairs that they felt their members and their financial strength merited.

The 1952 convention was therefore not, as most observers believed, a great victory for the national union forces, but rather, their ultimate decisive defeat. Made heady by MacDonald's astounding victory, they failed to realize that their triumph was almost irrelevant – more form than substance. The magnitude and shock of MacDonald's victory closed their minds to all else. Meanwhile the CIO unions were whittling away the powers of the secretary-treasurer, making him the captive rather than the captain of the new team. No more Conroys for them. It was, as Larry Sefton so astutely remarked at the convention, "a brand new" Congress. Though everyone owed "a debt of gratitude forever to the national unions" for their past contributions, it was the international unions with their overwhelming numbers which now controlled the Congress.[60]

Blinded in the euphoria of the MacDonald victory, the national union forces were rudely awakened on the following day to find themselves in a new, scarcely recognizable Congress. No longer could a strong secretary-treasurer successfully withstand the pressures of the international unions. At the 1952 convention the national union forces had made their last desperate, valiant gesture, had won a final remarkable victory, but in doing so they had lost the war. Down to defeat with them went the last lingering hopes for a purely Canadian national labour organization.

11
Conclusion

By the end of 1952 the basic conflicts within the Congress had been resolved. With the expulsion of the left-wing unions, the explosive Communist issue which for so long had tormented the Congress had been defused. With their victory at the 1952 convention, the international unions were now clearly in control of the Congress. This is not to say, however, that the voices urging autonomy for the Canadian labour movement had been stilled. On the contrary, many of the international union leaders, particularly Millard, were in the forefront demanding for their Canadian unions increased independence from the American parent organization. What it did signify, however, was that Congress policies – organizational, political, and economic – would now be completely in line with those agreed upon by the large international unions.

The Congress envisaged by Conroy and Mosher, a Congress in which the national affiliates and the chartered locals would be numerous, powerful and rich enough to withstand the incursions and override the demands of the international unions, proved chimerical. The resources of the international unions, as first Conroy and then MacDonald realized, were insurmountable. On the other hand, Conroy's foremost achievement, the attainment and guarantee of the complete autonomy of the Congress from the CIO, proved unassailable. Decisions made by the Congress executive and approved by the convention were binding on all CIO affiliates in Canada whether the CIO approved or not. For example, in 1952 the Congress decided to raise the monthly per capita tax on all affiliates to ten cents despite the formidable opposition of the CIO. For several years this decision caused a great deal of friction between the two organizations. The matter was finally settled only when the CIO gave in to Congress demands.[1] Though controlled by its CIO affiliates, the Congress none the less maintained its autonomy from the CIO.

With its internal dissensions largely reconciled, the Congress devoted most of its energy after 1952 to a merger with the Trades and Labor Congress.[2] Closer ties with the TLC had always been a primary Congress objective. At its very first convention, and at every subsequent convention, resolutions were passed calling for co-operation and joint action with the TLC. These were usually ignored by the TLC. An attempt by the Congress in 1941 to sponsor a meeting of representatives of the CIO, the AFL, and the TLC was rudely rebuffed by the TLC. Similarly, efforts on the part of the Congress to present joint legislative programs to the government were rejected, as were Congress requests to exchange fraternal delegates at conventions. At its 1944 convention, the Congress set up a permanent committee to meet with TLC representatives to discuss the question of unity between the two organizations. But all Congress efforts to hold meetings were spurned.[3]

By 1950 it seemed that the attitude of the TLC had changed. In a period of six months the two labour centres issued joint statements supporting the United Nations' position on Korea, calling on all their affiliates to support the strike of the seventeen railway unions, and warning the government against compulsory arbitration of this strike. The TLC even agreed to present a joint brief on price controls to the government and to set up a joint consultative committee with the Congress, the railway unions, and the Catholic trade union movement in Quebec. But, because it was not satisfied with the consultative committee and felt that it had gained little by joining it, at the end of 1951 the TLC withdrew.[4]

In 1953, the TLC was faced with an entirely new situation. The deaths of Philip Murray and William Green in late 1952 had removed two of the larger obstacles in the way of a remerger of the AFL and CIO. In April 1953 representatives of both these organizations met "for the purpose of exploring the possibility of achieving organic unity" between the two federations. This resulted in a "no raiding" agreement between the two. Soon afterwards the TLC publicly urged all its affiliates to desist from "raiding" CCL organizations in order to facilitate the "eventual" merger between them. And on 3 December 1953, the TLC executive set up an "exploratory" committee to hold talks with the Congress. Several days later the Congress executive named its own committee of Mosher, MacDonald, Burt, and Millard.[5]

The committee met together on 25 January, 11 February and 26 February 1954. The results of these unity committee meetings were meagre – agreement on a joint submission to the Government on unemployment and a no-raiding pact similar in every way to the one signed between the AFL and the CIO. But significantly, the committee also agreed that its ultimate objective would be a merger of their two organizations.[6]

The impetus to merge was further accelerated by the election of Claude Jodoin as president of the TLC and especially by the unanimous decision of the CIO at its 1954 convention to merge with the AFL. At the fourth and fifth meetings of the unity committee discussions were limited to the no-raiding agreement. At the sixth meeting, however, the question of the autonomy of the new Congress was raised. After much discussion, the persuasiveness of the CCL representatives won over the TLC delegation, and it was decided that the new Congress would follow the pattern set by the CCL in its relationship with the CIO rather than that between the TLC and the AFL. A statement of the principles of the new Congress was submitted by MacDonald at the following meeting and except for two points, pertaining to the activities of District 50 and the TLC's United Construction Workers, was unanimously approved.[7]

Indeed the activities of District 50 were threatening to disrupt the merger. Frank Hall, president of the powerful TLC Brotherhood of Railway and Steamship Workers, warned Jodoin that his union had "no desire to become associated with District 50 because of its complete lack of responsibility towards the labour movement." The building trades unions in the TLC also warned Jodoin that they would have nothing to do with the merger if District 50 was to become part of the new Congress.[8]

The problem of District 50 was discussed at the eighth and most bitter meeting of the unity committee. Representatives of the TLC building and railway unions aired their grievances against the "raids" of District 50 and reiterated that the District "presented the only barrier to the proposed TLC-CCL merger." In rebuttal, Barrett, who had refused to sign the no-raiding agreement, categorically denied all the allegations made against his union. Because no agreement was reached, it was decided to discuss the problem at the next unity meeting. But by that time the matter was no longer of any consequence, for in December 1954 the UMW refused to pay its per capita tax to the CCL, and it was quite obvious that it would not join the new Congress. Because of this, the TLC unions decided no longer to make an issue of District 50's "disruptive" activities.[10]

On 9 May 1955, the terms of the merger agreement were unanimously approved by the unity committee. These were ratified by the TLC at its convention in May and by the Congress at its convention in October. On 23 April 1956, the two Congresses met together in Toronto and created the Canadian Labour Congress. After nearly two decades of separation, the trade union movement in Canada was once again united.

The merger was perhaps inevitable. From the outset division in the labour movement had not been the result of a decision made by Canadians. Rather, it had been forced on them by developments in the United States. There had not developed in Canada that hostility and bitter rivalry between the two labour organizations that had racked the trade union movement below the border. The upshot was that the merger in Canada was, in Eugene Forsey's words, "a more perfect union," than that in the United States where the two labour bodies could not even agree on a name for their newly created organization. Thus, while the TLC unhesitatingly accepted the CCL's suggestion that the new labour centre be known as the Canadian Labour Congress, their two counterparts in the United States refused to give up their distinctive names.

In the history of the Canadian labour movement no event is more significant than the arrival of the CIO. It came into Canada in the one period in this century when it appeared as if Canadians might regain control of their own labour movement. But the advent of the CIO doomed that hope. Ironically, the CIO did not even want to come into Canada; it was dragged in. From the beginning, CIO activity in Canada was more the result of the forceful demands and activities of the Canadian workers than of the plans of the CIO hierarchy in the United States. Taking their cue from fellow workers in the United States, Canadian workers started their own organizing campaigns on behalf of the CIO. The reaction of the CIO leaders was, however, something less than encouraging: in fact, they urged Canadian workers to hold back.

Dismayed by the apparent apathy of the CIO, Canadian workers took matters into their own hands. All over the country tiny locals began springing up, calling themselves CIO, but the CIO in the United States had no knowledge of these locals. Throughout Canada, but especially in Ontario, small groups of dedicated men were organizing for the CIO, again without the CIO's knowing of them. Within a few months, the CIO found itself with scores of unions and hundreds of workers it did not want, and even worse, did not know what to do with.

For the workers of Canada, CIO was a magic name. Wherever they heard it, they flocked; whoever used it, they trusted. Canadian workers obviously felt that the CIO magic would rub off on them; what the CIO was achieving for its members in the United States, it would also achieve for its members in Canada. And even though the CIO was not yet ready to expand into Canada, Canadian workers insisted. Protesting, the CIO was dragged unwillingly into Canada. But even then it did little to help Canadian workers. It did not disown any of the unofficial CIO organizers in the country; but, on the other hand, neither did it assist them in any way. Indeed, it was on the assembly lines of Oshawa and Sarnia, and not in the union offices in Washington and Detroit, that industrial unionism in Canada was born. It was not John L. Lewis nor any of his representatives who brought the CIO to Canada; it was the body-shop workers in Oshawa and the foundry workers in Sarnia who were responsible.

Canadian workers had no hesitation at the time in joining an American union. Having just suffered through a ravaging depression, Canadians were understandably more concerned with material benefits than national identity. They felt they had no choice but to join forces with their fellow workers to the south. After all, their problems were the same, their traditions were similar and in many cases, their employers were identical. Above all, the CIO seemed to have more to offer them than any Canadian union. It had the personnel, the large treasury, and most important, the experience, to provide the Canadian workers with the organization they so desperately required.

Or so Canadians thought. But in fact, the personnel, the treasury and the experience were not provided by Americans; they were largely Canadian. All the CIO provided was its name. It seems quite clear that the major CIO unions in Canada – the UAW, Steel, UE, Mine-Mill, and the IWA – were basically organized and financed by Canadians with little, and often no help from their parent organizations in the United States. Naturally, there were times when financial and organizational assistance from the United States was indispensable. But it is also true that often Canadian funds poured across the border to the aid of insolvent CIO organizations in the United States. It was largely the SWOC check-off in Sydney, Nova Scotia, for example, that allowed its American parent organization to survive in 1940 when John L. Lewis broke with the CIO and stopped the flow of Mineworkers' funds into the SWOC treasury. Dues from the IWA in British Columbia and Mine-Mill in Northern Ontario were also vital in keeping their parent organizations afloat. The CIO had been founded with huge subsidies from the United Mine Workers and the Amalgamated Clothing Workers. In Canada, however, these unions were less generous. Their entire grant went for organization in the United States; there was little left for Canada.

Thus, from the outset, the CIO in Canada seems to have been largely the work of Canadians, not Americans.

If this analysis is correct – and all the evidence seems to support it – then it raises some interesting questions. If almost all the organizing for the CIO was done by Canadians; if almost all the money needed for this organization was provided by Canadians; and if almost all the leadership in the new unions was provided by Canadians; then who needed the CIO? What did the CIO do for Canadians that Canadians weren't doing for themselves? Was the CIO in fact necessary for the development of an industrial union movement in Canada?

The one deduction we can safely make is that, at the time, Canadian workers obviously believed that the CIO *was* necessary. For the Canadian workingman old traditions die hard. Because he felt that American unions had been essential in the past, despite the drastically changed situation of the 1930s, he obviously believed they were still essential. Caught up in the "continentalist" ideology, and in the belief in the superiority of things American, Canadian workers were preconditioned to join American rather than Canadian unions.

Unlike those of the AFL, the leaders of the CIO readily abdicated most of their responsibilities in Canada to local people. As a rapidly expanding organization in the United States, the CIO could spare neither the time nor the energy for the Canadian situation. As a result, organization in Canada was left largely in the hands of the Canadians themselves. The leaders of the CIO in Canada were mostly native-born, their experience was almost completely Canadian, and their interests were almost exclusively Canadian. At the outset they were scarcely concerned with labour developments in the United States. These factors combined to make the merger with the militantly nationalist All-Canadian Congress of Labour much easier to achieve. Ironically, however, though they had done much of the organizing for the CIO themselves, these men were extremely loyal to the American organizations. Whenever the interests of international and national unions clashed, invariably they supported the former.

Because of the initial strength of the ACCL forces within the new Congress, the merger turned out to be more of a coalition, with the nationalist ACCL elements pushing in one direction, the CIO in the other. As the CIO forces grew increasingly more powerful, however, the coalition soon became decidedly lop-sided. The strength of the CIO unions forced the Congress to follow paths inimical to the interests of the national unions. But at the same time, the Canadian-born leaders of the CIO made certain that the limited autonomy of their unions, as well as that of the Congress, would not be jeopardized by any dictates from the CIO.

Conventional wisdom has it that the relationship between the CIO and the CCL was between equals. As one noted student of the labour movement, Professor Paul Norgren, described it in 1951: "The CCL has been free of any domination by the CIO and the relationship between the two organizations has remained entirely amicable." After his exhaustive study of international unionism in Canada, John Crispo concluded that the CIO "appears never to have had ... designs ... to interfere in the affairs of the CCL," and that the CIO fully sympathized "with Canadian aspirations for independence."[11]

Unfortunately these analyses are simply not true. Between the CIO and the CCL, there was always a great deal of tension and animosity. One would have thought that the CIO should have stayed out of the CCL's affairs, since the development of CIO unions in Canada was largely the work of Canadians. But right from the beginning the CIO was insistent upon showing the flag in Canada – the American flag, that is. For a time it stubbornly refused to allow its unions in Canada to merge with the ACCL for fear they might sever their international connection. When the Canadian affiliates overcame this opposition the CIO then demanded that the newly created Congress devote all its energies to organizing workers into CIO unions. It also insisted that the CCL hand over to the appropriate CIO union its national and chartered unions and desist from organizing any more of these unions. This provoked a bitter squabble since the CCL received most of its revenue from its national and chartered unions and not from its affiliated CIO unions, most of whose revenues went to the United States. And whatever funds dribbled back across the border from CIO head-quarters in Washington to the CCL offices in Ottawa, the CIO insisted be used for solely CIO purposes. In addition, over Congress objections, the CIO de-manded that the CCL accept as affiliates all CIO unions in Canada, and that all jurisdictional disputes among Canadian CIO unions be settled in the Uni-ted States. After lengthy acriminious disputes, the CCL usually – but not always – got its way on all these matters.

The key man in warding off the designs of the CIO was the CCL's dynamic secretary-treasurer, Pat Conroy. He had been elected to this key position because he was a member of a CIO union – the United Mine Workers of America. But after a few short months in office he found himself spending a good deal of his time fighting the CIO. According to him, the aim of the CIO was to make the Canadian Congress of Labour its "satellite." Conroy felt that the Canadian labour movement had been for too long a satellite of American unions, and that it had finally arrived at a stage of its development where it needed a central labour body of independent decision making authority. It was his job, as he saw it, to give the CCL that authority.[12]

On the other hand the CIO was not prepared to give the Congress that authority, at least not without a fight. To the CIO, the CCL was no different from any CIO state council. Like any state council it was obliged to accept all CIO dictates. With the support of the national unions, Conroy desperately fought these CIO pretensions. Unfortunately, led by Millard, the international unions in the Congress usually sided with the CIO. Increasingly exasperated by the attitude of the CIO and its affiliates in the Congress, in 1951, frustrated beyond endurance, Conroy resigned. With his resignation, the fate of the national union movement was sealed. The centralizing efforts of the CIO had triumphed over the nationalist appirations of the CCL.

Because of these differences in outlook and the consequent bickering between the two factions, the Congress's organizing efforts were not as successful as they otherwise might have been. Mosher, Conroy, and their allies in the national unions demanded that more organization be undertaken on behalf of the chartered locals. Millard and his allies in the CIO unions called for more aggressive efforts amongst unorganized workers who fell within the jurisdictions of the international unions. There were perpetual disputes over the allocation of various Congress locals, the CIO unions demanding that they be turned over to the appropriate international union, the national unions that they remain chartered locals of the Congress.

Within the Congress inner circles there was also a constant power struggle between these two factions, climaxed by Mahoney's abortive attempt for the office of secretary-treasurer in 1952. Though Mahoney was defeated, by that time the international unions, whom he represented, had emerged triumphant. There seemed little either the Congress leadership or the national union forces could have done to change the result. The strength of the international unions was just too great to be overcome, most especially since the vast majority of Canadian workers were indifferent to the conflict. The question of American control of their unions did not disturb them as much as the question of higher wages, better working conditions, and more job security, all of which seemed dependent on the muscle provided by the American connection. And since most of them were working for American-owned companies, why should they be overly concerned if their unions were also American controlled?

Nevertheless, despite these internal pressures, the CCL did achieve a great deal to benefit the trade union movement in Canada. Under the terms of the merger agreement which created the Canadian Labour Congress in 1956, the AFL loosened its firm grasp over its Canadian affiliates and agreed to follow the pattern forced on the CIO by the Congress. The CLC was thus from the start, as the first paragraph of its constitution stipulated, an "autonomous Canadian Labour Centre with full powers over all labour matters in Canada." Most large AFL unions also followed the lead of the larger CIO unions and set up Canadian districts and national offices for their affiliates. Thus the struggle of Conroy and Mosher had not been in vain. As a result of their efforts, the international unions within the Canadian Labour Congress agreed to recognize Canada as a separate entity, to grant their Canadian affiliates a limited independence, and to treat their members in Canada differently from members in the United States. This was to be the CCL's crowning achievement.

To some, of course, the greatest contribution of the Congress to the Canadian labour movement was its expulsion of its "Communist" unions. Certainly, the expulsion of these left-wing unions, though hasty and somewhat crude, did significantly lessen the influence of the Communist party in the Canadian trade union movement. But it seems that this action was neither necessary nor wise.

At the time of their expulsions, the left-wing unions were relatively insignificant in both membership and influence within the Congress. They had neither the strength in numbers nor the influence to elect any of their adherents to the Congress executive nor to affect any of the decisions made by the CCL. Though they were "troublesome," "noisy," and did oppose many of the Congress policies, these were hardly sufficient causes to have them thrown out of the CCL. In most instances, the party people were good unionists, and the left-wing unions certainly provided the necessary services to their members. In fact, without the contributions and activities of these party people and their left-wing supporters, the task of organizing workers into the CIO and the CCL in the late 1930s and early 1940s would have been immensely more difficult.

Yet in the immediate post-war period these men – and their unions – who had done much to build and strengthen the industrial union movement in Canada were ruthlessly ejected. Caught up in the anti-Communist hysteria which hallmarked the late 1940s and early 1950s following the Gouzenko disclosures, and concerned about its image and what the affiliation of the "Communist" unions was doing to that image, the Congress patriotically decided to rid itself of its left-wing membership. This was accomplished without too much difficulty or even much soul-searching. The Communists had to go and ways were found to expel them. That these ways were brutal and perhaps even unconstitutional was irrelevant. What was important was that they achieved their purpose. By 1951, the Congress was "cleansed" and could then devote its energies elsewhere.

Though on the whole they have been rather badly maligned by historians and commentators on the period, there seems little doubt that the contribution of the Communists to the creation of the CIO in Canada was invaluable. They were activists in a period which cried for activity; they were energetic, zealous, and dedicated, in a period when organizing workers required these attributes. They helped build the CIO, and helped it grow until it was strong enough to do without them. They did the work that no one else was willing or able to do. Although there are many nasty things one can say about the Communists, undeniably in building a viable industrial union movement in Canada, theirs is a contribution not easily measured.

It was Communists under the able guidance of J.B. Salsberg who helped organize most of the CIO unions in Canada in the 1930s. The large CIO unions, Steel, Auto, Electric, Woodworkers, Mine-Mill, and Textile, were organized at the beginning by Communists and were all, at one time or another in their history, dominated by the party. Harold Pritchett, founder of the IWA, C.S. Jackson founder and still president of the Canadian UE, Tommy Church, George Anderson, and Harvey Murphy, the first organizers of Mine-Mill, Harry Hunter, Dick Steele and Harry Hambergh, the first organizers for the Steelworkers, and Alex Welch who helped start the Textile organization in Canada, were all active members or supporters of the party, as were a host of other nameless, young, dedicated organizers who spread out the length and breadth of Canada in the 1930s to bring unionism to the unorganized.

That the expulsions of the left-wing unions accomplished anything of benefit to the Congress is doubtful. Since the international unions and their national union adversaries had found unity in combatting these left-wing unions, and in little else, once the expulsions were completed the conflict between the two factions came out into the open, severely weakening the Congress. In addition, the ousted left-wing unions continued as independents, maintaining their memberships, and successfully withstanding Congress-sanctioned "raids." As successful independent organizations no longer restrained by the Congress, these unions wielded just as much influence in Canadian labour circles after their expulsion as before, and could more easily undertake those "subversive" activities which had caused them to be expelled from the Congress. Though Mine-Mill eventually merged with Steel, the UE still remains a powerful and viable union outside the Canadian Labour Congress. Certainly the short-term benefits to the Congress of expelling its bothersome left-wing unions were far outweighed by the long-term drawbacks to the Canadian labour movement of having a large group of workers barred from the mainstream of the trade union movement because of the political affiliation of their leaders.

The history of the Canadian Congress of Labour is studded with great successes and, at times, great failures. Its contributions to the Canadian trade union movement in the fields of collective bargaining, labour legislation, and political organization are significant, but are beyond the scope of this study.[13] Suffice it to say that under its leadership hundreds of thousands of unorganized and largely unskilled workers were brought into the trade union movement. It succeeded in organizing these workers where many previous attempts failed. Above all, it succeeded for the first time in establishing an industrial union movement in Canada. And though it failed to check the advance of American unionism into Canada, it found a way to accommodate it – to provide the Canadian workingman with the protection and power of the international unions he so desperately wanted, and yet, at the same time, to attain for the organized labour movement in Canada that degree of autonomy it so badly needed.

References

Abbreviations

ACW *Amalgamated Clothing Workers files*
BCFL *British Columbia Federation of Labour files*
CCF *Cooperative Commonwealth Federation papers*
CLC *Canadian Labour Congress files*
IWA *International Woodworkers of America files*
LRB *Labour Research Bureau files*
Mine-Mill *Mine, Mill and Smelter Workers files*
PAC *Public Archives of Canada*
PAO *Public Archives of Ontario*
UAW *United Automobile Workers papers*
UE *United Electrical Workers files*
UPW *United Packinghouse Workers files*
USW *United Steel Workers files*

Chapter 1

1 CLC, Minutes of the Executive Council, Trades and Labor Congress 1928-1931.
2 J.B. Salsberg; Tom McEwen; Harvey Murphy.
3 Communist Party of Canada, *Canada and the VII World Congress of the Communist International* (Toronto, 1935), 16-18.
4 Salsberg.
5 Proceedings, American Federation of Labor Convention, 1934, 174-5.
6 Salsberg.
7 J. Adams, The History of the United Steel Workers of America in Canada, MA thesis, Queen's University, 1952, 59-60.
8 *Steel Labor*, 5 Sept. 1936; 5 Dec. 1936, Salsberg; Harry Hunter.
9 *Labour Organization in Canada*, 1936 (Ottawa: Department of Labour), 174-5; Wayne State University, UAW Papers, Oral History Collection: John Eldon, pp. 1-3. *Star*, 8 Nov. 1936.
10 Milton Montgomery; *Star*, 4 March 1937; *Canadian Forum*, April 1937.
11 *Toronto Telegram*, March 5, 1937; *Star*, March 8, 1937.
12 *Canadian Comment*, May 1937; Arthur Schultz; Charles Millard.
13 Salsberg; Millard; *United Auto Worker*, May 8, 1967, letter from Hugh Thompson, written sometime in 1966, with some of Thompson's reminiscences of the strike.
14 *New Commonwealth*, March 1937; Millard.
15 PAO, Hepburn Papers, minutes of meeting, 18 March 1937, 3; Millard; *New Commonwealth*, 27 March 1937.
16 Hepburn Papers, minutes of meeting, 24 March 1937.
17 PAC, Lapointe Papers, Ontario Provincial Police Report to Chief Inspector, Criminal Investigation Branch, on CIO Meeting in Oshawa, March 25, 1937; Millard.
18 Hepburn Papers, minutes of meeting, 31 March 1937, 2.
19 *Ibid.*, 1 April, 2-5.
20 *Oshawa Times*, 3 April 1937.

21 Hepburn Papers, minutes of meeting, 5 April 1937, 1-3.
22 *Ibid.*, 6 April, 1.
23 Hepburn Papers, Hepburn to Mackenzie, 25 Feb. 1937; Mackenzie to Hepburn, 25 Feb. 1937; Hepburn to Roebuck, 26 Feb. 1937; Crerar to Hepburn, 4 March 1937; Confidential Report on Hugh Thompson made by Inspector Collins of the Department of Immigration for the Minister of Immigration, undated.
24 Hepburn Papers, minutes of meeting, 7 April 1937.
25 *Ibid.*, memo from Irwin to Nixon, 7 April 1937.
26 Hepburn Papers, Hepburn to Lapointe, 8 April 1937; Williams to Hepburn, 8 April 1937; Hepburn to Odette, 8 April 1937; Hepburn to Miss H.N. Ward, Assistant Deputy-Minister of Public Welfare; David Croll; Arthur Roebuck; *New York Times*, 9 April 1937.
27 Lapointe Papers, Lapointe to Hepburn, 8 April 1937; MacBrien to Hepburn, 8 April 1937; MacBrien to Officer-in-Command, RCMP, Toronto, 9 April 1937.
28 *Star*, 10 April 1937.
29 *Globe and Mail*, 10 April 1937; *Daily Clarion*, 9 April 1937.
30 *Star*, 12 April 1937.
31 *Canadian Forum*, June 1937; *Star*, 12 April 1937.
32 *Oshawa Times*, 12 April 1937.
33 Eamon Park; Millard; Salsberg; Fred Dowling.
34 Hepburn Papers, Hepburn to King, 13 April 1937; King to Hepburn, 13 April 1937; Hepburn to Senator Hardy, 16 Feb. 1937.
35 Hepburn Papers, Hepburn to Lapointe, 13 April 1937; Lapointe to Hepburn, 13 April 1937; Hepburn to Lapointe, 14 April 1937.
36 *Star*, 15 April 1937.
37 *Globe and Mail*, 16 April 1937; Hepburn Papers, secret reports from Constable Wilson, 12, 13, 14, 15, 16 April 1937.
38 Croll; Roebuck.
39 Hepburn Papers, Hepburn to Croll and

Roebuck, 14 April 1937; Croll and Roebuck to Hepburn, 14 April 1937. With Croll's resignation, Hepburn added his portfolios of Labour, Public Welfare, and Municipal Affairs to his own of Prime Minister and Provincial Secretary. This prompted one pundit to comment: "If anyone sees him talking to himself, he will be able to conclude that the Ontario Cabinet is having a meeting." *Lindsay Daily Warder*, 17 April 1937.

40 *Oshawa Times*, 16 April 1937; *Globe and Mail*, 17 April 1937.

41 *Oshawa Times*, 17 April 1937.

42 Hepburn Papers, statement of 17 April 1937.

43 *Star*, 19 April 1937; Millard.

44 Hepburn Papers, secret police reports from Constable C.W. Hitch, Timmins, 13, 14, 16 April, and from Inspector Creasy, Haileybury, 14 April warning that the "CIO would close down steel, coal, and railroad if there were a lockout in the gold mines;" H.P. Knox to Hepburn, 16 April 1937.

45 *New York Times*, 19 April 1937; *Union News*, May 1937.

46 *Star*, 19 April 1937.

47 *Oshawa Times*, 20 April 1937.

48 Millard; UAW special general executive board meeting, 19 April 1937, Washington.

49 *Oshawa Times*, 20 April 1937; Millard.

50 UAW executive meeting; Thompson Papers Martin to Thompson, 20 April 1937.

51 *Star*, 21 April 1937; Hepburn Papers, McIntyre to Hepburn, 21 April 1937; Hepburn to McLaughlin, 20 April 1937.

52 Hepburn Papers, minutes of meeting, 21 April 1937; McIntyre to Hepburn, 22 April 1937; Lorne to Hepburn, 22 April 1937; minutes of meeting, 22 April 1937.

53 Hepburn Papers, contract between General Motors and its employees, 21 April 1937; *Globe and Mail*, 26 April 1937.

54 *Daily Clarion*, 26 April 1937; *Star*, 26 April 1937.

55 *Financial Post*, 8 May 1937; McCullagh to McLaughlin, 18 Jan. 1943, quoted in B. Young, The Leadership League, MA thesis,

Queen's University, 1966, 206; McCullagh to McMaster, 18 Jan. 1943, 206.

Chapter 2

1 Mine-Mill, e.g. the secretary of Mine-Mill Local 239 in Sudbury wrote to Mine-Mill headquarters that organization amongst the miners was slow though he expected the "settlement of the Oshawa strike to help us." J.G. Munroe to J.M. Sherwood 11 April 1937; *Steel Labor*, April 1939; Millard; Salsberg.

2 CCF, Spry to Lewis, 30 April 1937.

3 Salsberg; Peter Hunter, From the Other Shore, (unpublished manuscript), Toronto 1965.

4 UE, Transcript of interview with Tim Buck, 3 Oct. 1960, 8.

5 UE, *Union Light*, 28 April 1937.

6 UAW, Thompson papers, file on Oshawa strike; *Star*, 21 April 1937; *Financial Post*, 24 May 1937 (article by Guy S. Cunliffe).

7 *Labour Gazette*, April-Sept. 1937; *Daily Clarion*, April to Sept. 1937.

8 *Financial Post*, 7 Aug. 1937; *Globe and Mail*, 2 Sept. 1937.

9 *Financial Post*, 26 June 1937.

10 UAW, Thompson papers, Lewis to Thompson, 15 Aug. 1937; *Financial Post*, 30 Oct. 1937.

11 E.E. Wooldon, AFL organizer, quoted in *Toronto Star*, 12 March 1937; *Financial Post*, 5 June 1937.

12 *New Commonwealth*, 11 Dec. 1937; USW Lewis to Barrett, 15 Sept. 1937.

13 *Steel Labor*, 21 Jan. 1938; USW, report of Silby Barrett to Ontario Conference of SWOC lodges, Toronto, 11-12 June 1938, 3.

14 USW, report of Dick Steele, Canadian Regional Secretary, 1.

15 *Ibid.*, report of Barrett, 1-2.

16 W. Galenson, *The AFL against the CIO* (Cambridge, Mass., 1960), 151.

17 *New Commonwealth*, 12 March 1938 and 9 Aug. 1938.

18 CCF, Jolliffe to Lewis, 24 Aug. 1938.

19 Salsberg.
20 USW, Barrett to Lewis, 19 Jan. 1939; Salsberg. UAW, Addes Papers, Millard to Addes, 1 Feb., 15 Feb., 30 Jan. 1939; UE, *Canadian Auto Worker Bulletin*, 11 Feb. 1939.
21 UE, Joyce (recording secretary, Local 195, UAW) to Haywood, 27 June 1940; Shultz; Millard.
22 USW, Millard to Thompson, 3 May 1939; Millard.
23 USW, Millard to Lewis, 24 April 1939; Millard to Brophy, 25 April 1939; Millard to Murray, 5 May 1939.
24 CCF, Jolliffe to Lewis, 24 Aug. 1938.
25 TLC Convention Proceedings, 1938.
26 USW, Steele to Murray, 14 Oct. 1938; Murray to Steele, 20 Oct. 1938; Jackson; Millard; Harold Pritchett.
27 AFL Convention Proceedings, Nov. 1938, Houston, 133; USW, Barrett to Lewis, 3 Dec. 1938; *Trades and Labor Congress Journal*, Feb. 1939; USW, Barrett to Lewis, 6 Feb. 1939.
28 CCF, notes by David Lewis of a conference with Millard, 11 Feb. 1939; Millard.
29 USW, Green to Buckley, 21 March and 2 April 1939; Buckley to Green, 24 March and 15 April 1939.
30 USW, Barrett to Lewis, 6 Feb. 1939.
31 USW, Joyce to Lewis, 31 May 1940; UE, resolution of Local 195, UAW, June 1939; USW, Burt to Barrett, 1 June 1939; Millard to Barrett, 5 June 1939; Millard to Thompson, 3 May 1939.
32 USW, Steele to Barrett, 10 May 1939; Salsberg; Jackson; USW, Millard to Barrett, 5 June 1939.
33 UE, minutes of the Coordinating Committee of the CIO, 27 June 1939.
34 USW, report of the CIO in Canada, 1939; UE, minutes of meeting of CIO, 12 July 1939, 2.
35 CLC, Toronto and District Labor Council files, Green to Noble, 12 May 1939.
36 UE, Barrett to Douglas, 21 Aug. 1939; *Star,* 22 Aug. 1939.
37 TLC Convention Proceedings, 1939.

Chapter 3

1 UE, report of the first conference of the Canadian Committee for the CIO, Ottawa, 4-6 Nov. 1939; USW, Barrett to John L. Lewis, 25 Oct. 1939.
2 USW, Millard to Haywood, 8 Nov. 1939.
3 UE, report of first conference.
4 *Ibid.,* submission of CCIO, 5 Nov. 1939, 27; USW, Millard to Haywood, 8 Nov. 1939.
5 PAO, Hepburn papers, Mosher to Hepburn, 24 April 1937; *Canadian Unionist,* April 1937, 273.
6 Dowd, 4 Jan. 1967; *Canadian Unionist,* May 1937, 323-4 and Aug. 1937, 64.
7 USW, report on the CIO in Canada, June 1939, 4; CLC Archives, Barrett to Lewis, 12 Nov. 1938; USW, minutes of the Amherst Steelworkers Conference, 4-5 Mar. 1939; CLC, Barrett to Mosher, 24 Nov. 1938; Mosher to Barrett, 5 Dec. 1938.
8 CLC, Mosher to Barrett, 28 Nov. 1939; 23 Dec. 1939.
9 CCF, Lewis to Winch, 16 Feb. 1939, Lewis to MacInnes, 21 Dec. 1939; CLC, Millard to Murray, 28 Nov. 1939.
10 CLC, Millard to committee members of CIO, 5 Dec. 1939; memorandum of understanding between ACCL and CCIO, 30 Nov. 1939.
11 *Star,* 7 Dec. 1939; CLC, E.H. Rowe (CCIO recording secretary) to Dowd, 20 Dec. 1939.
12 CLC, Taylor to Dowd, 20 Dec. 1939.
13 CLC, Dowd to Salverson, and Mosher to Cohen, 12 Dec. 1939; minutes of executive board meeting of ACCL, 28 Dec. 1939; Taylor to Dowd, 20 Dec. 1939.
14 USW, Millard to Haywood, and Millard to Murray, 13 Jan. 1940.
15 USW, Millard to Murray, 13 Jan. 1940; CCL, e.g. Dowd to Stevenson, 18 Jan. 1940.
16 *London Free Press,* 5 Feb. 1940; CLC, Mosher to Taylor, 22 Feb. 1940; Millard to Mosher, 14 Feb. 1940; Mosher to Millard, 21 March 1940.
17 *Toronto Clarion,* 1 May 1940; Salsberg;

CLC, Millard to Mosher, 13 May 1940; Mosher to Millard, 15 May 1940.

18 USW, Haywood to Millard, 20 May 1940; Millard to Haywood, 25 May 1940.

19 USW, secretary, Local 195 UAW, to Haywood, 30 May 1940; Haywood to Joyce, 10 June 1940; Joyce to Haywood, 27 June 1940; Burt to Thomas, 19 July 1940; Burt to Millard, 19 July 1940; Millard to Durocher, 18 Aug. 1940.

20 CLC, Barrett to Mosher, 9 April 1940; Millard to Barrett, 25 July 1940.

21 CLC, Millard to Dowd, 18 Aug. and 4 Sept. 1940; USW, Millard to CIO unions in Canada, 10 Aug. 1940.

22 CLC, Dowd to Cohen, 20 Dec. 1939; Cohen to Mosher, 26 Dec. 1939; Mosher to Cohen, 27 Dec. 1939; Jackson.

23 CLC, Cohen to Dowd, 26 June and 1 July 1940; minutes of executive meeting of ACCL, 8 Sept. 1940, 24.

24 ACW, minutes of special meeting of all executive and joint board delegates, 11 Nov. 1939; minutes of joint board meeting, 19 Sept. 1940; Spivak.

25 CCF, Cotterill to Lewis, 14 Sept. 1940.

26 CCF, Lewis to Jolliffe, 5 Sept. 1940; Lewis to Millard, 5 Sept. 1940.

27 *Canadian Forum*, Oct. 1940.

Chapter 4

1 D.R. Kennedy, *The Knights of Labor in Canada*, MA thesis, University of Western Ontario, 1936, chap. 4.

2 J. Adams, The History of the United Steel Workers of America in Canada, MA thesis, Queen's University, 1952, 37.

3 Statutes of Nova Scotia, 1937, Trade Union Act, c. 6, s. 12.

4 Millard; USW Murray to Millard, 8 Feb. 1940.

5 USW, Barrett to Lewis, 28 Dec. 1939.

6 Salsberg; Millard; Harry Hunter.

7 USW, Murray to Millard, 6 Oct. 1939.

8 Millard; USW, Millard to Murray, 8 Nov. 1939.

9 USW, Millard to Murray, 27 Feb. 1940; Murray to Millard, 12 March 1940.

10 USW, D. McDonald to Hunter, 11 May 1940; report of Canadian region to SWOC convention, 21-4 May 1940.

11 USW, Murray to Millard, 23 July 1940; Millard to Pressman, 5 June 1940.

12 USW, Steele to Murray, 8 June 1940; CCF, Millard to Lewis, 7 June 1940.

13 USW, Steele to Murray, 8 June 1940; Salsberg; USW, Steele to all SWOC lodges in Canada, 8 June 1940.

14 USW, Millard to McDonald, 17 June and McDonald to Millard, 24 June 1940.

15 USW, Bob Ward to Barrett, 26 June, to Murray, 24 June, to Barrett, 26 June 1940.

16 USW, Millard to McDonald, 27 June 1940; Barrett to all SWOC lodges in Canada, 3 July 1940; Millard to J. Smith (secretary Local 1817), 9 July 1940; Millard to Murray, 15 July 1940; Sweeney to Millard, 25 July 1940; Millard to Barrett, 25 July 1940.

17 USW, Millard to Murray, 30 Aug. 1940.

18 USW, Millard to Hunter and Hambergh, 17 Sept. 1940; Millard to Barrett, 10 Sept. 1940; Ward to all Steel lodges, 24 Sept. 1940.

19 USW, resolution of meeting, 29 Sept. 1940, 1; Ward to Murray, 8 Oct. 1940.

20 CLC Taylor to Dowd, 29 Oct. 1939; USW, Millard to McDonald, 17 June 1940; CLC, Taylor to Dowd, 16 Oct. 1940; Campbell to Algoma Union members, 23 Sept. 1940; Taylor to Dowd, 16 Oct. 1940.

21 USW, Millard to McDonald, 11 Nov. 1940.

22 USW, Hambergh to all SWOC lodges, 26 Nov. 1940; UE, Hunter to all SWOC lodges, 16 Dec. 1940.

23 CLC, Mackenzie to Lewis, 15 Nov. 1940; USW, Hambergh to all SWOC lodges, 26 Nov. 1940; Millard.

24 USW, Millard to Clowse, 4 Jan. 1941, and 20 Dec. 1940.

25 USW, McDonald to Millard, 13 Jan. 1941; Millard to McDonald, 22 March 1941; McDonald to Carey and Thomas, 7 Feb. 1941; McDonald to members of SWOC in Canada, 10 Feb. 1941.

26 USW, Hunter to McDonald, 19 Feb. 1941; Hambergh to McDonald, 20 Feb. 1941; e.g. A. Shepherd (Local 1111) to McDonald, 3 March 1941; McDonald to Hunter and Hambergh, 4 March 1941.

27 USW, Burt to McDonald, 10 March 1941; McDonald to Burt, 27 March 1941.

28 USW, Millard to Haywood, 17 March 1941; Millard to McDonald, 22 March 1941.

29 USW, Millard to McDonald, 22 March 1941; Mackenzie to all SWOC locals, 26 March 1941.

30 USW, minutes of proceedings of the Wages, Hours and Policy Conference, SWOC Canadian Region, 19-20 April 1941; McDonald to Hague, 22 April 1941.

31 USW, Millard to McDonald, 23 April 1941; minutes of Wages etc. Conference, report on organizational progress.

32 USW, Hunter to Millard, 5 June 1941; Millard to Hunter, 6 June 1941; Hunter to all SWOC lodges, 7 June 1941.

33 Salsberg. Hunter.

34 Salsberg.

35 USW, Millard to Haywood, 16 Sept. 1940; Millard to Thompson, 24 May 1939; Millard.

Chapter 5

1 USW, Millard to Haywood, 16 Sept. 1940; CLC, Dowd to Haywood 18 Sept. 1940.

2 UE, verbatim minutes, executive council meeting of CCL, 5 Nov. 1940, 1; CLC, minutes, executive committee, 13 Sept. 1940.

3 CLC, executive council meeting, 13 May 1941; Dowd to Mosher, 31 Dec. 1940; Ottawa Journal, 20 Dec. 1940; Susner (CCL organizer) to Mosher, 22 Jan. 1941.

4 Jackson; UE, Shop Stewards' Councils to all unions, 29 April 1941.

5 CCF Archives Shultz to Lewis, 26 March 1941; USW, Millard to McDonald, 21 March 1941.

6 UE, Millard to Jackson, 15 April 1941; Jackson to Millard, 25 April 1941; CLC, Jackson to Dowd, 10 May 1941.

7 CLC, Dowd to Jackson, 11 March 1941; Jackson to Dowd, 17 March 1941; Dowd to Carlin, 20 March 1941.

8 CLC, executive committee, 12 May 1941; executive council, 13 May 1941, 1-7; LRB, Report of national [Congress] executive council meeting, CCL, 13 May 1941, by Nigel Morgan, 2.

9 CLC, Conroy to Dowd, 30 June and to Mosher, 2 July 1941.

10 Steel Labor, 30 Aug. 1940; USW, resolution of Ontario Executive of SWOC, Ward to Murray, 8 Oct. 1940.

11 USW, Hunter to Murray, 10 April 1941; Hunter to Millard, 30 June 1941.

12 USW, conference of SWOC delegates to CCL convention, 7 Sept. 1941, 1-2; CLC, Barrett to all SWOC locals, 4 Oct. 1941.

13 CLC, Mosher to Barrett, 14 Aug. 1941; Barrett to Mosher, 21 Aug. 1941; Mosher to Barrett, 28 Aug. 1941.

14 CCL, proceedings 1941 convention.

15 CLC, Mosher to King, 1 Sept. 1939; Mosher to King, 6 June 1940.

16 CCL, executive committee, 4 Nov. 1940; Council, 5 Nov. 1940; USW, Millard to A.J. Hillis (chairman, NLSC), 25 April 1941; CLC, Millard to Mosher, 14 May 1941; Millard to Dowd, 24 May 1941; Mosher to McLarty, 21 April 1941; Dowd to Millard, 22 April 1941.

17 CLC, Mosher to King, 21 March 1941; executive committee, special meeting, 14 Dec. 1941; USW, Millard to all SWOC locals 17 Dec. 1941; CLC, executive committee, 20 Nov. 1942; Council, 21 Nov. 1942; Bengough and Mosher to King, 27 Nov. 1942.

18 PAC, Cabinet War Committee, Secret Minutes, 5 May 1941. The CNA delegation included representatives of the Steel Company of Canada, the National Steel Corporation the Otis-Fensom Elevator Company, and the Howard Smith Paper Mills Limited.

19 CLC, Dowd to Conroy, 13 Jan. 1941; Conroy to Dowd, 24 Jan. 1941; Dowd to Conroy, 28 Jan. 1941; CCF, Gargrave to Conroy, 18 Sept. 1941; Lewis to Gargrave, 30 Aug. 1941.

20 CLC, Millard to Conroy, 19 Jan. 1942; Conroy to Millard, 20 Jan. 1942.
21 CCF, Margaret Sedgewick to Lewis, 10 July 1941; Lewis to Sedgewick, 4 Sept. 1942.
22 CCL convention, 13-17 Sept. 1943, 53-6; CCF, Lewis to MacInnis, 21 Sept. 1943.
23 CLC, executive committee, special meeting, 11 Feb. 1944; executive committee CCL, 8 June 1944.
24 CLC, Conroy to Mosher, 2 July 1944; 25 June 1945; Conroy to Andras, 3 Jan. 1946; Conroy to Mosher, 29 June 1944.
25 CCF, Lewis to Conroy, 8 July 1944.
26 CLC, Jackson to Conroy, 27 June 1944; UE, statement of district 5 executive board of UE, 9 Sept. 1944; CLC, Livett to Conroy, 21 July 1944; minutes of PAC-CCL, 11, 12 Aug. 1944; Proceedings, CCL convention, 16-20 Aug. 1944, 53-5.
27 CLC, Park to Mosher, 28 October 1944; *Globe and Mail*, 28 Oct. 1944.
28 USW, press statement by Park, 30 Oct. 1944; CLC, Conroy to Jackson, 2 Nov. 1944; Mosher to Conroy, 2 Nov. 1944; Jackson to Conroy, 3 Nov. 1944; Conroy to Jackson, 13 Nov. 1944; Mosher to Conroy, 8 Nov. 1944; Conroy to Jackson, 27 Dec. 1944 (Conroy drew up the statement); UE press release, 2 Jan. 1945.
29 CLC, minutes of PAC meeting, 16 Nov. 1944, p. 3.
30 CLC, minutes of PAC meeting, 16 Jan. 1945, 2; Millard to Conroy, 22 Jan. 1945; Burt to Andras, 20 Feb. 1945; Mosher to Conroy, 22 Jan. 1945.
31 G. Horowitz, *Canadian Labour in Politics* (Toronto, 1963), 99-105; CLC, PAC organization report by Park, 3 March 1945; CCF, Lewis to Robinson, 12 Dec. 1944; Robinson to Lewis, 27 Dec. 1944.
32 CLC, PAC report, Jan. 1946; Conroy to Andras, 3 Jan. 1946; Millard to Mosher, 23 Jan. 1946; Mosher to Millard, 29 Jan. 1946.
33 Proceedings, CCL convention, 23-29 Sept. 1946, 70-81.
34 CLC, Conroy to Millard, 6 Aug. 1943.
35 Proceedings, CCL convention, 1942, financial statement, 60-73.
36 CLC, proceedings of the commission to investigate into the affairs of affiliated and chartered locals and the Vancouver Labour Council, 18 Jan: 1943.
37 *Vancouver Sun*, 30 Dec. 1942. – 6 Jan. 1943; CLC, Stephen to Mosher, 6 Jan. 1943.
38 CLC, Mosher to MacAuslane, 3 Jan. 1943; memorandum re Congress constitution to Gowling, Mactavish, and Watt, 4 Jan. 1943; Gowling to Dowd, 8 Jan. 1943; Mosher to MacAuslane, 3 Jan. 1943; CLC executive committee, 8 Jan. 1943.
39 CLC, T.G. Mackenzie to Conroy and McGuire, 18 Jan. 1943.
40 CLC, bulletin 4, Shop Stewards' Committee, 3 March 1943; Conroy and McGuire to manager of Royal Bank of Canada, Main and Hastings, 25 Jan. 1943.
41 USW, Nemetz to Millard, 18 Oct. 1943; CLC, O'Brien to Mosher, 9 Oct. 1943; Mosher to O'Brien, 13 Oct. 1943; 21 Oct. 1943.
42 CLC, O'Brien to Mosher, 2 Nov. 1943; Millard to Conroy, 28 Oct. 1943; O'Brien to Mosher, 2 Nov. 1943; CCF, Gargrave to Lewis, 11 Nov. 1943.
43 CLC, Mosher to O'Brien, 16 Nov. 1943; BCFL, minutes of BC Shipyard Federation, 15-16 Jan. 1944.

Chapter 6

1 For histories of Mine-Mill see: M. Wright, *It Takes More Than Guns: A Brief History of the IUMMSW* (Denver, 1944); R. Carlin, *I Know Mine Mill: Do You?* (Toronto, 1961); V. Jensen, *Heritage of Conflict* (Ithaca, 1950); V. Jensen, *Non-Ferrous Metal Mining Unionism* (Ithaca, 1954).
2 Mine-Mill, J.B. Munroe to Robinson, 23 June 1937; Munroe to Sherwood, 19 June 1937; Munroe to Robinson, 9 July 1937; Robinson to Munroe, 28 June 1937; Bob Carlin. See also W.J. McAndrew, Gold Mining Trade Unions and Politics: Ontario – the 1930's, MA thesis, University of British Columbia, 1969.

3 CLC Archives executive committee, CCL, 31 March – 3 April 1941; Lewis to Dowd, 27 April 1941; Robinson to Mosher, 5 May 1941.

4 CLC, Conroy to Dowd, 18 Nov. 1940; executive committee, CCL, 20-22 Oct. 1941; Conroy to Mosher, 11 Oct. 1941; Conroy to Haywood, 24 Oct. 1941; Dowd to Lewis, 15 Nov. 1941.

5 CCF, Coldwell to King, 27 Nov. 1941; CLC, Conroy to King, 15 Dec. 1941, 30 Dec. 1941, 13 Jan 1942; Simpson (president, Local 240 MMSW) to King, 29 Nov. 1941; CCF, King to Coldwell, 16 Dec. 1941; CCL King to Simpson, 6 Dec. 1941; King to Conroy, 8 Jan. 1942; *Northern News*, Kirkland Lake, 19 Dec. 1941.

6 CCF, Park to Lewis, 30 Dec. 1941; press release by mine-operators, 29 Dec. 1941; Kirkland Lake strike committee bulletin, 15 Feb. 1942; local 240 to friends, "Remember Kirkland Lake," 16 Feb. 1942.

7 Carlin; *Sudbury Star*, 25 Feb. 1942; CLC, leaflet entitled "Murder Will Out" issued by rank-and-file Sudbury miners.

8 CLC, Emerson to Conroy, 4 March 1942; CCL, executive committee, 27 Feb. 1942; CLC, Conroy to Haywood, 5 March 1942.

9 CLC, Carlin to Conroy, 16 Dec. 1943, 28 Dec. 1943. CCF, Kidd to Lewis, 14 April 1944.

10 Jensen, *Non-Ferrous Metal Mining Unionism*, 51-108; Robinson himself was probably not a Communist; CLC, Conroy to Carlin, 19 July 1943; Conroy to Carlin, 19 Jan. 1944; Carlin to Conroy, 26 Jan. 1944.

11 CLC, Ralph Carlin to Conroy, 30 March 1944; CCF, Kidd to Lewis, 14 April 1944; USW, Conroy to Millard, 4 April 1944; CLC, Millard to Conroy, 11 April 1944.

12 Jensen, *Non-Ferrous Metal Mining Unionism*, the vote was usually 6-6 or 7-5; Carlin; USW, Millard to Conroy, 15 Dec. 1945. CLC, Carlin to Conroy, 30 Aug. 1944.

13 Proceedings IUMMSW 1946 convention, 408-25; CLC, CIO report to Phillip Murray by committee appointed to investigate the break within the IUMMSW, 16-17 May

1947; Jensen, *Non-Ferrous Metal Mining Unionism*, 200-9.

14 Carlin.

15 USW, Millard to Conroy, 22 Jan. 1946.

16 CCF, Ames to Lewis, 13 Dec. 1946; 14 April 1947; USW, Millard to Bittner, 20 March 1947; Millard to Appelbe (USW representative), 20 Mar. 1947; CLC, Ralph Carlin to Conroy, 29 July 1947.

17 CLC, Harry Rushton (secretary Local 240) to Travis, 29 Sept. 1947; Travis to Rushton, 23 Oct. 1947; Ralph Carlin to Dowd, 24 Oct. 1947.

18 USW, Ralph Carlin to Millard, 19 Oct. 1947; Millard to Ralph Carlin, 23 Oct. 1947.

19 *Timmins Press*, 9 Dec. 1947; CLC, Ralph Carlin to Conroy, 9 Dec. 1947; Conroy to Ralph Carlin, 22 Dec. 1947.

20 CLC, Ralph Carlin to Conroy, 11 March 1948.

21 CLC, Conroy to Millard, 8 Jan. 1948; Conroy to Coldwell, 19 Dec. 1947; CCF, Kidd to Lewis, 18 Jan. 1948; Millard to Lewis, 2 Jan. 1948.

22 CLC, Rhodes to Conroy, 11 Feb. 1948; J. Shedden to Conroy, 2 Feb. 1948.

23 *Globe and Mail*, 17 and 23 Feb. 1948.

24 CLC, Clark to Mosher, 25 Feb. 1948; e.g. Clark to Murray, 26 Feb. 1948;Murray to Clark, 27 Feb. 1948, to Conroy, 27 Feb. 1948; Buckmaster to Mosher, 1 March 1948; Rosenblum to Mosher, 2 March 1948; Fadling to Mosher, 1 March 1948.

25 CLC, executive council CCL, 3-4 Mar. 1948.

26 CLC, Robinson and Carlin to Mosher, 3 March 1948, to Murray, 3 Mar. 1948; Conroy to Murray, 9 Mar. 1948.

27 CLC, e.g. Fadling (IWA) to Conroy, 17 March 1948; Matles (UE) to Conroy, 20 March 1948; USW, Murray to Millard, 18 March 1948; CLC, Ralph Carlin to Conroy, 11 Mar. 1948; e.g. local 695 to Conroy, 15 Mar. 1948; *Sudbury Star*, 12 Mar. 1948.

28 CLC, Memo from M.M. Maclean (Department of Labour) to Conroy, 28 March 1948.

29 CCF, Jolliffe to Coldwell, 2 April 1948; CLC,

MacLean to Conroy, 2 April 1948; Conroy to Clark, 2 April 1948. *Timmins Daily Press* 13 March 1948.

30 USW, B. Sefton to Conroy, 28 April 1948; CLC, J. Russell to Conroy, 4 April 1948; Conroy to Russell, 6 April 1948.

31 CLC, Ralph Carlin to Conroy, 13 April 1948; Clark to Local 241 officers, 17 April 1948; Ralph Carlin to Mosher, 25 April 1948. Ralph Carlin admitted that the members had "got out of hand" because of their "confusion, bitterness and disappointment."

32 CLC, Clark to Mosher, 8 May 1948; Mosher to Clark, 11 May 1948.

33 CLC, Dowd to Clark, 8 June 1948; Clark to Dowd, 27 June 1948; Ralph Carlin to Conroy, 20 June 1948; Barrett to Ralph Carlin, 17 June 1948; Conroy to all Congress affiliates, 8 July 1948.

34 USW, Millard to Carlin, 12 April 1948; CCF, memorandum on Carlin and other members of the Sudbury CCF, 23 July 1948; Morden Lazarus (secretary Ontario CCF) to Carlin, 8 April 1948, quoted in *The Case for Sudbury*, distributed by the "Elect Carlin Committee," 1948.

35 USW, Millard to Carlin, 12 April 1948; Millard to Conroy, 13 April 1948.

36 CCF, Brewin to Johnson (president Ontario CCF), 28 April 1948; memorandum on Carlin ... ; *Case for Sudbury*, 14-17.

37 USW, Millard to Mosher, 29 July 1948; CLC, Mosher to Millard, 30 July 1948, 9 Aug. 1948.

38 CLC, Mosher to McGuire to Conroy, 10 Aug. 1948; Clark to Dowd, 20 Aug. 1948; memo, Clark to Wright, 29 July 1948; Wright to Clark, 30 July 1948; Carlin to Mosher, 18 Aug. 1948.

39 The *Union*, 30 Aug. 1948; USW, Millard to McDonald, 26 Aug. 1948.

40 BCFL, e.g. Carlin to Pritchett, 30 Aug. 1948; Moffitt (president BC district) to officers and delegates of BCFL, 2 Sept. 1948.

41 CLC, Mosher to Carlin, 1 Sept. 1948; Doherty to Conroy, 2 Sept. 1948; Mosher to Doherty, 10 Sept. 1948.

42 USW, Millard to MacDonald, 26 Aug. 1948; CLC, Vachon (Timmins) to Conroy, 11 Oct. 1948; Shedden (Port Colborne) to Conroy, 23 Sept. 1948; B. Sefton to Mosher, 30 Aug. 1948; Millard to Conroy, 10 Feb. 1948; Sefton to Mosher, 30 Aug. 1948, Mosher to Sefton, 1 Sept. 1948.

43 CLC, Clark to Conroy, 22 Sept. 1948; Clark to Shedden, 22 Sept. 1948. Mine-Mill – CCL conference, 27 Sept. 1948.

44 Proceedings CCL convention, 1948, 13-16.

45 CLC, executive committee CCL, 16 Oct. 1948. CLC, Conroy to Clark, 28 Oct. 1948; Conroy to all CCL executive members, 5 Nov. 1948; Mosher and Conroy to Clark, 2 Nov. 1948; Mosher to Shedden, 28 Oct. 1948.

46 CLC, *District Roundup*, district 8, MMSW, 5 Nov. 1948, 1; Conroy to Shedden, 25 Oct. 1948; Shedden to Conroy, 27 Oct. 1948; Mosher to Shedden, 28 Oct. 1948; USW, Sefton to Conroy, 28 Dec. 1948.

47 CLC, Carlin to Conroy, 5 Nov. 1948, 6 Nov. 1948; Conroy to Carlin, 9 Nov. 1948; Burt to Conroy, 9 Nov. 1948; Conroy to Burt, 11 Nov. 1948.

48 Only the Mine-Mill local in Port Colborne had been granted a Congress charter. Persistent requests from Mine-Mill locals in the Ottawa Valley, Niagara Falls, Timmins, and British Columbia, had been turned down with the advice that they stay in their union and "clear up the conditions which caused them to rebel". CLC, Conroy to Ralph Carlin, 9 Nov. 1948; Conroy to Burt, 11 Nov. 1948.

49 CLC, executive council CCL, 14 Dec. 1948; Conroy to Clark, 22 Dec. 1948.

50 CLC, Clark to Murray, 30 Dec. 1948; Clark to Conroy, 30 Dec. 1948.

51 USW, Sefton to Conroy, 28 Dec. 1948; CLC, LeBlanc (president, Local 241 Timmins) to Mosher, 31 Dec. 1948.

52 CLC, executive council CCL, 11 Jan. 1949; Mosher to Carlin, 14 Jan. 1949; USW, press release USW, 13 Jan. 1949; *Timmins Press,* 15 Jan. 1949; USW, Sefton to Millard, 18 Jan. 1949.

53 *Welland-Port Colborne Evening Tribune*, 15 Jan. 1949.
54 USW, Millard to Conroy, 24 Jan. 1949; CLC, Conroy to all affiliates, 7 Feb. 1949; Mosher and Conroy to CCL executive, 14 Feb. 1949.
55 CLC, *A Report: The Case For Mine-Mill*, Bob Carlin, 18 Feb. 1949, 3-8; radio script, Bob Carlin over station CKGB, 26 Feb. 1949; USW, Behie to Millard, 1 March 1949.
56 CLC, executive council CCL, 24 March 1949; Dowd to Carlin, 30 March 1949.
57 USW, Millard to Conroy, 4 May 1949; CLC, Conroy to Ralph Carlin, 25 May 1949.
58 CLC, Bob Carlin to fellow trade unionists, 5 Oct. 1949; USW, Millard to CIO committee investigating activities of the IUMMSW, 16 Dec. 1949, 8; Clark to officers of CCL and delegates to the convention, 27 Sept. 1949; USW, Millard to CIO committee ... [on] IUMMSW, 8.
59 USW, Millard to Hague, 16 Dec. 1950; Millard to MacDonald, 13 April 1950; as well, Barrett continued to snipe against Steel, and in 1950, sent a telegram to Harvey Murphy in Trail opposing "the method which Steel has taken in regard to raiding lead and rock miners." CCL, Barrett to Murphy, 1 March 1950.
60 CLC, Conroy to Millard, 6 Oct. 1950; Both Steel and the Congress charged that Mine-Mill was favoured by the large corporations – INCO and COMINCO – because it was a weaker union than Steel.
61 CLC, report of CIO committee investigating activities of IUMMSW, 15 Feb. 1950; Carlin; Salsberg.
62 CLC, CIO investigating committee ... [on] IUMMSW, 16.

Chapter 7

1 Salsberg; Tom McEwen.
2 Pritchett; IWA, Proceedings of first general convention of Federation of Woodworkers, 18-20 Sept. 1936, 34-6.
3 IWA, Federation of Woodworkers, report of second semi-annual convention, 20-22 Feb. 1937, 6; V. Jensen, *Lumber and Labor* (New York), 1945, 200-5.
4 *Timberworker*, 9 July 1937; IWA, Proceedings of special convention of the Federation of Woodworkers, 15 July 1937.
5 *Timberworker*, 19 Oct. 1940.
6 Paul Phillips, *No Power Greater*, (Vancouver 1967), 105-15. IWA, Proceedings 1939 Convention, p. 6; Proceedings, emergency conference, IWA, BC district, 1 Nov. 1942, 10-11; District 1, 1944 convention, 18.
7 CLC, Conroy to Haywood, 20 Sept. 1943; Conroy to Lowery (IWA president), 20 Sept. 1943; USW, Millard to Conroy, 27 Oct. 1944; CLC, memo, Conroy to Mosher, 29 Jan. 1945; UPWA, Tallman to Dowling, 17 Aug. 1945.
8 Phillips, *No Power Greater*, 131; BCFL, O'-Brien, Pritchett, and MacLeod to all CCL locals in BC, 5 Sept. 1944.
9 CLC, O'Brien to Mosher, 9 Jan. 1945; CCF, F.J. McKenzie to Lewis, 15 March 1945; McKenzie to Lewis, 29 March 1945; Lewis to McKenzie, 22 March 1945.
10 CLC, MacAuslane to Conroy, 2 June 1947; UPWA, Tallman to Dowling, 17 Aug. 1945; USW, Park to Mahoney, 15 Nov. 1947; CLC, Tallman to Conroy, 23 Jan. 1947; Conroy to Tallman, 27 Jan. 1947.
11 USW, Park to Millard, 18 Feb. 1947; CLC, Mahoney to Conroy, 14 June 1948; Millard.
12 CLC, Conroy to Mahoney, 13 Nov. 1947; USW, Millard to Baskin, 1 Nov. 1937; Park to Mahoney, 17 Nov. 1947.
13 *B.C. Lumber Worker*, 20 Oct. 1947; IWA, Mosher to Pritchett, 20 Oct. 1947; CLC, Mosher and Conroy to E.J. Melsness (secretary District 1), 13 Nov. 1947; Dalskog to Mosher and Conroy, 17 Nov. 1947; Conroy to Radford, 12 Dec. 1947; Dowd to Pritchett, 9 Dec. 1947.
14 CLC, Radford to Conroy, 3 Dec. 1947; IWA, *Information,* Nov. 1947.
15 CLC, Mahoney to Conroy, 4 Dec. 1947.
16 CLC, Radford to Conroy 7, 16, 28 Jan. 1948.

17 USW, Millard to Conroy, 22 May 1945; IWA, Proceedings BC district convention, 6-7 Jan. 1945, 74-5.

18 *Ibid.*, 3-5 Jan. 1948, 22-108; *Vancouver Sun*, 5 Jan. 1948.

19 *B.C. Lumber Worker*, 28 Jan. 1948; CLC, Radford to Conroy, 28 Jan. 1948; USW, Mahoney to Conroy, 16 Jan. 1947.

20 USW, Mahoney to Conroy, 3 Jan. 1948; CLC, Conroy to Mahoney, 9 Jan. 1948; Conroy to Radford, 31 Jan. 1948.

21 CLC, Radford to Conroy, 22 Jan. 1948; Conroy to Radford, 10 Feb. 1948; Mahoney to Conroy, 26 Feb. 1948; USW, Mahoney to Cotterill, 13 Feb. 1948.

22 CLC, Conroy to Radford, 25 Feb. 1948; USW, Mahoney to Conroy, 25 March 1948.

23 CLC, Conroy to Mahoney, 2 March 1948; *B.C. Lumber Worker*, 24 March 1948 (in one local, the "White Bloc" received only 4 of the 267 votes cast; CLC, Radford to Conroy, 17 March 1948.

24 CLC, verbatim excerpts from a speech by Harvey Murphy, 8 April 1948; USW, statement by Mahoney to Labour Lobby conference, 9 April 1948; minutes, legislative action committee (Lobby), 8-9 April 1948, 2; *Vancouver Sun*, 9 April 1948.

25 CLC, Mahoney to Conroy, 9 April 1948.

26 USW, Mahoney to Cotterill, 10 April 1948; Mahoney to Cotterill, 13 April 1948; CLC, Mahoney to Conroy, 13 April 1948.

27 USW, Conroy to Mahoney, 14 April 1948; Mahoney to Conroy, 17 April 1948; CLC, Conroy to Mahoney, 22 April 1948.

28 USW, Mahoney to Mosher and members of executive council, 16 April 1948; CLC, Mahoney to Mosher, 5 May 1948.

29 CLC, report of trial committee re: charges against Pritchett and Murphy.

30 CLC, Mahoney to Conroy, 3 July 1948; Mosher to Pritchett and Murphy, 25 Aug. 1948.

31 BCFL, minutes BCFL executive council, 28 Aug. 1948; USW, Mahoney to Conroy, 2 June 1948; BCFL, executive council BCFL, 12 June 1948; CLC, Conroy to Mahoney, 29 June 1948; USW, Mahoney to Conroy, 2 July 1948.

32 USW, Mahoney to Conroy, 27 July 1948; CLC, Mahoney to Mosher, 26 Aug. 1948; Mosher to Mahoney, 27 Aug. 1948.

33 USW, Mahoney to Conroy, 26 Aug. 1948; CLC, Mosher to Mahoney, 27 Aug. 1948.

34 USW, e.g. Mahoney to Conroy, 16 and 26 Aug. 1948; Mahoney to Millard, 30 Aug. 1948; Mosher to Mahoney, 27 Aug. 1948; CLC, Mahoney to Mosher, 30 Aug. 1948; Dowd to Mahoney, 1 Sept. 1948.

35 USW, Mahoney to Conroy, 7 Sept. 1948; CLC, O'Brien to all locals of IUMMSW in BC, 30 Aug. 1948.

36 BCFL, Proceedings fifth annual convention BCFL, 4-5 Sept. 1948, 9-141.

37 USW, Mahoney to Park, 9 Sept. 1948; CLC, Mahoney to Conroy, 7 Sept. 1948.

38 USW, Mahoney to Tallman, 9 Sept. 1948.

39 USW, Mahoney to Conroy, 7 Sept. 1948; Mahoney to Cameron, 8 Sept. 1948.

40 USW, Conroy to Mahoney, 11 Sept. 1948; CLC, Mahoney to Conroy, 7 Sept. 1948.

41 LRB, report and financial statements for the period ending Dec. 14, 1946 and Dec. 13, 1947, BC District 1, by Riddell, Stead, Graham and Hutchison, 12 May 1948; USW, Mahoney to Conroy 24 June 1948.

42 LRB, auditors report, 4-7; Pritchett; Emil Bjarnson (whose Trade Union Research Bureau did much of the union's auditing claims that the missing invoices were inadvertently destroyed); Nigel Morgan confirms that none of the district officers had much "bookkeeping experience" and therefore did not realize that invoices had to be kept).

43 USW, Mahoney to Millard, 2 July 1948; Mahoney to Conroy, 25 June 1948; IWA, resolutions re organization policy from BC districts 1 and 2; USW, Mahoney to Millard, 2 July 1948.

44 CLC, Mahoney to Conroy, 2 July 1948.

45 *B.C. Lumber Worker*, 30 June 1948; IWA, Dalskog to Carl Winn (IWA secretary-treasurer), 10 July 1948; CLC, Mahoney to Conroy, 2 July 1948.

46 CLC, Dalskog to Conroy, 12 July 1948; USW, Mahoney to Conroy, 15 July 1948; CLC, Dalskog to Conroy, 29 July 1948.

47 USW, Mahoney to Conroy, 13 July 1948; IWA, brief presented by Local 357 IWA, 15 July 1948; USW, Mahoney to Conroy, 13 July 1948.

48 CLC, Chappell to Conroy, 19 July 1948; IWA, international executive board, investigating committee report, 6 Oct. 1948, 2.

49 USW, Mahoney to Chappel, 4 Nov. 1948. Chappell complained to Mahoney and Conroy that he was not consulted about the report and that it was therefore not as "strong" as it should have been. CLC, Chappell to Conroy, 6 Nov. 1948; USW, Chappell to Mahoney, 27 Oct. 1948.

50 B.C. Lumber Worker, 21 July 1948.

51 USW, Mahoney to Conroy, 16 Aug. 1948; Fadling to Conroy, 26 Aug. 1948.

52 CLC, Conroy to Mahoney, 27 Aug. 1948; USW, Mahoney to Conroy, 30 Aug. 1948; Conroy to Mahoney, 11 Sept. 1948.

53 B.C. Lumber Worker, 15 Sept. 1948; USW, Mahoney to Conroy, 15 Sept. 1948; Mahoney to Fadling, 12 Sept. 1948.

54 Mahoney to Conroy, 20 Sept. 1948.

55 CLC, Dalskog to Conroy, 1 Sept. 1948; USW, Mahoney to Conroy, 2 Sept. 1948; CLC, Mosher to Dalskog, 8 Sept. 1948; IWA, Dalskog to all CCL unions in BC, 13 Sept. 1948.

56 USW, Mahoney to Mosher, 15 Sept. 1948; Fadling to Mahoney, 19 Sept. 1948; CLC, Mahoney to Conroy, 20 Sept. 1948.

57 USW, Mahoney to Conroy, 17 Sept. 1948; radio script, Mahoney, 20 Sept. 1948; CLC, Mahoney to Conroy, 27 Sept. Morgan; Murphy. Voice of the IWA. 24 Sept. 1948.

58 Pritchett; Morgan; Bjarnson; McEwen.

59 CLC, Mahoney to Conroy, 6 Oct. 1948; Vancouver Sun, 30 Sept., 1-4 Oct. 1948.

60 Alsbury; Salsberg; Pritchett; Radford; Morgan; Murphy.

61 B.C. Lumber Worker, 6 Oct. 1948.

62 Vancouver News Herald, 4-7 Oct. 1948.

63 CLC, Dalskog to Conroy, 8 Oct. 1948; Vancouver Sun, 15-20 Oct. 1948.

64 CLC, Mahoney to Conroy, 26 Oct. and 5 Nov. 1948; Conroy to Mahoney, 6 Nov. 1948.

65 CLC, Mahoney to Conroy, 26 Oct. 1948; USW, Mahoney to Conroy, 17 Jan. 1949; Conroy to Mahoney, 24 Feb. 1949; Mahoney to Conroy, 1 March 1949; CLC, Claude Ballard (IWA assistant director of organization) to Harvey Ladd (IWA rep. in eastern Canada), 28 Jan. 1949.

66 IWA, minutes Local 1-71, 1 Oct. 1948; cheque 4361 endorsed to Mine-Mill strike fund; minutes Local 1-71, $9,000; Local 1-217, $4,500; Local 1-80, $14,524.30; District Council, $400.00; Murphy.

67 CLC, Hartung to Murphy, 30 Oct. 1948; Murphy to Hartung, 1 Nov. 1948; Clark to Mosher, 6 Dec. 1948; Hartung to Murphy, 5 Nov. 1948; Murphy to Hartung, 12 Nov. 1948; USW, Murray to Germer, 8 March 1949.

68 CLC, digest of evidence re charges that CIO affiliates have aided and abetted the secession movement against IWA in BC, March 1949; USW, Mahoney to Germer, 22 March 1949.

69 CLC, Digest of Evidence; findings of the commission, May 1949.

70 BCFL, O'Brien to members of BCFL, 6 Nov. 1948.

71 Quoted in Western Canadian Lumber Worker, Sept. 1962.

72 B.C. Lumber Worker, 30 Sept. 1948.

73 Canadian Tribune, Sept. 1948.

Chapter 8

1 Salsberg (who claims that he was consulted on most of the UE's important decisions); Hunter.

2 Jackson; UE, notes for opening speech 25th annual convention UE, Jackson, 1962.

3 Salsberg. Harris is an admitted member of the Communist Party. Jackson is not, though he is closely associated with the party.

4 Even twenty years later, Jackson still maintained that the "phony war took on an entirely new meaning with the invasion of the

Soviet Union by the Hitler Nazis." Notes, Jackson, 1962, 1.

5 *The Detonator* (UE Local 521), 12 Feb. 1943; UE *Policy in Progress*, Jackson, 31 Jan. 1943, 10-11.

6 CLC, Jackson to executive council, 24 Feb. 1942; to Dowd, 6 March 1942, to Mosher, 15 Mar. 1942.

7 CLC, *Backstage at Windsor*, labour correspondent cooperative press association, 1946, 1-2.

8 UAW, R.J. Thomas collection, executive board meeting UAW, 10-11 Sept. 1945; Burt's position was that "the only way to do a job with the Ford Company" was to have everyone come out on strike.

9 CLC, special executive council CCL, 26 Sept. 1945.

10 Millard; Schultz; the Congress felt that the UAW should have waited until Ford rejected the decision, thus giving the union a tactical victory with the government and the public; instead, Roy England, Local 200 president, dramatically tore the decision to shreds in front of newspaper photographers.

11 UAW, Special Ford Strike Bulletin: report of the deliberations of the special conference between officials of the Ford Motor Company of Canada, officials of the UAW-CIO, and representatives of the federal and provincial governments, 15-17 Oct. 1945.

12 UAW, Thomas collection, executive board meeting UAW, 26, 28, 1945.

13 Leslie Morris, LPP, *The Big Ford Strike*, Jan. 1946, 3; USW, Millard to Murray, 20 Nov. 1945.

14 USW, Millard to Mosher, 21 Nov. 1945, to Murray 2 Nov. 1945; *Canadian Tribune* 5 Jan. 1946.

15 Horowitz, *Canadian Labour in Politics* (Toronto 1968), 110-15.

16 Quoted in D. Moulton, *The Ford Strike*, Thesis, Glendon College, 1972, 5.

17 Salsberg; CLC, Millard to Conroy, 31 Dec. 1945; CCF, Park to Lewis, 9 Feb. 1946.

18 USW, Millard to Burt, 3 Dec. 1945; Millard to Conroy, 31 Dec. 1945; Millard to Mosher, 21 Nov. 1945.

19 CLC, executive council CCL, 13-14 Feb. 1946.

20 USW, Millard to Murray, 16 Feb. 1946; CLC, executive-council CCL, 12 June 1946; Jackson to executive council, 12 June 1946.

21 CLC, Jackson to Mosher, 27 Dec. 1945; Mosher to Forsey, 3 Jan. 1946; Forsey to Mosher, 3 Jan. 1946.

22 CLC, Jackson to Conroy, 1 April 1946; executive council CCL, 7 April 1946; Congress circular letter, 10 April 1946.

23 CLC, Jackson to Conroy, 3 Nov. 1947; Murray to Conroy, 11 July 1947; Conroy to Jackson, 30 July 1947.

24 CLC, Rhodes to Mosher, 25 Nov. 1948; Mosher to Jackson, 26 Nov. 1948; UE, *Canadian News*, 3 Dec. 1948; Rhodes to Conroy, 7 Dec. 1948.

25 CLC, E.R. Evans (CCL representative) to Conroy, 6 Dec. 1948; Conroy to Rhodes, 10 Dec. 1948.

26 CLC, executive committee CCL, 13 Dec. 1948; Dowd to Jackson, 15 Dec. 1948; UE, district 5 statement re Sovereign Potteries, 1-3.

27 *Welland-Port Colbourne Tribune*, 31 Jan. 1949. The decision to withdraw had been made at a Council meeting, on the grounds that the WFTU was a "Communist organization."

28 OFL proceedings, 18, 19 Feb. 1947; UE *News*, 25 Feb. and 4 March 1949.

29 CLC, Cleve Kidd (OFL secretary) to Mosher, 15 March 1949.

30 CLC, minutes of executive committee, 23 March 1949; council, 24 March 1949; CLC, CCL press release, 15 April 1949.

31 UE, Jackson to all UE locals, 6 April 1949; CCL, investigating committee hearing, 14 April 1949; UE, *Welfare of the Congress*, 14 April 1949.

32 CLC, report of investigating committee, 11 May 1949; UE, district council meeting, 30 April – 1 May 1949.

33 CLC, MacGuire to Conroy, 13 May 1949.

34 Dowd; Dowling; UE, Jackson to UE staff, 5 July 1949; CLC, executive committee 4 July 1949; executive council, 5 July 1949; UE, Jackson to all UE locals, 6 July 1949.

35 UE, Jackson to UE staff and business agents, 5 July 1949.

36 CLC, Jackson to Conroy, 6 July 1949; UE, Statement re suspension of UE officers, 6 July 1949; UE News, 8 July 1949; CLC, Conroy to Jackson, 8 July 1949.

37 UE News, 29 July 1949; UE, Harris to all local national and international unions, 11 Aug. 1949; CLC, Burt to all local unions, 16 Aug. 1949.

38 UE, report of district 5 officers, 1949. minutes annual district council meeting district 5, 19-20 Sept. 1949.

39 CIO News, 7 Nov. 1949.

40 CLC, Haywood to Conroy, 15 Nov. 1949; Conroy to Mosher, 8 Nov. 1949; Morton to Mosher, 12 Nov. 1948.

41 UE News, 18 Nov. 1949; CLC, Jackson to Conroy, 14 Nov. 1949; Kidd to Mosher, 23 Nov. 1949; Conroy to Rhodes, 8 Nov. 1949.

42 CLC, Mosher to Jackson, 18 Feb. 1949; Rhodes to Mosher, Millard to Mosher, Barrett to Mosher, all 18 Nov. 1949; UPW, e.g. Mosher to Dowling, 16 Nov. 1949.

43 CLC, e.g. McGuire to Mosher, 22 Nov. 1949; Chappell to Mosher, 18 Nov. 1949; Barrett to Mosher, 18 Nov. 1949; USW, Millard to Mosher, 18 Nov. 1949.

44 CLC, MacAuslane to Mosher, 21 Nov. 1949; Burt to Mosher, 22 Nov. 1949.

45 CLC, Rhodes to Mosher, 21 Nov. 1949; Mosher to Rhodes, 25 Nov. 1949; UE News, 18 Nov. 1949.

46 Dowd; during this entire episode, Conroy was in Europe attending a meeting of the ICFTU.

47 CLC, Mosher to members of the executive council, 1 Dec. 1949.

48 Jackson; CLC, Jackson to Mosher, 2 Dec. 1949.

49 CLC, Dowd to Jack Williams, Dec. 2 1949; O'Donnell (IUE representative) to Dowd, 5 Dec. 1949; Mosher to Jackson, 5 Dec. 1949; Emspak to Conroy, 2 Dec. 1949; Dowd to Emspak, 5 Dec. 1949.

50 CLC, Press Release, 5 Dec. 1949; CCL executive committee meeting, 18 Jan. 1950.

51 CLC, MacAuslane to Dowd, 8 Dec. 1949; Burt to Mosher, 6 Dec. 1949.

52 CLC, Mosher to Burt, 8 Dec. 1949.

53 CLC, Jackson to Mosher, 7 Dec. 1949 (The relevant parts of the constitution were article 2, section 9, and article 11, section 2); Mosher to Jackson, 9 Dec. 1949.

54 CLC, Jackson to Mosher, 10 Jan. 1950; Mosher to Jackson, 11 Jan. 1950; UE, district executive board to Mosher, 6 Jan. 1950.

55 CLC, executive committee, 18 Jan. 1950.

56 CLC, executive committee, 4 July, 20-22 Sept. 1950.

57 CLC, 6 UE appeal, 25 Sept. 1950.

58 E.g. Peterborough Examiner, 27 Sept. 1950, called for UE members to overthrow its Communist leadership; Ensign (a Catholic diocesan paper), 14 Jan. 1950.

59 CLC, Jolliffe and Lewis: memorandum on IUE campaign in Canada 3 Nov. 1949 to 30 April 1950, 2 May 1950.

60 USW, Millard to Carey, 21 Feb. 1952; CLC, T.J. Fitzpatrick (IUE representative) to Joe Mackenzie, 28 Nov. 1950; CLC, Donald MacDonald to Carey, 24 Jan. 1952.

61 Winnipeg Tribune, 13 March 1951; CLC, Borgford to Conroy, 14 March 1951; Mosher to Conroy, and Conroy to Mosher, 16 March 1951.

62 CLC, executive committee CCL, 9 April 1951; Mosher and Conroy to Haddow, 13 April 1951; Dowd to Ben Gold, 13 April 1951.

63 CLC, appeal of IFLWU, 17 Sept. 1951.

64 Millard, Dowling, and two others who prefer not to be named, who were all in the forefront in expelling the left-wing affiliates, today regret their haste.

65 CLC, Burt to Conroy, 15 Dec. 1946. Burt.

66 CLC, Mosher to Burt, 30 Oct. 1941; USW, Millard to Burt, 3 Feb. 1942; Mosher to Thomas, 7 Jan. 1942.

67 CCF, Lewis to Jolliffe, 9 March 1944.

68 USW, Millard to Burt, 3 Dec. 1945.

69 CLC, Mosher to Chappell, 9 Nov. 1947.

70 CLC, Millard to Conroy, 25 Nov. 1949; e.g. Conroy to Reuther, 18 Feb. 1948; Reuther to Conroy, 21 Sept. 1948. Burt.

71 CLC, Conroy to Reuther, 29 Oct. 1948; to Burt, 29 Oct. 1948.

72 USW, Conroy to Millard, 29 Oct. 1948; *Ford Facts*, 21 Oct. 1948; CLC, Millard to Conroy, 2 Nov. 1948.

73 CLC, Conroy to Burt, 16 Nov. 1950; *Canadian Tribune*, 13 Nov. 1950. *United Automobile Worker*, Canadian ed. Oct. 1951. Burt.

Chapter 9

1 *Canadian Unionist*, 19 Oct. 1940, 15; *ibid.*, 1941 Jan. 18-19; USW, SWOC Canadian region policy conference, 20 April 1941.

2 CLC, Dowd to Haywood, 14 Nov. 1940; Mosher to Burt, 12 Nov. 1940; Mosher to Haywood, 20 Dec. 1940; Mosher to Millard, 13 Dec. 1940; Mosher to Conroy and to Millard, Dec. 13 1940.

3 CLC, Mosher to Murray, 17 Jan. 1941.

4 CLC, Mosher to Murray, 21 Jan. 1941. In a letter to Len DeCaux, editor of the *CIO News*, Dowd asked that references to the Congress in CIO publications be kept at a minimum since "these indicate a closer connection between the Congress and ... the CIO than actually exists." 25 Nov. 1940.

5 CLC, Haywood to Mosher, 19 Feb. 1941.

6 CLC, Mosher to Haywood, 1 March 1941.

7 CLC, Haywood to Mosher, 10 March 1941.

8 Proceedings, CCL convention, 1941, 9-10, 57-81.

9 USW, Millard to MacDonald, 7 Nov. 1941; Salsberg.

10 USW, Millard to Clowes, 27 June 1941; CLC, Mosher to Conroy, 12 Dec. 1940; Dowd to Conroy, 20 Dec. 1940; Conroy to Dowd, 18 Dec. 1940.

11 CLC, Mosher to Millard, 21 March 1941; Dowd to Mosher, and Mosher to Dowd, 25 Feb. 1941.

12 CLC, Millard to Mosher, 14 May 1941; to Dowd, 20 June 1941, to Mosher, 30 Oct. 1941; Dowd to Mosher, 26 Sept. 1941.

13 CLC, Conroy to Dowd, 29 Oct. 1941, to Haywood, 24 Oct. 1941; 29 Oct. 1941; Haywood to Conroy, 29 Dec. 1941.

14 CLC, Conroy to Haywood, 2 Jan. 1942, to Millard, 3 Jan. 1942.

15 CLC, Millard, Spivak, and Conroy to Haywood, 7 Jan. 1942; J.R. Bell (CIO comptroller) to Conroy, 21 Jan. 1942; Conroy to Bell, 23 Jan. 1942; Carey to Conroy, 15 Mar. 1942.

16 CLC, Conroy to Haywood, 6 Jan. 1942, April 21 1942; Conroy to Haywood, 30 May 1942.

17 CLC, Mitchell to Conroy, 18 June 1942; Burt to Conroy, 29 June 1942, to Mitchell, 24 June 1942; Conroy to Millard, 30 June 1942; Burt to Conroy, 20 June 1942; Conroy to Burt, 22 July 1942.

18 CLC, Mosher to Murray, 21 Oct. 1942.

19 CLC, Conroy to Jackson, 17 Nov. 1942; Conroy to Burt and Millard, 21 Oct. 1942; to Burt, 21 Oct. 1942.

20 CLC, Burt to Conroy, 27 Oct. 1942; Conroy to Burt, 4 Nov. 1942; Conroy to Jackson, 5 Nov. 1942.

21 CLC, McDonald, Thomas, and Jackson (for Fitzgerald) to Conroy, 19 Dec. 1942.

22 CLC, Conroy to Burt and Millard, 19 and 21 Dec. 1942, to Millard and Jackson, 29 Dec. 1942; USW, McDonald to Millard, 27 Nov. 1942; Millard to McDonald, 1 Dec. 1942.

23 UE, Jackson to Morgan, 31 Dec. 1942;

24 CLC, Fitzgerald to Conroy, 6 Jan. 1943; Jackson to Conroy, 14 Jan. 1943, 22 March 1943.

25 CLC, Haywood to Conroy, 21 June 1943; Conroy to Haywood, 8 July 1943, 11 May 1944; Haywood to Conroy, 19 May 1944; Conroy to Haywood, 9 June 1944; Haywood to Conroy, 16 June 1944.

26 CLC, Mosher to Conroy, 6 Feb. 1943.

27 CLC, J.C. Murphy (organization director NATE) to Conroy, 22 Dec. 1943; 25 Jan. 1944; Conroy to Robson, 31 Dec. 1943; Millard to Conroy, 31 Jan. 1944.

28 CLC, Murphy to Conroy, 22 Feb. 1944; Haywood to Conroy, 19 May 1944; Conroy to Haywood, 9 June 1944; Haywood to Conroy, 16 June 1944; Conroy to Haywood, 21 July 1944.

29 CLC, Barrett to Lewis, 15 Oct. 1942.

30 CLC, Conroy to Murray, 16 Oct. 1942; Barrett to Conroy, 20 Dec. 1942; Haywood to Conroy, 29 Oct. 1942.
31 USW, Millard to Haywood, 13 Aug. 1942; CLC, Mosher to Conroy, 17 Aug. 1943.
32 CLC, Conroy to Barrett, 13 Nov. 1943.
33 CLC, Conroy to Haywood, 12 Nov. 1943; Haywood to Conroy, 13 Dec. 1943.
34 CLC, Conroy to Haywood, 29 Aug. 1944.
35 CLC, Haywood to Conroy, 5 Sept. 1944.
36 USW, Millard to Murray, 16 March 1945; Conroy to Millard, 21 March 1945.
37 CLC, Conroy to Haywood, 26 May 1945.
38 CLC, Haywood to Conroy, 31 May 1945; Conroy to Haywood, 14 June 1945.
39 CLC, Haywood to Conroy, 20 June 1945.
40 USW, Millard to Conroy, 28 June 1945.
41 CLC, Conroy to Haywood, 26 May 1945.
42 CLC, Millard to Conroy, 23 July 1945; USW, Millard to Conroy, 9 Aug. 1945; CLC, executive committee, 21 Aug. 1945.
43 CLC, Conroy to Mosher, 5 Oct. 1945.
44 CLC, Conroy to Haywood, 2 May 1950.
45 CLC, Haywood to Conroy, 21 Dec. 1945; 4 Jan. 1946; Conroy to Haywood, 27 Dec. 1945; Haywood to Conroy, 10 June 1946; Conroy to Haywood, 12 June 1946; Conroy to Haywood, 30 Sept. 1946.
46 USW, Millard to Conroy, 27 Dec. 1947; CLC, Conroy to Mosher, 30 Dec. 1947.
47 CLC, e.g. Conroy to Murray, 21 Oct. 1948; 30 Nov. 1948.
48 USW, Conroy to Millard, 27 April 1949; CLC, Carey to Conroy, 27 May 1949.
49 CLC, Conroy to Millard, 3 May 1949; executive committee, 4 July 1949; Conroy et al. to Carey, 5 July 1949.
50 USW, Millard to McDonald, 6 July 1949; CLC, Burt to Reuther, 22 July 1949; USW, Millard to McDonald, 8 Nov. 1949.
51 CLC, Millard to Conroy, 16 Nov. 1949; Conroy to Carey, 3 Oct. 1950.
52 CLC, Carey to Conroy, 29 Dec. 1950; Conroy to Carey, 22 Jan. 1951; USW, Millard to Murray, 16 Jan. 1951.
53 USW, Millard to Murray, 18 Dec. 1950; CLC, Conroy to Chappell, 16 Oct. 1951, to Millard, 30 March 1951.

Chapter 10

1 CLC, Conroy to Burt, 31 March 1944.
2 Mahoney threatened to resign his Congress appointment in BC unless Conroy kept McAuslane away from him (USW, Mahoney to Conroy, 2 July 1948. Similarly Millard threatened to resign from the Congress executive if McAuslane were elected to it (CLC, Millard to Mosher, 28 Sept. 1949).
3 CLC, Conroy to Millard, 21 April 1950.
4 USW, Millard to Conroy, 2 Dec. 1948; Millard to MacDonald, 10 May 1949; Burt to Millard, 3 Feb. 1946.
5 USW, Millard to Haywood, 14 June 1946.
6 CLC, Conroy to Millard, 10 June 1946; USW, Millard to Mosher, 30 Sept. 1946; Millard to Haywood, 14 June 1946.
7 USW, Millard to Murray, 28 June 1948; Millard to Conroy, 26 Oct. 1948; CLC, Jackson to Conroy, 9 Sept. 1948; Mosher and Conroy to Jackson, 10 Sept. 1948.
8 USW, Conroy to Pomeroy (local secretary), 22 Feb. 1950; CLC, Conroy to Millard, 23 Feb. 1950; USW, Millard to McDonald, 24 Feb. 1950; CLC, Millard to Conroy, 6 March 1950.
9 CLC, decision of the jurisdictional committee; Mosher to Dow, 30 March 1950; USW, Millard to McDonald, 3 April 1950.
10 CLC, Burt to Conroy, April 15, 1950. USW, Millard to Reuther, to Conroy, to McDonald, all 19 April 1950.
11 CLC, Conroy to Millard, 21 April 1950.
12 CLC, Burt to Conroy, 5 May 1950; UAW, international executive board meeting, 24-29 April 1950; CLC, Burt to Mosher, 26 May 1950; Barrett to Mosher, 30 May 1950.
13 USW, McDonald to Millard, 8 May 1951; Bill Sefton to Millard, 2 Dec. 1950; CLC, minutes executive council CCL, 12 April 1951; USW, Millard to MacDonald, 2 Sept. 1951; CLC, Conroy to Chappell, 10 Oct. 1951.

14 CLC, survey of trade union organization in the textile industry, Feb. 1941.

15 CLC, Conroy to Williams, 19 Dec. 1941; Millard to Conroy, 17 Dec. 1941; to Haywood, Dec. 11, 1941.

16 CLC, Conroy to Millard, 21 Oct. 1943; minutes of Textile Workers conference, 22 April 1944; Millard to Dowd, 6 June 1944; executive committee, 12 Oct. 1944.

17 CLC, Rowley to Conroy, 3 Aug. 1948; "Mr. Sam Baron and the TWUA in Canada", by the Canadian District UTWA (AFL) July, 1948; transcript radio broadcast by Val Bjarnson (UTWA representative) on CKPC, Brantford, 9 July 1948; CLC, "An Answer to a Smear Campaign," TWUA, 8 Sept. 1948; Baron to Conroy, 26 July 1948.

18 CLC, Baron to Mosher, 18 Oct. 1950; Rieve to Conroy, 12 Aug. 1950; Conroy to Rieve, 16 Aug. 1950.

19 CLC, Rieve to Baron, 27 Sept. 1950.

20 CLC, Baron to the Canadian members of TWUA, 19 March 1951, 16; Globe and Mail, 29 Jan. 1951.

21 CLC, Rieve to all Canadian locals, 13 Feb. 1951, 21 Feb. 1951; e.g. Baron to all Canadian locals, 22 Feb. 1951; Rieve to all Canadian joint boards, 6 March 1951; Baron to Canadian members of TWUA, 19 March 1951.

22 Star, 10 March 1951.

23 Globe and Mail, 3 April 1951; CLC, Daoust to Mosher, 20 March 1951; Mosher to Daoust, 30 March 1951.

24 CLC, statement prepared by Mosher and read by Dowd at Textile Workers conference, 31 March – 2 April 1951.

25 CLC, Rieve to Mosher, 16 April 1951.

26 CLC, Mosher to Conroy 19 April; Conroy to Mosher, 19 April 1951; Dowd; McGuire.

27 CLC, Conroy to Rieve, 19 April 1951.

28 CLC, Mosher to Rieve, 27 April 1951.

29 CLC, Baldanzi to Mosher, 27 April 1951; Baron to Mosher, 24 April 1951; Duffy and Watson (London) to Mosher, 27 April 1951; Burt to Mosher, 3 May 1951.

30 CLC, Rieve to Mosher, 7 May 1951; Rieve to Conroy, 7 May 1951.

31 Dowling; Millard; USW, Millard to Murray, 25 Sept. 1951; Millard to Mosher, 28 Sept. 1951.

32 J.E. McGuire; Dowd.

33 USW, Millard to Murray, 25 Sept. 1951; Millard; Dowling; Alsbury.

34 USW, Millard to Murray, 25 Sept. 1951.

35 Proceedings, CCL convention, 17-21 Sept. 1951, 9.

36 CLC, executive council CCL, 22 Sept. 1951, 30 Aug. 1951, 12 Nov. 1951. One telegram in six words stated what others must have felt: "Conroy or chaos. Won't you reconsider." Jim MacDonald (CCL representative in Nova Scotia) to Conroy, 22 Sept. 1951; USW, Murray to Millard, 2 Oct. 1951; Millard to Mosher, 4 Oct. 1951.

37 CLC, Mosher to Millard, 4 Oct. 1951; USW, Millard to Mosher, 28 Sept. 1951; Millard to Murray, 28 Sept. 1951; Globe and Mail, 23 Sept. 1951; CLC, executive committee CCL, 11 Nov. 1951; McCloy to all CCL locals in Alberta, Oct. 1951.

38 Globe and Mail, 24 Sept. 1951. Financial Times, 5 Oct. 1951.

39 CCF, Lewis to Ingle, 27 Dec. 1951.

40 USW, Millard to Murray, 25 Sept. 1951.

41 Globe and Mail, 1 May 1952; Canadian Packinghouse Worker, June 1952; Murray Cotterill, Star, 20 May 1952.

42 Canadian Railway Employees Monthly, Feb. 1952, 41; Ottawa Journal, 3 March 1952; USW, Millard to Mosher, 3 March 1952.

43 CLC, Mosher to Millard, 4 March 1952; Canadian Railway Employees Monthly, March 1952, 71.

44 Globe and Mail, 23 Sept. 1951.

45 J.E. McGuire's private papers, CBRE executive board meeting, 3rd meeting, 19 March 1942; McGuire.

46 McGuire's private papers, CBRE executive board meeting, 25 Jan. 1950, 7 April 1950; McGuire.

47 CLC, Mosher to national executive board of CBRE, 4 March 1952; CLC, McGuire to national executive board of CBRE, 4 March 1952, accompanied by a letter from his doctor; Ottawa Journal, 24 March 1952.

48 CLC, CBRE press release, 24 March 1952; executive council CCL, 26 March 1952.
49 *Ottawa Citizen*, 28 March and 1 April 1952.
50 CBRE convention, proceedings, 1952.
51 USW, Dowling to Millard, 8 May 1952.
52 *information*, Jan. 1953, 3; CLC, executive council CCL, 3 June 1952; executive council, 15 Jan. 1952; CLC, Rhodes to Burt, 4 Feb. 1952; jurisdiction committee to Mac-Donald, 27 March 1952; Mosher to Millard, 19 Feb. 1952.
53 USW, Millard to Mosher, 4 April 1952; CLC, Mosher to Millard, 17 April 1952.
54 USW, Millard to Mosher, 16 April 1952; CLC, Mosher to Millard, 18 April 1952.
55 CLC, Millard to MacDonald, 13 Sept. 1952. The man was Spivak (Spivak; Millard).
56 CLC, Millard to MacDonald, 13 Sept. 1952.
57 *Ibid;* Dowling.
58 CLC, Proceedings, CCL convention, 22-26 Sept. 1952, 4; *Globe and Mail*, 20, 27 Sept. 1952. *Financial Post*, 27 Sept.-4 Oct. 1952.
59 *The Oshawaworker*, 16 Oct. 1952.
60 Proceedings, CCL convention, 1952, 81-83.

Conclusion

1 CLC, Carey to all international unions, 30 Oct. 1952; Carey to MacDonald, 12 June 1953; CIO executive board meeting, 22-7 March 1954.
2 E. Forsey, "The Movement towards Labour Unity in Canada," *Canadian Journal of Economics and Political Science,* Feb. 1958.
3 CLC, Mosher to Moore, 18 Dec. 1941; Moore to Mosher, 19 Dec. 1941; Conroy to Daoust, 11 Jan. 1943; Bengough to Conroy, 22 Jan. 1943; Conroy to Bengough, 19 Dec. 1945; Bengough to Conroy, 28 March 1946; Conroy to Bengough, 11 June 1943; Ben-gough to Conroy, 15 June 1943; Mosher to Bengough, 4 Dec. 1944, 10 April 1947; Bengough to Conroy, 19 April 1947.
4 CLC, Bengough to Conroy to all affiliates, 29 Aug. 1950; Aug. 31, 1950; Bengough to Conroy, 20 and 27 Feb. 1951.
5 CLC, interim report and recommendations of the Joint Committee on Labour Unity, AFL-CIO; 1 June Carey to Mosher, 1953; Gordon Cushing to MacDonald, 7 Dec. 1953; MacDonald to Cushing, 16 Dec. 1953.
6 CLC, MacDonald to Carey, 5 March 1954; USW, Millard to MacDonald, 7 April 1954.
7 CLC, minutes 4th meeting of TLC-CCL unity committee, 8 Nov. 1954.
8 CLC, minutes 5th meeting unity committee, 16 Dec. 1954; minutes 6th meeting unity committee, 24 Jan. 1955.
9 CLC, Hall to Jodoin, 14 March 1955; Cushing to MacDonald, 18 March 1955.
10 CLC, minutes 8th meeting unity committee, 18, 19 April 1955. Dowd to Cushing 30 April 1955. The Congress expelled the UMW in Dec. 1955 and refused to allow District 26 to affiliate with the new Congress on a provincial basis (executive committee, 13 Dec. 1955).
11 P. Norgren, "The Labour Link between Canada and the United States," in A.E. Kovacs, ed., *Canadian Labour Economics* (Toronto, 1961), 37. J. Crispo, *International Unionism: A Study in Canadian-American Relations* (Toronto, 1967), 111-112.
12 Private correspondence, Conroy to the author, 11 March 1970.
13 See G. Horowitz, *Canadian Labour in Politics* (Toronto, 1968), on political influence. The various books and articles by John Crispo, Eugene Forsey, and Stuart Jamieson cover some aspects of the other contributions of the CCL to the Canadian labour movement.

Bibliography

PRIMARY SOURCES

Archival Collections

Public Archives of Canada. Cooperative Commonwealth Federation Papers; Lapointe Papers; War Cabinet Minutes, 1939-41
Province of Ontario Archives: Hepburn Papers
Labor History Archives, Wayne State University. United Automobile Workers of America Papers
University of British Columbia Library, Special Collections Division. International Union of Mine, Mill and Smelter Workers Papers

Private Collections

Amalgamated Clothing Workers. Files and correspondence of the ACW in the Labour Lyceum building in Toronto
British Columbia Federation of Labour. Files and correspondence in the basement of the BCFL offices in Vancouver
Canadian Labour Congress. Files and correspondence of the Canadian Congress of Labour, the Trades and Labor Congress and the All-Canadian Congress of Labour in the CLC offices in Ottawa and in storage at the Hill the Movers' warehouse in suburban Ottawa. Most of these have now been moved to the Public Archives of Canada.
International Woodworkers of America. Files and correspondence in the IWA headquarters in Vancouver
Labour Research Bureau. Files and correspondence pertaining to the British Columbia labour movement in the basement of the LRB office in Vancouver

United Electrical Workers. Files and correspondence in the UE head office in Toronto
United Packinghouse Workers. Files and correspondence in the basement of the UPW headquarters in Toronto
United Steel Workers. Files and correspondence in the USW head office in Toronto

Government Publications

Canada, Department of Labour, *Labour Gazette* 1936-56 (published monthly)
Canada, Department of Labour, *Labour Organization in Canada* 1936-56 (published annually)

Convention Proceedings

All-Canadian Congress of Labour, 1927-39
British Columbia District #1 International Woodworkers of America, 1944-9
British Columbia Federation of Labour, 1944-8
Canadian Brotherhood of Railway Employees, 1936-56
Canadian Congress of Labour, 1940-55
Canadian Labour Congress, 1956
Congress of Industrial Organization, 1936-56
International Woodworkers of America, 1937-49
Ontario Federation of Labour, 1946-50
Trades and Labor Congress of Canada, 1936-55
United Electrical Workers, District 5, 1942-50
United Steel Workers, Canadian Region, 1942-56

Interviews

Stewart Alsbury, (New Westminster, B.C. 1967); Emil Bjarnson, (Vancouver, 1967); George Burt, (Kingsville, Ontario, 1972); Bob Carlin, (Sudbury, 1967); Murray Cotterill, (Toronto, 1971); Senator David Croll, (Toronto, 1963); Norman Dowd, (Ottawa, 1966); Fred Dowling, (Toronto, 1967); Mike Fenwick, (Toronto, 1971); Senator Eugene Forsey, (Ottawa, 1967); Harry Hunter, (Hamilton, 1966); C.S. Jackson, (Toronto, 1967); William Kashtan, (Toronto, 1971); Oscar Kogan, (Toronto, 1972); William Longridge, (Toronto, 1971); Bruce Magnuson, (Toronto, 1971); William Mahoney, (Toronto, 1971); J.E. McGuire, (Ottawa, 1967); Charles Millard, (Toronto, 1967); Milton Montgomery, (Hamilton, 1967); Nigel Morgan, (Vancouver, 1967); Harvey Murphy, (Vancouver, 1967); Eamon Park, (Toronto, 1967); Harold Pritchett, (Burnaby, B.C., 1967); Bob Radford, (Vancouver, 1967); Senator Arthur Roebuck, (Toronto, 1963); Ross Russell, (Toronto, 1967); J.B. Salsberg, (Toronto, 1967);

Arthur Schultz, (Toronto, 1967); Paul Siren, (Toronto, 1972); Sol Spivak, (Toronto, 1966); Muni Taub, (Toronto, 1971); Bob Ward, (Toronto, 1967)

Newspapers and Periodicals

British Columbia Lumber Worker, 1944-9
Canadian Forum, 1936-56
Canadian Packinghouse Worker, 1952-6
Canadian Railway Employees Monthly, 1936-56
Canadian Tribune, 1940-7
Canadian Unionist, 1936-56
Daily Clarion, 1936-8
Financial Post, 1936-56
Ford Facts, 1943-50
Glace Bay Gazette, 1942-4
International Woodworker, 1942-9
Labor Statesman, 1944-9
New Commonwealth, 1936-40
New York Times, 1936-9
Oshawa Times, 1936-40
Pacific Advocate, 1936-40, 1945-50
Peterborough Examiner, 1946-50
Steel Labor, 1936-56
Sudbury Star, 1940-7
Toronto Globe and Mail, 1936-56
Toronto Star, 1936-56
Trades and Labor Congress Journal, 1936-56
United Autoworker (Canadian edition), 1939-56
UE News, 1941-51
Vancouver Sun, 1942-9
Welland–Port Colbourne Tribune, 1947-9
Windsor Star, 1943-8

SECONDARY SOURCES

Books and Articles

Bernstein, I. *The Lean Years: A History of the American Workers, 1920-1932.* Baltimore 1966 – *Turbulent Years: A History of the American Workers, 1933-1941.* Boston 1970
Carlin, R. *I Know Mine-Mill, Do You?* Toronto 1961
Crispo, J. *International Unionism: A Study in Canadian-American Relations.* Toronto 1967

Forsey, E. "The Movement Towards Labour Unity in Canada: History and Implications," *Canadian Journal of Economics and Political Science,* XXIV, 1, Feb. 1958

Galenson, W. *The* AFL *against the* CIO. Cambridge, Mass. 1960

Greening, W.E. and MacLean, M.M. *It Was Never Easy.* Ottawa 1961

Horowitz, G. *Canadian Labour in Politics.* Toronto 1968

Jamieson, S. *Industrial Relations in Canada.* Toronto 1957

– *Times of Trouble: Labour Unrest and Industrial Conflict in Canada, 1900-66.* Ottawa 1971

Jensen, V. *Heritage of Conflict.* Ithaca, NY, 1950

– *Lumber and Labor.* New York 1945

– *Non-Ferrous Metals Industry Unionism, 1932–1954.* Ithaca, NY, 1954

Kampelman, Max. *The Communist Party vs. the* CIO. New York 1957

Lipton, C. *The Trade Union Movement in Canada 1827–1959.* Montreal 1966

Logan, H.A. *Trade Unions in Canada.* Toronto 1948

Morris, Leslie. *The Big Ford Strike.* Toronto 1946

Morris, J.O. *Conflict within the* AFL. Ithaca, NY 1958

Phillips, P. *No Power Greater.* Vancouver 1967

Robin, Martin. *Radical Politics and Canadian Labour 1880–1930.* Kingston, Ontario 1968

Saposs, David. *Communism in American Unions.* New York 1959

Starobin, Joseph. *American Communism in Crisis, 1943-1957.* Cambridge, Mass. 1972

Wright, M. *It Takes More Than Guns: A Brief History of the* IUMMSW. Denver 1944

Young, Walter. *The Anatomy of a Party: The National* CCF, *1932-61.* Toronto 1969

Theses and Unpublished Manuscripts

Adams, J. "The History of the United Steel Workers of America in Canada." MA thesis, Queen's University, 1952

Armstrong, M.M. "The Development of Trade Union Political Activity in the CCF." MA thesis, University of Toronto, 1959

Bjarnson, E. "Collective Bargaining in the Coal Mining Industry of Canada 1828-1938." MA thesis, Queen's University 1965

Cahan, J.F. "A Survey of Political Activities of the Ontario Labour Movement." MA thesis, University of Toronto, 1945

Forsey, Eugene. "The History of Canadian Trade Unionism 1812-1902." 1971

Hunter, Peter. "From the Other Shore." 1965

Kennedy, D.R. "The Knights of Labor in Canada." MA thesis, University of Western Ontario, 1956

McAndrew, W.J. "Gold Mining Trade Unions and Politics: Ontario in the 1930's." MA thesis, University of British Columbia, 1969

Montague, J.T. "Trade Unionism in the Meat Packing Industry." MA thesis, Toronto, 1950

Moulton, D. "The Windsor Ford Strike." Senior thesis, Glendon College, York University, 1972

Williams, C.B. "Canadian American Trade Union Relations–A Study of the Development of Binational Unionism." PhD thesis, Cornell, 1964

Young, B. "The Leadership League." MA thesis, Queen's University, 1966

Index